Islamic Medical Wisdom

The Tibb al-A'imma

Islamic Medical Wisdom

The Tibb al-A'imma

CONTENTS

Preface	vii
Introduction	xxv
TIBB AL-A'IMMA	1
INDEX OF AFFLICTIONS	186

PREFACE

The present is the first English translation of a text in the Twelver Shi'i prophetic medical tradition. As such it will prove of both interest and importance to specialists and non-specialists alike. The former include those pursuing study of various aspects of Islamic history and civilization in general and especially students of the history of Islamic medicine. The latter include both those wishing greater awareness of the Twelver Shi'i faith and heritage in general, and those desirous of greater familiarity with practical dimensions of the faith in particular.

For these audiences a fuller appreciation of this text is perhaps best achieved by some discussion of the place of the prophetic medical tradition within the context of the history of Islamic medicine.

Western-language scholars have generally defined Islamic medicine as composed of two distinct and dichotomous traditions, pre-Islamic Galenic medicine and prophetic medicine. Galenic medicine is understood to have become available to Islamic medical writers and practitioners as Greek scientific texts were translated into Arabic, beginning especially in Baghdad In the early 3rd/9th century. Supported by the Abbasid caliphs and other wealthy benefactors, over the next two hundred years the translation movement made much of Greek philosophy and science available in Arabic, the lingua franca of Islamic civilization.

Briefly and broadly speaking, the essence of the Galenic medical system was humoral pathology: equilibrium of the four humours (*al-akhlat*) — blood, phlegm, yellow bile, and black bile — produced well-being, while disequilibrium produced illness, the specificity of which depended on the affected humour. Together with the doctrines of the elements, temperaments, qualities, and faculties, the Galenic medical system presupposed a system of therapy aimed at maintaining or restoring equilibrium in the body by changes in diet, environment, activity, and by use of external medications.

Among the early Islamic-period adherents of the Galenic medical system were some of those philosopher/physicians best-known today. These included, for example, Abu Zakariyya Yuhanna b. Masawayh (d. 243 A.H./857 AD.), his student Hunayn b. Ishaq (d. 259/873), himself one of the foremost of the translators, Abu Bakr Muhammad b. Zakariyya al-Razi (latinized as Rhazes) (d. 311/923), 'Ali b. al-'Abbas al-Majusi (often known as Haly Abbas) (d. between 380/982 and 385/995), Abu 'Ali al-Husayn b. 'Abd Allah b. Sina (latinized as Avicenna) (d. 428/1037), and 'Ala' al-Din Ali b. Abu al-Hazm al-Qurashi, Ibn al-Nafis (d. 687/1288).[i]

Western scholars have identified these and other medical writers of this period as part of a broader period of cultural effervescence characteristic of the later years of the 'Abbasid caliphate, and explained this 'golden age' of Islamic civilization in terms both of the translation movement and the socio-economic and political stability marking these years.

---

[i] This brief overview relies heavily on Manfred Ullmann, *Islamic Medicine* (Edinburgh: Edinburgh University Press, 1978), 7f, 41f, 55f; Michael W. Dols' introduction to his *Medieval Islamic Medicine, Ibn Ridwan's Treatise 'On the Prevention of Bodily Ills in Egypt'* (Berkeley and London: University of California Press, 1984), 3-24; and J. Christoph Burgel, "Secular and Religious Features of Medieval Arabic Medicine', in *Asian Medical Systems: A Comparative Study,* Charles Leslie, ed. (Berkeley and Los Angeles: University of California Press, 1972), 44-62.

Preface

According to this analysis Islam's 'golden age' began its decline in the 6th/12th century precisely because the lack of originality and spontaneous creativity at the basis of Islam's cultural vitality finally revealed itself and the 'Abbasid caliphate also met its political, not to say also its socio-economic end, with the Mongol destruction of Baghdad in 656/1258. This inherent lack of creativity similarly asserted itself vis-a-vis Islamic medicine; ultimately Islamic medicine is seen to have involved less an interest in, and efforts to supplement, Greek medicine than better arrangement of the Greek material. [ii]

As Galenic medicine declined the second, dichotomous tradition in Islamic medicine is said to have increasingly asserted itself. This was the prophetic medical tradition.[iii] Prophetic medicine is generally depicted as having arisen to counter the authority of the Greek-based medical tradition by positing that knowledge and certainty in medicine, as in religion and philosophy, could only be attained through revelation.

[ii] According to Ullmann 'the Arabs had received Greek medicine at the last stage of its development and could do no other than assume that this system was perfect and final' Burgel wrote that 'Arabic medicine.... [lacked] an evolutionary conception of science', and identified the decline in Islamic medicine as part of a broader dissolution of the 'scientific impetus' which was a feature of the later Abbasid period. See Ullmann, *Ibid.* 22; Burgel, *ibid*, 53-54, and note 5 below. In their adherence to the 'golden age' concept both were echoing E.G. Browne who had characterized 'Arabian science' and 'Arabian medicine' as 'for the most part Greek in origin... and only in a very small degree the product of the Arabian mind.' See Browne's *Arabian Medicine* (Cambridge: Cambridge University Press, first published 1921, reprinted 1962), 2, and also 5-6.

[iii] In Arabic, either *Tibb al-Nabi* (the medicine of the Prophet) or *al-tibb al-nabawi* (prophetic medicine).

Preface

However, although ostensibly based on the Qur'an and the statements and actions attributed to the Prophet Muhammad (d. 11/632)[iv], most writers have followed Browne in citing and accepting the criticism of prophetic medicine by Ibn Khaldun (d. 809/1406), who characterized the tradition as 'definitely no part of divine revelation but something customarily practised among the Arabs [before the rise of Islam]'. As such, according to J. Christoph Burgel prophetic medicine was 'quackery piously disguised'. Nevertheless, with the influence of Galenic medicine on the decline, prophetic medicine is said to have been attracting increasing attention by the 7th/13th and 8th/14th centuries.[v]

[iv] For an introduction to this literature, see J.Robson's *'Hadith'* in *EI/II*, 3 (Leiden: Brill 1971) 23-28, and also G.H.A. Juynboll, *Muslim tradition: Studies in chronology, provenance and authorship of early hadith* (Cambridge: Cambridge University Press, 1983).

[v] See Browne, *ibid*, 11-14, especially 13-14; Burgel, *ibid*, 50, 60, citing Browne, *ibid*, 13-14. See also Ullmann, *ibid*, 5. The citation from Ibn Khaldun is from Fazlur Rahman, *Health and Medicine in the Islamic Tradition, Change and Identity* (New York: Crossroad, 1989), 33. See also *ibid*, 42f for additional causes for the rise of the prophetic tradition. On Rahman, see also notes 14, 15 below. Burgel, in a tone perhaps implicitly accepted by many scholars, also described 'so-called prophetic medicine', astrology, alchemy, and magic as 'looked upon as sciences by the great majority, and even by most of the scholars. Nevertheless, they were hothouses of irrationalism, the rational disguise making them only the more harmful'. As such, they were 'enemies' of 'rational thought', 'harmful' to the 'essentials of science', and were the 'spiritual forces... most potent in paralyzing the scientific impetus of the golden age.' See Burgel, *ibid*, 54. Although Cyril Elgood did not cite Ibn Khaldun, he depicted 'the story of Arabian Medicine [as]... one of continual rebellion by the doctors against the system of thought imposed upon them by the theologians' and the basis of prophetic medicine as pre-Islamic practices. See his 'Tibb ul-Nabi or Medicine of the Prophet', *Osiris* 14 (1962), 37.

Preface

Prophetic medical writings discussed in greatest detail by Western language scholars include the chapters on medical questions in the *Sahih* - the collection of hadith complied by Abu 'Abd Allah Muhammad b. Isma'il al-Bukhari (d. 256/870) - the treatise of the Shafi'i scholar Shams al-Din Abu 'Abd Allah Muhammad b. Abu Bakr, Ibn Qayyim al-Jawziya (d, 750/1350-51), that of Shams al-Din Abu 'Abd Allah Muhammad b. Ahmad al-Dhahabi (d. 748/1347-48), and that of Jalal al-Din 'Abd al-Rahman b. Abu Bakr al-Suyuti (d.911/1505).[vi]

More dynamic visions of the course of science and medicine in the pre-modern Middle East are, nevertheless, both possible and desirable. Initially the contributions of non-Muslims might be recognised by more widely incorporating the term 'Islamicate', as developed by Marshall G. Hodgson.[vii]

[vi] For his discussion of prophetic medicine, Burgel's main source was the *Sahih*. See Burgel, *ibid.* 54-9. On Ibn Qayyim, see Basim F. Musallam in his *Sex and Society in Islam* (Cambridge: Cambridge University Press, 1983), 50, and Rahman, *ibid*, 43, 51-2, 112-113. Ibn Qayyim's *Al-Tibb al-Nabavi* is to be translated by Penelope Johnstone of the Oriental Institute, University of Oxford. On al-Dhahabi, see Rahman, *ibid*, 43f. Elgood translated al-Suyuti's essay in his "Tibb-al-Nabbi". On the authorship of this essay see Hakim Altaf Ahmad Azmi, 'A New Manuscript of Prophet's Medicine by Jalal al-Din al-Suyuti', *Studies in History of Medicine and Science*, IX (1985), Nos. 3-4, 95-112. Names of other writings and writers in this tradition can be found in Elgood, *ibid*, 40-5; idem, 'The Medicine of the Prophet', *Medical History*, 6 (1962), 146-53; Azmi, *ibid*, 95-97; Rahman, *ibid*, 41f.

[vii] See Hodgson's *Venture of Islam: Conscience and History in a World Civilisation*, 3 vols. (Chicago: University of Chicago Press, 1974). The term has already been used by Emilie Savage-Smith in her *Islamicate Celestial Globes, their History, Construction, and Use* (Washington D.C.: Smithsonian Institute Press, 1985). Of the adherents to medicine mentioned above, Hunayn b.Ishaq was, for example, a Nestorian Christian as was his teacher Yuhanna b. Masawayh. Al-Majusi was from an Iranian Zoroastrian family. It ought to be recognized that while humoral medicine did not necessarily involve the sort of 'scientific' investigation – in anatomy, for example – which became a widespread feature of

Preface

Once adopted, such a framework of reference must entail the discarding of such terms as 'Arabian Science' and 'Arabian medicine': developments in science and medicine — not to say other spheres of culture as well — can no longer be traced to something intrinsically Arab. Indeed, the very notion of the "golden age', no longer explicable in terms of something inherent to *Arab* or *Islamic* society, itself is revealed as inherently tendentious.[viii]

In searching for an alternative causal theory of developments in Islamicate science and medicine, the social specificity of different medical texts and their authors is perhaps the most useful and relevant starting point. Awareness of such works as the texts listed above and their authors mainly derive from the fact of their having been written down. The actual influence of the ideas in these texts in their own time must, however, be gauged with care. The audiences for the lengthy, comparatively technical Galenic medical texts were likely confined mainly to other medical practitioners and writers educated in this tradition, and court patrons and contemporary socio-economic and political elites to whom these authors frequently dedicated their texts. All these were

---

Western medical theory and practice only in the last century, humoral theories of illness and wellness did necessitate continual efforts to delineate variations in the environment, or medications, for example, to restore humoral balance.

[viii] On the use of the terms 'Arabian Science' and 'Arabian medicine', see note 2 above. The 'golden age' concept is itself an element of a larger agenda peculiar to the discipline of Oriental studies, wherein Arab/Muslim society is portrayed as the repository, via the translation movement, of the accomplishments of Greek civilization until the latter was recaptured by Europe. According to this conceptualization that recapture was, in turn, the basis of the Renaissance. Of the secondary source authors listed above, Browne (*ibid*, 2-3) was the first to have detailed the notion of 'Arab society' as such a repository. See also Ullmann, *ibid*, 22.

Preface

predominantly urban-based. Throughout the pre-modern period, however, the bulk of the population— Muslim and non-Muslim alike— was certainly rural and illiterate. The extent to which this majority was aware of, let alone actually exposed to, details of the concepts and 'techniques' discussed by adherents to the Galenic tradition must therefore be considered at best unclear, and at worst quite limited.

The extent of the influence of the prophetic medical tradition is less apparent. Larger compilations of *hadith* containing sections on medical questions, in al-Bukhari's *Sahih*, for example, were clearly directed to different audiences than treatises specifically on prophetic medicine, such as that of Ibn Qayyim al-Jawziya and al-Dhahabi, wherein the authors offered both arguments — including those for the validity of the prophetic over the Galenic legacy — and selected *hadith*.[ix] As such the latter may have been the product of a contest with the Galenic tradition for urban hearts and minds.

Nevertheless, and most likely as a result of prejudice against the tradition, Western scholars have yet to undertake the systematic, comparative study of different prophetic texts, instead generally portraying the prophetic tradition in relatively static and uncompromising terms. Moreover, those very few prophetic medical texts examined to date originate from within Sunni Islam. To date the Shi'i Muslim prophetic medical tradition has yet to attract the attention of scholars in the field.

Briefly, Twelver Shi'i Islam may be differentiated from the majority Sunni branch of Islam by its recognition of members of the family of the Prophet Muhammad, beginning with, and through the line of, 'Ali b. Abu Talib (d. 40/661) — the Prophet's cousin and son-in-law — as having been divinely designated to govern the

---

[ix] See, for example, the arguments of Ibn Qayyim and al-Dhahabi as cited by Rahman in his *Health and Medicine*, 42-3.

Preface

Muslim community and as being in as direct contact with Allah as the Prophet himself for the purpose of guiding the community. Their statements and actions are therefore regarded as divinely-inspired, and constitute both a commentary on and an extension of the revelation. The twelfth and last of this line, Muhammad b. al-Hasan, disappeared in 260/874, while still quite young. He is to reveal himself at the end of time and bring judgement to the world and justice and vindication to believers. The Twelver Shi'a have been always been a numerical minority in Islam. In the 10th /16th century, however, Twelver Shi'ism became the established faith in Iran. It remains so, and the Twelvers are now the majority faith in Iran, Iraq, Bahrain, and Lebanon. There are also sizeable Twelver communities in India. Pakistan, the Gulf states, and the USSR.[x]

There is no dearth of Twelver Shi'i medical texts. Agha Buzurg al-Tehrani (d. 1389/19 70) in his massive bibliography of Twelver texts, *al-Dhari'a ila tasanif al-Shi'a*, devoted several pages to listing texts on medicine completed from the earliest years following the disappearance of the Twelfth Imam up to the last century.[xi] In his introduction to the present work, Muhammad Mahdi al-Sayyid Hasan al-Khirsan lists the authors of a number of such texts. As al-Khirsan notes, the earliest of these were probably compilations of *hadith* on medical subjects transmitted from the Imams - similar to the Sunni *Sahih*. Some later texts appear to be

---

[x] For an introduction to Shi'i Islam and Twelver Shi'ism in particular, see Moojan Momen, *An Introduction to Shi'i Islam: The History and Doctrines of Twelver Shi'ism* (New Haven and London: Yale University Press, 1985). The very early history of the faith is discussed in detail by S. Husain M. Jafri, *Origins and Development of Shi'a Islam* (London and New York: Longman, 1979). A useful introduction to Twelver law, its major periods, and key personalities, is Hossein Modarressi Tabataba'i, *An Introduction to Shi'i Law: a bibliographical study* (London: Ithaca Press, 1984).

[xi] Agha Buzurg al-Tehrani, *Al-Dhari'a ila tasanif al-Shi'a* (Tehran and Najaf, 1353-98q), 15: 135-44.

Preface

arguments supplemented by *hadith* citations - as the treatises of Ibn Qayyim and al-Dhahabi. A number of these texts are extant today.

There are also the 'four books' of Twelver *hadith*,[xii] not to mention other early compilations of narratives. Because these works contain transmissions from the Imams on many different subjects, they might usefully be examined for transmissions relevant to rnedical subjects. To date, however, there has been no effort to examine any of these sources with a view to detailing and analyzing what is distinctly Twelver Shi'i about this genre of literature, let alone undertaking a comparison with similar works in the Sunni tradition.

The present text, *The Medicine of the Imams*, is a collection of statements of the Imams compiled by Abu 'Atab 'Abd Allah and al-Husayn, the sons of Bistam b. Sabur, Bistam himself was a companion of the sixth Imam Abu 'Abd Allah Ja'far b. Muhammad al-Sadiq (d. 148/765) and the seventh Imam Abu al-Hasan Musa b. Ja'far al-Kazim (d. 183/799).[xiii] Probably because, despite the wealth of Shi'i material, it is one of the few such texts to be published, this compilation is the only Twelver medical work to have attracted notice in the field, and then only recently. Solely based on the present work Rahman characterised the Shi'a, in contrast with the Sunni, as encouraged to bear the 'pain and discomfort of disease' and seek the assistance of a doctor 'only if disease threatens to become incurable and pain unbearable'. According to Rahman, the Shi'a 'underplay the natural cures and

---

[xii] These four are *al-Kafi* by Muhammad b. Ya'qub al-Kulayni (d. 329/941), *Man la Yahduruhu al-Faqih* of al-Shaykh al-Saduq, Muhammad b. 'Ali al-Qummi, mentioned in al-Khirsan's introduction, and *Tahdhib al-Ahkam* and *al-Istibsar*, both by Abu Ja'far Muhammad b. al-Hasan al-Tusi (d. 460/1067). See also notes 16 and 29 below.

[xiii] On the present text, see al-Tehrani, *ibid*, 15:139-40. The publication history of the text is discussed at the end of al-Khirsan's introduction and in note 14.

Preface

emphasize the value of suffering'. Such tendencies, he argued, were 'undoubtedly connected with the passion motif and the stress on martyrdom, of which Sunni Islam has little trace'. [xiv]

The late Michael W. Dols, in an essay review of the book in which Rahman offered this analysis, proposed a more eclectic definition for prophetic medicine than has hitherto been available. Dols characterized the prophetic tradition as a: blend of three distinct elements . . .: the folk medicine of the Arabian bedouin, the borrowing of Galenic concepts that had become common parlance (such as humours, temperaments, and qualities), and the overarching principle of divine or supernatural causation. [xv]

An initial appraisal of the present text suggests Dols' is a more appropriate analysis than that of Rahman and that, indeed, all three forms of medicine found favor within the Shi'i community, Parallels with the pre-Islamic medical practice and theory as discussed by Ullmann, for example, are readily apparent in these narratives. There is clear evidence of some anatomical knowledge: many of the major organs are mentioned in these texts. Ullmann

---

[xiv] Rahman, *ibid*, 37-8, citing only pp.16, 6 of the Arabic text of the present work, corresponding to al-Khirsan's introduction. There al-Khirsan is not actually citing any narratives but the statements of two later Twelver scholars, Muhammad Baqir al-Majlisi – who died not in 1800, the date given by Rahman, but in 1110/1699 – and the late 4th/10 century scholar al-Shaykh al-Mufid. Rahman's Arabic edition of the text was published in Najaf in 1965. The edition on which the present translation was made was published in Beirut.

[xv] Michael W. Dols, 'Islam and Medicine', a review of Fazlur Rahman, *Health and Medicine in the Islamic Tradition*, in *History of Science*, xxvi (1988), 421. In her forthcoming 'Islamic Medicine' in *An Encyclopaedia of Arab Science*, R. Rashed, ed. (London: Routledge, 1991), Emilie Savage-Smith suggests the prophetic tradition flourished alongside the 'Greek-based tradition but probably serving a different part of the community', and dismisses suggestions that the former was a 'threat to "scientific" or "rational" medicine'.

mentioned the use of animal urine[xvi] and human blood as curatives, and references to both appear in the present compilation. Various herbal combinations, soups, animal fat, sugar,[xvii] and honey appear as medicaments. There is also evidence of belief that magical properties had been conferred on such otherwise innocuous elements as the water of the Zamzam well or the soil of the grave of one the Imams. Such pre-Islamic supernatural forces as the 'evil eye' were also seen as a danger in the Islamic period.

The overall emphasis on preventative medicine, abstaining from certain foods, for example, and such cures as cupping and cauterization — which Ullmann suggested were strongly criticized by the Prophet — also feature in some of these hadith. There is also clear evidence of a 'theory of contagion' or transmission of illness that Ullmann suggested was in evidence in pre-Islamic and early Islamic Arabia, as witnessed in the narrative transmitted from Imam Ja'far al-Sadiq from the Prophet advising against 'looking at the afflicted'.[xviii]

The humoral-basis which was a feature of the Greek medical system is also in evidence in these narratives. There are, for example, references to maladies being related to, if not also caused by, black and yellow bile, and phlegm. The narratives are replete with lists of medicaments designed to alleviate such afflictions. There are also references to climate, for example, as a factor in illness and wellness. Although there is no formal mention of the

---

[xvi] References to urine in the Qur'an can be found in A.J. Wensinck's *A Handbook of Early Muslim Tradition* (Leiden: Brill, 1927), which might also be consulted for references to different medical subjects, including other remedies and curatives.

[xvii] The different forms of sugar are discussed in J. Ruska's 'Sukkar', *EI*, 4 (Leiden: Brill, 1934), 501-10.

[xviii] Ullmann, *ibid*, 1-5, 86-7.

Preface

humours themselves, the 'natural constituents' are mentioned. The presence in these narratives of the third of the three components mentioned by Dols, the belief that illness and wellness could also be the result of divine intervention, as well as that of Satan and the jinn, is also clearly in evidence as the number of prayers, invocations, and supplications attest.

There are also narratives which offer a more complex view of medical theory and practice. There is, for example, the occasional *hadith* in which references occur to more than one of these three forms of medicine. In the case of the treatment for phlegm in the two narratives transmitted by Hariz b. Ayyub al-Jurjani and Muhammad b. al-Sirraj, for example, both recitation of the Qur'an and herbal-based remedies are said to be effective.

Given the references to all three forms of theory and practice in these narratives and the apparent parallels with the Sunni-based prophetic medical tradition as it has been discussed to date, a systematic, comparative study of the Sunni and Shi'i prophetic medical traditions would seem to be merited. The Sunni texts which are already available might be the basis of preliminary study. Al-Suyuti referred similarly somewhat imperfectly to the humoral conceptualization in his treatise.[xix]

Both al-Suyuti's essay and the narratives in the present text address many of the same afflictions, such as the 'evil eye', colic, or leprosy.[xx] Locating such references in the present compilation

---

[xix] See Elgood, 'The Medicine of the Prophet', 50, where al-Suyuti discussed the humoral system in more detail than in the present compilation, but substituted the spleen for the black bile, although noting that 'Spleen is sometimes called Black Bile'.

[xx] The various terms applied to leprosy are discussed by Michael W. Dols in his 'Djudham', *EI* /II, suppl., Fasc. 5-6 (Leiden: Brill, 1982), 270-74. It seems apparent that references to 'the evil disease' in the present compilation are also references to a form of skin disorder.

Preface

has been facilitated by the inclusion of an index of maladies and afflictions. Al-Suyuti's essay also contains a list of the properties of foods and drugs arranged alphabetically according to their Arabic equivalents. This list might be cross-referenced with the lists of curatives and Arabic terms appended to the present text, and comparison of the proposed remedies undertaken.

Comparisons with texts written by Islamicate adherents to the Galenic system might also usefully be undertaken. The narratives in the present compilation contain many references to eyes and eye-care, for example. In the narrative transmitted by 'Abd Allah b. Bistam the remedy called 'the healing' is said to be beneficial for *rih al-sabal*, a condition which figures in the works of both Yuhanna b. Masawayh and Ibn al-Nafis.[xxi]

The specifically pharmacological material in this compilation and other prophetic texts would also appear to merit comparison both with similar material in other prophetic texts, as has been suggested, but also with elements of Greek pharmacology which became available in Arabic during the 'Abbasid period in such works as the *Aqrabadhin* of Abu Yusuf Ya'qub b. Ishaq al-Kindi (d. ca. 256/870). Mention of the beneficial properties of 'Armenian clay' in the present compilation, for example, does have precedent in the works of both Galen and the *materia medica* of Dioscorides. Some of the terms which appear herein may be corrupted versions of other terms, owing to some confusion among practitioners of this tradition, or may have meaning other than that given in the present translation. As such, these terms perhaps merit special attention. *Al-Kundus*, for example, could also be soapwort as well

---

[xxi] On Ibn Masawayh, see Max Meyerhoff, 'The History of Trachoma Treatment in Antiquity and During the Arabic Middle Ages', *Bulletin of the Ophthalmological Society of Egypt* (Cairo), 29 (1936), 40; Emilie Savage-Smith, 'Ibn al-Nafis's *Perfected Book on Ophthalmology* and His Treatment of Trachoma and its Sequelae', *Journal for the History of Arabic Science*, 4 (1980), 166.

Preface

as *sneezewort*, as given herein. The sole reference to mercury (*al-zaybaq*) may in fact be a misprint for *al-zanbaq*, jasmine. *asarawan* may be a misprint for *asarun*, that is 'asarabacca' (Asarum europaeum). *abarfiyun* may be a rnisprint for *afarbiyun* (euphorbium). [xxii]

There are, nevertheless, elements distinct to the Twelver Shi'i faith evident in these narratives. The controversy surrounding the authenticity of the Qur'an surfaces in the narrative transmitted from Ibrahim al-Baytar concerning the sura *al-Falaq* (113) and the sura *al-Nas* (114) and whether or not these two had been included in the version of the Qur'an of the Prophet's companion 'Abd Allah b. Ghafil, Ibn Mas'ud (d. 32-3/652-653).[xxiii]

[xxii] On al-Kindi, see Martin Levey, translator, *The Medical Formulary or Aqrabadhin of al-Kindi translated with a study of its material medica* (Madison and London: The University of Wisconsin Press, 1966). On 'Armenian clay', see Ullmann, *ibid*, 25, 12. In addition to al-Kindi, the following references have been used in the translation of the terms and remedies given herein: Martin Levey, *The Medical Formulary of al-Samarqandi and the relation of early Arabic simples to those found in the indigenous medicine of the Near East and India* (Philadelphia: The University of Pennsylvania Press, 1967); J.L. Schlimmer, *Terminologie Medico-Pharmaceutique* (Tehran: University of Tehran Press, 1970, reprint of 1874 edition); Alfred Siggel, *Arabische-Deutscher Worterbuch* (Berlin, 1950); and, less reliable, A.K. Bedevian, *Illustrated Polyglotic Dictionary of Plant Names* (Cairo, 1936). Other useful glossaries can be found in Dols, *Medieval Islamic Medicine*, 153-66; Savage-Smith, *Ibn al-Nafis*, 182-7; Azmi, *ibid*, 107-11; al-Shaykh al-Rais Ibn Sina, *al-Risala al-Wahiyya*, Mahmood Suwaysi ed. (Tunis: University of Tunis, 1975), 118-244; Hakim Mohammad Said, *Al-Biruni's Book on pharmacy and material medica*, edited with an English translation (Karachi, 1973). It will be seen that these sources frequently offer conflicting translations for names of plants and herbs. Arabic terms are given in parentheses only at the first occurrence of the word, and are indexed for the first page only. If several Arabic terms are translated by one English term, the different Arabic terms may be indexed more than once.

[xxiii] On Ibn Mas'ud, see J.-C. Vadet's 'Ibn Mas'ud', in *EI/II*, 4 (Leiden: Brill, 1971), 873-5. Given Ibn Mas'ud's apparently Shi'i tendencies, Imam Ja'far's

Preface

The issue of the existence of a peculiarly Twelver attitude to illness and wellness has already been raised with the reference to Rahman's characterization of the Shi'a as being 'advised to bear the pain and discomfort of disease' and summon a physician only in the last resort, and his ascription of this attitude to 'the passion motif and the stress on martyrdom'.[xxiv]

A less cursory, more detailed examination of these narratives than that undertaken by Rahman suggests there is little basis for such a generalization. The numerous forms of herbal remedies — the same 'natural cures' Rahman suggested Shi'i prophetic medicine disavowed— the many preventative prescriptions, as well as the numerous prayers, invocations, and supplications recorded in these narratives overwhelmingly attest to the desire for wellness and the importance given to knowledge of the means to attain it. The occasional advice to avoid physicians ought not to be confused with, or interpreted as, a desire for death, let alone martyrdom, but might reflect the suspicion of the illiterate majority of a form of treatment outside their experience.

Nevertheless, even in this compilation there are references to the Imams' approval of physicians' advice, such as the narrative transmitted from 'Abd Allah b. Bistam himself from Imam Ja'far

---

disavowal of Ibn Mas'ud's reading of the Qur'an suggests an effort to minimize differences between Sunni and Shi'i in accord with the Imam's quietist tendencies. For an introduction to the Twelver position on the authenticity of the Qur'an, see Etan Kohlberg's 'Some Notes on the Imamite Attitude to the Qur'an', in S.M. Stern, et al, eds., *Islamic Philosophy and the Classical Tradition* (Oxford: Cassirer, 1972), 209-24.

[xxiv] Rahman, *ibid*, 37. Clearly here Rahman is exhibiting the conventional tendency in Oriental studies to ascribe an attitude of fatalism to Islam and Muslims, but considering it to be a particularity of the Shi'a as opposed to the ostensibly more enlightened Sunnis.

Preface

al-Sadiq wherein the Imam approved of a drink proposed by a physician which involved raisins and honey. Two narrations from Imam Ja'far concerning citron contain only a hint of disagreement with the advice preferred by physicians.

Perhaps the least obvious but most distinctively Shi'i feature to these narratives is the transmitters themselves. These personalities are indexed separately and merit some attention. Among their number are some individuals already known to scholars in the field. Hisham b. al-Hakam, for example, is well-known among scholars of the Twelver Shi'a as a rationalist companion of Imam Ja'far al-Sadiq.[xxv] Others of these individuals had more problematic careers. Also well-known, but with something of a checkered career, for example, is al-Mufaddal b. 'Umar al-Ju'fi who figures repeatedly in these narratives but whom some later biographers disavowed.[xxvi] Al-Mu'alla b. Khunays is described by al-Najashi as 'weak'[xxvii], and Muhammad b Sinan al-Zahiri is said by al-Najashi to have transmitted narratives from many 'weak' individuals.[xxviii] It would seem that while the non-medical narratives from these and other individuals might be troublesome, their medical narratives were deemed acceptable.

[xxv] See W. Madelung's article on him in *EI*/II, 3; 496-98, and also Momen, *ibid*, 65, 67, 73.

[xxvi] On al-Mufaddal, see W. Madelung, 'Khattabiyya, *EI* /II, 4: 1132-3; Momen, *ibid*, 53. The biographer Abu al-'Abbas Ahmad b. 'Ali al-Najashi (d. 450/1058-9) described him as 'corrupt' in his *Rijal al-Najashi* (Qum, 1407), 416. See also the article on him in the biographical work by Muhammad b. 'Ali al-Ardabili, *Jami' al-Ruwaat* 2 (Qum, 1403), 258-60. The latter was a student of the above-mentioned Muhammad Baqir al-Majlisi.

[xxvii] Al-Najashi, *ibid*, 417. See also al-Ardabili, *ibid*, 2:247-50.

[xxviii] Al-Najashi, *ibid*, 338; al-Ardabili, *ibid*, 2:88-9.

Preface

Clearly, however, further research on these transmitters and their transmissions would be useful. Where possible it would be especially useful, for example, to trace the narratives in the present compilation to the earlier collections in which they appeared originally, thus better understanding the purpose and intended audience of that original collection.[xxix] Interestingly, where the traditionists include references to individuals other than their coreligionists, mistakes appear to occur. The sole reference in the present compilation to Yuhanna b. Masawayh refers to him also as 'Abu Hafan' by which he is not known in conventional biographies.[xxx]

The paucity of our knowledge of the nature and influence of the prophetic tradition in Islamicate medicine, and Twelver Shi'i prophetic medicine in particular, is clear. The publication of the English translation of this compilation of Twelver medical hadith ought to be the occasion for commencing the reconsideration of the prophetic medical tradition, both for scholars in the field and others interested both in Islamicate history as well as in the theory and practice of Twelver Shi 'ism in particular. The Muhammadi Trust is to be thanked for its contribution to this process.

Andrew J. Newman

The Wellcome Unit for the History of Medicine

The University of Oxford

[xxix] On the earliest collections of Twelver narrations, see Etan Kohlberg, 'Al-Usul al-Arba'umi'a', *Journal of studies in Arabic and Islam*, 10 (1987), 128-66.

[xxx] See J.-C. Vadet's article on him in *EI*/II, 3: 872-3, and also Ibn Abi Usaybi'ah, *'Uyun al-Anba' fi Tabaqat al-Atibba* (Beirut, 1401/1981), 2:123-37.

INTRODUCTION

The Imams of the Ahl al-Bayt, peace be upon them, were as concerned with treating the body as they were with treating the soul, and their regard for the soundness of the body was similar to their regard for the refinement of the soul.

They were physicians of the soul and the body, and Muslims would consult them for their physical illnesses as they would for curing their spiritual sicknesses. This collection of hadith is ample evidence of that. The Imams, peace be upon them, were not merely conveyors of religious regulations and legislation, but were leaders committed to caring for the Muslims, equally concerned — if such a term is correct — with the health of their bodies and their beliefs, such that they encouraged the learning of medicine (*al-tibb*). In his comprehensive statement on the divisions of knowledge ['Ali b. Abu Talib (d, 40/661)] Amir al-Mu'mimin, peace be upon him, combined it [medicine] with the knowledge of jurisprudence (*al-fiqh*), saying: 'There are four kinds of knowledge: jurisprudence for religions, medicine for bodies, grammar for languages, and [study of] the stars to recognise the seasons.'

Much has been related from the Imams in collections [of *hadith*] on medicine and preserving good health, just as there are more descriptions of various remedies related from them. Here for the reader are a small number of their sayings which are general rules for preserving health and physical well-being:

Amir al-Mu'minin said to his son, al-Hasan [b. 'Ali b. Abu Talib (d. 49/669)], peace be upon him: 'Shall I teach you four general principles so that you may have no need of medicine?' Al-Hasan replied: 'Yes indeed, O Amir al-Mu'minin.' He said: 'Do not eat unless you are hungry, cease eating while you still have a desire to eat, chew your food well, and, after you awaken from sleep, relieve yourself If you practise these measures, you will not require medicine'.

Amir al-Mu'minin 'Ali, peace be upon him, also said: 'The Qur'an contains a verse which sums np all medicine: *"Eat and drink but do not be prodigal."' (Qur'an 7:31).*

Zarr b. Hubaysh said that 'Amir al-Mu'minin related four statements on medicine which, had they been uttered by Galen and Hippocrates, a hundred pieces of paper would have been decorated with their words. These were: 'Guard against the cold (*al-bard*) at its onset, and face it at its end, for its effect on the body (*al-badan*) is similar to its effect on trees. Its onset withers them and its end causes them to leaf.'

He also said: 'There is no healthiness with gluttony'.

Al-Baqir, [the fifth Imam, Abu Ja'far Muhammad b. 'Ali (d. 117/735)], peace be upon him, said: 'The medicine of the Arabs is of seven kinds: cupping (*al-hujjama*), administering clysters (*al-huqna*), steam baths (*al-hammam*), inhaling medications through the nose (*al-su'ut*), vomiting (*al-qay'*), taking honey (*al-'asal*), and, the final remedy, cauterization (*al-kayy*). Sometimes, added to that is [the application of] lime (*al-nura*).'

Al-Sadiq [the sixth imam, Abu 'Abd Allah Ja'far b, Muhammad (d 148/765)], peace be upon him, said: 'If people eat moderately, their bodies will be healthy.' He also said: 'Three things make a person fat, and three things make him lean. As for those that make one fat, they are an excess of steam baths, smelling sweet scents, and wearing soft [i.e. fine] clothes. Those that make one lean are the excessive eating of eggs (*al-bayd*), diarrhoea (*al-ishal*), and filling the belly (*al-butn*) with food.'

Introduction

Abu Hafan — Yuhanna b. Masawayh, the well known Christian physician — related that Ja'far b. Muhammad, peace be upon him, had said: 'The natural constituents (*al-taba'i'*) [of the body] are four: blood (*al-dam*), which is the slave — and sometimes the slave kills the master; wind (*al-rih*), which is the enemy— if one door is closed to him he comes to you from another; phlegm (*al-balgham*), which is the king, and endeavours to deceive; and bile (*al-mirra*), which is the earth - when it shakes, it shakes those on it.' Ibn Masawayh [also] said: 'Ali drew upon what Galen felt to give this description.'

Al-Sadiq, peace be upon him, said: 'Walking causes the patient to suffer a relapse. When my father [i.e. al-Baqir] fell ill he was dressed and carried to fulfil his need, that is, to perform the ablution (*al-wudu'*). He would say: "Walking causes the patient to suffer a relapse."'

Al-Kazim [the seventh Imam, Abu al- Hasan Musa b Ja'far (d. 183/799)], peace be upon him, said: 'Stay away from the treatment of physicians (*al-attiba'*) as long as you are well, for it is similar to building — a little of it leads to much.' He also said: 'Abstaining from certain foods (*al-lahmiyya*) is the chief medication. The abdomen (*al-ma'ida*) is the house of illness. Accustom (the body) to what you are used to.'

Abu al-Hasan, peace be upon him, said: 'There is no medication which does not stir up an illness, and there is nothing more beneficial for the body than withholding from it all except what it requires.'

Al-Ridha' [the eighth Imam, Abu al-Hasan 'Ali b. Musa (d. 203/818)], peace be upon him, said: 'Had the dead person been massaged, he would have lived. Why did you disclaim that?'

They, peace be upon them, said: 'Avoid medications as long as your body can bear the illness. When it cannot bear the illness, then take medications.'

Introduction

These are some of the things mentioned by the Imams, peace be upon them, regarding medical treatment, and they summarise the general principles and fundamentals of preserving health. Cautioning against gluttony is the basis of treatment, moderation in eating according to the needs and soundness of the body, the requirement for rest and calm after suffering from an illness, abstaining from certain foods, accustoming the body to routine, cautioning against using medications without need and more than is necessary, explaining the natural constituents and elements of the body and, in fact, even pointing to artificial respiration, etc., is all general medical advice and does not apply to a particular individual or country, or to a particular era.

The medical treatments related from the Imams in this book of ours, and others, contain medical preparations and prescriptions of specific proportions and particular qualities. They sometimes deal with particular cases, observation of the condition of the patient, the climate (*al-taqs*) of his province and the soil (*al-turba*) of the place where he lives. The answer of one of the Imams in reply to the patient's question, and the medication, may have been given after considering the above-mentioned points. This is a matter which should be taken into account, since variations in the climate and seasons of different countries require specific treatment for certain patients. For example, it would not be correct to use a medical treatment of the same proportion and quality for a hot country as for a cold country, and vice versa.

That, then, may have been the reason for the variations in some medical prescriptions, or in the ones whose significance is not known. Our distinguished ancient and modern scholars have mentioned that. Here are some of their statements on the subject for the reader:

Introduction

Al-Shaykh al-Saduq, Muhammad b. 'Ali b. Babawayh (d. 381/991-2), may Allah be pleased with him, said: "Our view on the reports on medicine is that they comprise the following: those based on the climates of Mecca and Medina, which cannot be applied to other climates; those related by the Imam based on his knowledge of the disposition of the questioner, and he would not have known his disposition if he were not more knowledgeable about it than he; those forged by opponents to give the sect a bad name among the people; those which were overlooked by the transmitters: those which were partly memorised, and partly forgotten; and those narrated about honey, that it is a cure for all illnesses. The latter is correct, but the meaning of it is that it is a cure for every cold illness. [Similarly] those mentioned about washing with cold water (*al-ma'*) for those with hemorrhoids; that is, if the hemorrhoids (*al-bawasir*) arc as a result of the heat, etc."

Al-Shaykh Mufid Muhammad h. Muhammad b. al-Nu'man (d. 413/1022) may Allah be pleased with him, said: 'Medicine is correct (*sahih*), and knowledge of it is established (*thabit*), and is through revelation (*al-wahy*). The religious scholars have only taken it from the Prophets. There is no way of gaining knowledge of the true nature of the illness except aurally, and no way of recognising the remedy except by being granted success [by Allah]. It is established that the way to that the latter is hearing it from the One who has knowledge of the Unseen.

It is narrated that the two al-Sadiqs [the Imams Ja'far al-Sadiq and Musa al-Kazim], peace be upon them, explained the statement of Amir al-Mu'minin, peace be upon him, that "The abdomen is the house of illness, abstaining from certain foods is the chief medication, and each body is accustomed to its conditioning" [as meaning that] something which may be beneficial for an illness which affects certain people in one region may kill others in the same region who use it for that same illness. What is suitable for

Introduction

people with one habit is not suitable for those whose habits differ, etc.'

Al-Shaykh Majlisi Muhammad Baqir b. Muhammad Taqi (d.1111/1699), may Allah be pleased with him. said: 'Certain medications which are unsuitable for the illness [may be used] as a trial and a test, so that the sincere believer whose faith is strong can be distinguished from the one who claims to follow Islam or one whose conviction is weak. If the believer uses it it benefits him not because of his particular qualities and his natural disposition, but because of his having turned to the One from whom it came, and because his faith and the sincerity of his adherence, as in the case of [an individual's] benefiting from the soil of the grave of al-Husayn [b. 'Ali b. Abu Talib (d. 61/680)] peace be upon him, and from invocations [*al-'udhat*) and supplications (*al-ad'iya*).'

This is supported by the fact that we found a group of sincere Shi 'a whose actions and medical treatments are based on reports narrated from the Imams, peace be upon them. They did not consult a physician and they were healthier and lived longer than those who did consult physicians and medical practitioners (*al-mu'alajun*). Similarly there are those who pay no attention to the positions of the stars, nor consult astrologers, but put their trust in their Lord and seek protection from ill-omened times, and from the evil of trials and enemies with Qur'anic verses and prayers. They are in better circumstances, more prosperous, and more hopeful than those who in matters both small and great take recourse to choosing times, and by that seek protection from evils and afflictions.

There is another aspect of this book of ours which will attract the reader's attention, and will perhaps arouse his curiosity. He will ask: What is the point of mentioning invocations, prayers, and charms (*al-ruqqa*) in this book? What has this to do with bodily medical treatment?

Introduction

We must stop for a moment with the reader to look together at the effect of these on treating the body. The Imams of the Ahl al-Bayt, peace be upon them, in their surpassing men in knowledge — knowledge in its widest and most inclusive sense — relied on an inexhaustible source: they learnt it from the Messenger of Allah, blessings of Allah be on him and his family. He in turn learnt it through revelation from the One who brought into existence illnesses and medications, diseases and cures.

Undoubtedly they [the Imams] understood the illnesses of the souls as well as the illnesses of the body and their outward symptoms, for they described cures [to heal] the soul of its piercing pains and its stifling agonies just as they described medications for the other diseases of the body. The best physician is one who can diagnose the illness, recognise its progress and cause, and prescribe treatment for its cure.

Many illnesses are the result of psychological suffering, due to anxiety, sorrow, agitation, loneliness, fear, etc. These certainly affect the body. This is evident, and I do not think any will deny it. How can we, when every day we experience trials and difficulties which cause anxiety and distress? If their psychological effects intensify, we experience its symptoms in the body, such as headaches, fever and other ailments arising from nervous tension and nervous breakdowns. These symptoms and illnesses are a definite result of those psychological sufferings, though they do not result from them alone but have other causes as well.

Therefore there is no objection — indeed it is good— to treat the illness through psychological and spiritual means, in order to put an end to the suffering and to cleanse its point of origin. In this way the soul is freed of its problems peacefully, trusting in the Regulator of its affairs who has knowledge of its good, and from Whom the probity and the remedy is sought. When the expected healing comes about, the sufferings of the soul subside and it is at rest. When the soul is tranquil and composed, well-being pervades the afflicted parts of the body as a direct result.

The reader cannot disavow psychological and spiritual medicine and the extent of the influence of both in treating many internal and mental illnesses, even skin disorders and endemic and genetic diseases. How many testimonies of this have we read and heard which have been wholly confirmed by modern science? Therefore, why should the Imam, who wishes for the good health of a Muslim afflicted with an illness caused by psychological suffering which persists in spite of treatment, not help him to hasten his recovery? Why, seeing that the symptoms of the patient arc a compound of psychological ailments and physical symptoms, should he not treat the soul and the body at the same time?

He would prescribe, for example, a preparation of drugs for healing the body, and then heal the soul with the blessing of the verses from the Noble Qur'an, or with one of the Names of Allah, the Sublime, or with an invocation seeking protection in Allah, the Sublime, imploring Him through the angels near to Him, or His Prophets who have brought the Message, or His honoured servants.

Let us look at the prescriptions of this kind of treatment. Are they anything other what we have described and which we ignore when seeking a cure, though they are the source of healing? The Mighty Qur'an has verses which clearly state that it is a healing for the believers. These include, for example, the statement of Allah, the Mighty and Sublime:

O men, now there has come to you an admonition from your Lord, and a healing for what is in the breasts, and a guidance, and a mercy to the believers (10:57); and the Sublime and Exalted's statement: And We send down, of the Qur'an, that which is a healing and a mercy to the believers; and the unbelievers it increases not, except in loss (17:82); and His statement, Blessed be

Introduction

His Name: If We had made it a barbarous Qur'an, they would have said, Why are its signs not distinguished? What, barbarous and Arabic? Say: To the believers it is a guidance and a healing. (41:44)

The Qur'an also has many commands to pray and ask for help, besides its other noble verses and mighty secrets, which the Imams of the Ahl al-Bayt, peace be upon them, knew and had learnt from the Messenger of Allah, blessings of Allah be on him and his family. No one was more knowledgeable about the secrets of the Qur'an and the sources of its blessings than they, for it had been revealed to their forefathers and their house, and they were its guardians. 'No one understands the Qur'an except those to whom it was addressed.'

By seeking healing in the verses of the Noble Qur'an, seeking protection with the Names of Allah, the Exalted, and seeking intercession through it, and praying to Him, it was endeavoured to purify the soul of its impurities, solve its difficulties and problems, and cure its pains.

Praying itself, being conditional on the serenity and tranquility of the soul, is not merely humility and submission or defeatism in the face of bitter reality — as it is mistakenly described. On the contrary, it is returning to the realm of reality itself, and abiding forever in it. Which of us will deny that, or will not believe it, even if he experiences it only once in his life? He is afraid of every fearful thing, seeks refuge from every reprehensible thing, and asks for more good from the One in whose Hand is the regulation of the affairs and the decree. From Him he hopes for deliverance from his problems, freedom from his pains, and security in his repose. So why should we not experience a spiritual joy at the effects of prayer when we turn to and use it as a natural remedy?

Introduction

In addition to their being mentioned in the Noble Qur'an, what confirms the fact that these prayers, invocations, and treatments are psychological cures, is that, if used, most of them are guaranteed to be followed by success. This assurance and guarantee of well-being is in itself the best psychological treatment, causing the patient to experience a sense of tranquility and to seek it in the words of those verses, prayers and invocations.

THE INTEREST OF THE COMPANIONS IN THE MEDICINE OF THE IMAMS

The authors of the biographies of the Imams' companions and the transmitters of their *hadith* have referred to many writings on medicine. There are more references to such individuals having written 'a book on medicine' than a book on any other subject. When we examine the external evidence we find this [phrase] refers to 'transmitted medicine'. At the same time the biographies of these personalities show they were interested in *hadith* of the Ahl al-Bayt. They collected the *hadith* into special books and classified them according to their particular subject matter, one of which was medicine.

There were also reports transmitted from some of those books on medicine into certain collections of *hadith* which are extant. These *hadith* were authentic in the view of the authors, and were from the Ahl al-Bayt and related to medicine. There is no evidence linking many of those writers to the physicians of their time, or indicating they had learnt and obtained their information from the physicians or studied under them. Had that been so, the biographers would have mentioned it, as they did in the biographies of many who had been influenced by Greek or Indian medicine, or who had acquired knowledge from the ancient medical writings.

Introduction

Thus, we can say that their compilations were medical narrations transmitted from the Imams of the Ahl al-Bayt. We will now list those who collected such reports and mention a few of those authorities who were concerned with collecting the *hadith* of the Ahl al-Bayt on the subject of medicine:

1. Ahmad b. Muhammad b. al-Husayn b. al-Hasan Du'l al-Qummi, d. 350/958-9.

2. Abu 'Abd Allah Ahmad b. Muhammad b. Sayyar al-Basri, secretary to the family of Tahir. He lived in the time of Imam al-'Askari [the eleventh Imam, Abu Muhammad Hasan b. 'Ali (d. 260/873-3)], peace be upon him. [Ahmad b. 'Ali b. Ahmad] al-Najashi (d. 450/1058-9) has related his book via three intermediaries. Some hadith on medicine have been narrated from him by al-Saduq in *al-Khisal,* al-Barqi [Ahmad b. Muhammad b. Khalid (d. late third/ninth century)] in his *Al-Mahasin*, and other authors, based on his chain of transmitters from the Imams, peace be upon them.

3. Al Husayn b. Bistam b. Sabur al-Zayyat — one of the compilers of the present book.

4 Abu Ahmad 'Abd al-'Aziz b. Yahya b. Ahmad b. 'Isa al-Jaludi, Shaykh Abu'l-Qasim Ja'far b. Muhammad b. Qulawayh, d. 367/977-9.

5. 'Abd Allah b. Bistam b. Sabur al-Zayyat- - the second of the compilers of this book.

6. 'Abd Allah b. Ja'far b. al-Husayn b. Malik b. Jami' al-Humayri, one of the transmitters of hadith of the third and fourth centuries [/ninth and tenth centuries] and author of the book *Qurb al-Isnad*, published by the al-Haydariyya press, and others.

7. Abu'l-Hasan 'Ali b. al-Hasan b. Faddal b. 'Umar b. Ayman al-Fathi.

8. Abu'l-Hasan b. 'Ali b. al-Husayn b. Musa b. Babawayh al-Qummi, d. 329/941, Shaykh of Qumm and father of al-Shaykh al-Saduq. The latter authored *Man la yahduruhu al-faqih*, one of the four *hadith* collections. Al-Najashi narrated on his authority from his Shaykh 'Abbas b. 'Umar al-Kuludhani, and his chain of transmission was excellent.

9. Abu Ja'far Muhammad b. Ahmad b. Muhammad b. Raja' al-Bajali al-Kufi. who died in 266/880 on his return from Mecca.

10. Abu Ja'far Muhammad b. Ahmad b. Yahya b. 'Imran b. 'Abd Allah b. Sa'd b. Malik al-Ash'ari al-Qummi, the author of *Nawadir al-Hikma*, well known as Dabba Shabib.

11. Abu 'Abd Allah Muhammad b. 'Ubayd Allah al-Jannabi al-Barqi, known as Majilawayh.

12. Abu'l-Hasan Musa b. al-Hasan b.'Amir b. 'Imran b. 'Abd Allah b Sa'd al-Ash'ari al-Qummi.

13. Abu'l-Nadr Muhammad b. Mas'ud b. Muhammad b. 'Ayyash al-Sulami al-Samarqandi.

A number of personalities who came after the companions of the Imams, peace be upon them, also collected these *hadith*. The names of a few of them are:

1. Al-Sayyid Abu Muhammad Zayd b. 'Ali b. al-Hasan al-Husayni, a student of al-Shaykh [Muhammad b. Hasan] al-Tusi [d. 460/1067] and teacher of the father of Muntajab al-Din ['Ali b. Ubayd Allah (d. after 585/1189)], the latter being the author of *Al-Fihrist*.

Introduction

2. Al-Shaykh Ahmad b Salih al-Biladi al-Bahrani al-Jahrami al-Maskan, d. 1124/1712. He wrote the *Al-Tibb al-Ahmadi* in which he cited traditions narrated about medicine. Al-Shaykh Yusuf [b. Ahmad] al- Bahrani (d. 1186/1772) said in *Lu'lu' al-Bahrayn*: 'I have a copy of this'; and he said: 'I saw in a copy of it in his handwriting that he was born in 1057/1656.'

3. Al-Sayyid 'Abd Allah Shubr al-Kazimi, d. 1242/1827. He wrote a book on the medicine of the Imams which our Shaykh [Agha Buzurg al-Tehrani] al-Razi [d. 1389/1970] mentioned in his *Al-Dhari'a* (xv:140), and said: 'It is approximately 11,000 verses [in length]. He collected a book of medical traditions which is twice [the size of] his first book.'

4. Muhammad Qasim b. Ghulam 'Ali, the physician. He composed a book on the medicine of the Imams, of which his [own] copy can be found in the Radawiya Library.

5. Muhammad Sharif b. Muhammad Sadiq al-Khawatunabadi. He composed a commentary on *Tibb al-A'imma*, the *Sharh Tibb al-Nabi*, and another commentary, *Sharh Tibb Al-Ridha'*. All of them are mentioned in his book *Hafiz al-Abdan*, which he wrote in 1121/1709.

6. Al-Sayyid Mahmud, whose father was Sarkhi, a contemporary. He wrote the *Mafatih al-Sihha*, in which he expounded on the medicine of the Prophet, blessings of Allah be on him, the medical treatment of [Imam] Al-Ridha', peace be upon him, and that of the Imams, peace be upon them. It is published in Persian.

Introduction

THE SONS OF BISTAM

These were al-Husayn and Abu 'Atab 'Abd Allah, the two sons of Bistam b. Sabur al-Zayyat of Nisabur. Of them al-Najashi wrote:

Al-Husayn b. Bistam — [Ahmad b. Muhammad b. al-Hasan al-Jawhari] Abu 'Abd Allah b. 'Ayyash [Ibn 'Ayyash] said: 'He is al-Husayn b. Bistam b. Sabur al-Zayyat, He and his brother, Abu 'Atab, compiled a book on medicine. It is very useful and beneficial and deals with medicine based on foods and their benefits, charms and invocations.' He said: 'Al-Sharif Abu l-Hasan Salih b. al-Husayn al-Nawfali narrated [this book] from my father from both Abu 'Atab and al-Husayn.'

'Abd Allah b. Bistam Abu 'Atab, the brother of al-Husayn b. Bistam, previously mentioned in the section on al-Husayn — who, with his brother, composed a book on medicine. He is 'Abd Allah b. Bistam b. Sabur al-Zayyat.'

The *Rijal* of al-Najashi provides a biography of their father and his brothers: Bistam b. Sabur al-Zayyat Abu l-Husayn al-Wasiti, was a trustworthy *mawla*, and his brothers Zakariyya, Ziyad and Hafs were all trustworthy. They narrated *hadith* on the authority of [Imam] Abu 'Abd Allah and [Imam] Abu al-Hasan, peace be upon them. Abu al-'Abbas - that is Ibn 'Uqda [Ahmad b. Sa'id b. 'Uqda] - and others have mentioned them in writings on transmitters of *hadith*. He composed a book which a number of people have narrated from him. 'Ali b. Ahmad told us that Muhammad b. al-Hasan narrated the book from 'Ali b. Isma'il from Safwan from Bistam.'

The two of them transmitted reports in their book from of a group of people. Together they narrated reports from Muhammad b. Khalaf, describing him as being one of the religious scholars of the family of Muhammad, and from Ahmad b. Ribah, the physician. Al-Husayn alone narrated from 'Abd Allah b. Musa. His brother, 'Abd Allah, narrated, on his own, from a number of people, who were: Ibrahim b. al-Nadr, one of the children of Maytham al-Tammar ('Abd Allah narrated from him and said: 'We were together in Qazwin'), Ibrahim b. Muhammad al-Awdi, Ishaq b. Ibrahim, 'Abd Allah b. Ibrahim, Muhammad b. Razin, Muhammad b. Isma'il b. Hatim al-Tamimi, Muhammad b. Zurayq, Abu Zakariya Yahya b. Abu Bakr Adam, and Kamil.

It is clear from this that the two brothers were from a learned family which transmitted the *hadith* of the Ahl al-Bayt, and were regarded as trustworthy people in narrations. Al-Najashi hesitated in narrating the report of Ibn 'Ayyash, in spite of the fact that the latter was a friend of both himself and his father, because of a tradition of his Shaykhs which regarded him as being a weak transmitter, and he asked for God's mercy for him after that. [However,] neither their book nor the authors themselves ought to be denigrated or considered weak because of that. Indeed Ibn 'Ayyash has well known books from which our associates have transmitted *hadith* and which they have accepted.

Al-Sayyid Hasan al-Sadr, may Allah have mercy on him, mentioned him [Ibn 'Ayyash] in his *Ta'sis al-Shi'a* and praised him greatly. His narrations are regarded as acceptable, and among them is his narration of the present book by these two individuals.

In view of the small number of its copies and the fact that it was published only once several years ago, on the instructions of the late Ayat Allah al-Sayyid al-Burujirdi [d. 1380/1961], may Allah encompass him with His mercy, it was published again in Iran, along with two other books. He, may Allah have mercy on him, confined himself in his introduction to citing al-Najashi, pointing out that there was nothing in that report which would lead him to consider the book unsound.

Introduction

We have quoted the comment of al-Najashi for the reader, and there is clearly nothing to indicate that. The fact that the book was not mentioned [by al-Najashi] is not sufficient to consider it unsound.

This is particularly so, since our distinguished Shaykhs have narrated from it and have agreed with its being narrated and have quoted from it in their books. We direct the reader to consult [for example,] *Al-Fusul al-Muhimma* by al-Shaykh al-Hurr al-'Amili [d. 1104/1693], may Allah have mercy on him. He has included selections of it in various chapters of works related to medicine and similar topics. Al-Shaykh al-Majlisi, may Allah be pleased with him, has also cited much from this book in various chapters of [vol. XIV of] his *Bihar al-Anwar*.

Professor Muhammad Kazim al-Katabi may Allah give him success, has requested that the book be reprinted so that it is easily available. He is deserving of thanks and worthy of prayer for — may Allah reward him with the best reward. We are grateful to him. Praise be to Allah for His success and His guidance, and we ask Him to accept from us and from him. He is the One Who gives success and fulfillment.

Muhammad Mahdi al-Sayyid Hasan al-Khirsan

al-Najaf al-Ashraf

7 Rabi' al-Thani, 1375/1956

TIBB AL-A'IMMA

Tibb al-A'imma

In the Name of Allah, the Merciful the Compassionate

Praise be to Allah, as it befits Him to be praised, and the blessings of Allah be on Muhammad and his Family, the good, the pure, the chosen ones.

INTRODUCTION TO BOOK

This book comprises the medicine of the Ahl al-Bayt peace be on them.

Abu 'Atab and al-Husayn, the sons of Bistam, narrated from Muhammad b. Khalaf of Qazvin — one of the scholars of the Ahl al-Bayt — from al-Hasan b. 'Ali al-Washsha' from 'Abd Allah b. Sinan from his brother Muhammad from Ja'far al-Sadiq from his father from his grandfather from al-Husayn b. 'Ali, peace be upon them, who said:

'Amir al-Mu'minin, peace be upon him, visited Salman al-Farisi and said: "O Abu 'Abd Allah, how is your illness?" He replied: "O Amir al-Mu'minin, praise be to Allah, I complain to you of much distress." Amir al-Mu'minin said: "Do not be distressed, O Abu 'Abd Allah, for there is not one of our Shi'a afflicted with a pain (*waja'*), but that it is for a sin previously committed by him, and the pain is a purification for him." Salman replied: "If it is as you say then there is no recompense in it for us except to be purified." 'Ali, peace be upon him, said: "O Salman, there is recompense in it for you in enduring it patiently and beseeching Allah, magnified is His Name. For, by praying to Him in these two ways, He will credit you [with] good deeds and raise you by degrees. As for the pain, it is especially for the purification and expiation of sins." He [al-Husayn] said: Salman kissed his forehead and wept, saying: "Were it not for you, O Amir al-Mu'minin, who would distinguish these things for us?"

Abu 'Atab 'Abd Allah b. Bistam narrated from Muhammad b. Khalaf from al-Washsha' from 'Abd Allah b. Sinan from his brother Muhammad b. Sinan, who said that Ja'far b. Muhammad, peace be upon him. said: 'There is no one who, when fearing affliction, precedes it with prayer except that Allah turns away that affliction from him. Do you not know that Amir al-Mu'minin, peace be upon him, said: "The Prophet, blessings of Allah be upon him and his family, said: 'O 'Ali.' He replied: 'At your service, O Messenger of Allah.' He said: 'Prayer repels affliction, and that has been conclusively established.'"'

Al-Washsha' said: I asked 'Abd Allah b. Sinan: 'Is there a particular prayer for that?' He replied: 'I asked al-Sadiq, peace be upon him, about that and he said: "Yes, the oppressed Shi'a have a particular prayer for every illness. Those endowed with perception have no particular prayer, for the prayer of those endowed with perception is not veiled."'

'Abd Allah b. Bistam narrated from Muhammad b. Khalaf from al-Washsha' who said: Al-Ridha', peace be upon him, said to me: "If one of you falls ill, let him permit the people to call on him, for the prayer of each one will be answered." Then he said: "O Washsha'". I replied: "At your service, my lord and master." He said: "Have you understood what I told you?" I replied: "O son of the Messenger of Allah, yes." He said: "You did not understand. Do you know who 'the people' are?" I replied: "Yes indeed. The community (*umma*) of Muhammad, blessings of Allah and peace be upon him and his family." He said: "'The people' are the Shi'a."

Abu 'Abd Allah al-Husayn b. Bistam narrated from Muhammad b. Khalaf from al-Hasan b. 'Ali from 'Abd Allah b. Sinan from his brother Muhammad b. Sinan from al-Mufaddal b. 'Umar, who said: I heard al-Sadiq, peace be upon him, say on the authority of al-Baqir, peace be upon him: 'When a believer falls ill, Allah reveals to the companion at his left hand: "Do not record a single sin against my servant as long as he is in my custody, and in my hold." And He reveals to the companion at his right hand: "Write for my servant on his page of good deeds what you would record for him when he was well."'

THE MEASURE OF REWARD FOR EACH ILLNESS

Abu 'Atab narrated from Muhammad b. Khalaf — and I think al-Husayn [b. Bistam] also related to us — from al-Washsha' from 'Abd Allah b. Sinan from Muhammad b. Sinan from al-Sadiq, peace be upon him, who said: "One night's sleeplessness during an illness that afflicts a believer is [equal to] a year's worship."

From him from Ja'far b. Muhammad, peace be upon him, from 'Ali b. al-Husayn, peace be upon him, from his father, peace be upon him, who said: 'I heard the Messenger of Allah, blessings on him and his family, say "One night's fever expiates a year's sins."'

By this chain of transmitters from 'Abd Allah b. Sinan, who said: I was in Mecca and had kept secret something no one but Allah, the Mighty and Sublime, knew. When I arrived in Medina, I called on Abu 'Abd Allah al-Sadiq, peace be upon him. He looked at me, then said: "Ask Allah's forgiveness for that which you have concealed and do not make known." I said: "I ask Allah's forgiveness." He ['Abd Allah b. Sinan] said: The medial vein (*al-'irq al-madini*) on one of my feet (*al-rijl*) had become prominent. When I bid him [al-Sadiq] farewell— that was before the vein became prominent— he said to me, "Whosoever suffers and is patient, the decree of Allah credits him with a reward of a thousand martyrs."

'Abd Allah b Sinan said: When I reached the second stage [on the return journey] the vein became prominent, and I continued suffering for months. When I performed the Hajj the next year, I called on Abu 'Abd Allah, peace he upon him, and said to him: "Invoke Allah's protection for my foot." I told him that this foot was paining me. He replied: "Never mind this foot. Give me your healthy foot and Allah will heal you." So I stretched the other foot out before him and he invoked Allah's protection over it. When I stood up and bid him farewell and reached the second stage, the vein became prominent in the foot. I said: "By Allah, he did not protect it, but only caused an affliction." I suffered for three nights, then Allah, the Mighty and Sublime, cured me and the invocation benefited me.

The invocation is: "In the Name of Allah, the Merciful, the Compassionate: O Allah, I ask You by Your Pure, Immaculate, Most Holy and Blessed Name, by Which whoever asks of You, You grant him, and by Which whoever calls on You, You answer him, to bless Muhammad and his family, and to heal the suffering in my head (*al-ra's*), my hearing (*al-sam'*), my sight (*al-basar*), my belly, my back (*al-zahr*), my hand (*al-yad*) my foot, my body (*al-jasad*), and in all my organs (*al-a'da'*) and limbs (*al-jawarih*). Surely You are Gracious to whomsoever You will, and You are Powerful over all things."

He said: Al-Khazzaz al-Razi narrated from Faddala, from Aban b. 'Uthman from Abu Hamza al-Thumali from al-Baqir, peace be upon him, from Amir al-Mu'minin, peace be upon him, who said: 'Whosoever is afflicted with a pain in his body, let him invoke protection for himself and say: "I take refuge in the Might of Allah and His Power over things. I seek protection for myself in the Omnipotent of the heavens. I seek protection for myself in the One with Whose Name no disease harms. I seek refuge for myself in the One Whose Name is a blessing and a cure." If he recites that, no pain or illness will afflict him.'

'Ali b. Ibrahim al-Wasiti narrated from Mahbub from Muhammad b. Sulayman al-Awdi from Abu Jarud from Abu Ishaq from al-Harith al-A'war, who said: I complained to Amir al-Mu'minin, peace be upon him, of aches and pains in my body. He said: 'When anyone of you suffers [from pain], let him recite: "In the Name of Allah and by Allah, and blessings of Allah on the Messenger of Allah and his family. I take refuge from the evil that I suffer in the Might of Allah and His Power over what He wills." If he recites that, Allah will turn away the affliction from him, if He, the Exalted, wills.'

FOR PAIN IN THE HEAD

Sahl b Ahmad narrated from 'Ali b. Nu'man from Ibn Muskan from 'Abd al-Rahman al-Qusayr from Abu Ja'far al-Baqir, peace be upon him, who said: 'Whoever suffers from a complaint of the head, let him put his hand on it and recite seven times: "I take refuge in Allah, in Whose trust is that which is on the land and in the sea, in the heavens and the earth, and He is the All-hearing, the All-knowing." He will be relieved of the pain.'

Hariz Abu Ayyub al-Jurjani narrated from Muhammad b. Abu Nasr from Tha'laba from 'Amr b. Yazid al-Sayqal from Ja'far b. Muhammad b. 'Ali b. al-Husayn b. 'Ali b. Abu Talib, peace be upon him, that he [al-Sayqal] said: I complained to him of a pain in my head, and of my suffering from it night and day.

He [Ja'far b. Muhammad] said: 'Place your hand on it and say seven times: "In the Name of Allah, with Whose Name nothing on the earth or in the heavens causes injury. He is the All-hearing, the All-knowing. O Allah. I seek refuge in You from that which Muhammad, blessings on him and his family, sought refuge for himself." [The pain] will subside, by the authority of Allah, the Exalted.'

Tibb al-A'imma

'Ali b. 'Urwa al-Ahwazi, a narrator of the teachings of the Ahl al-Bayt, peace be upon them, narrated from al-Daylami from Dawud al-Raqqi from Musa b. Ja'far, peace be upon him, that he [Dawud] said: I said to him; "O son of the Messenger of Allah, I suffer constantly from a complaint in my head, and sometimes it keeps me awake at nights and distracts me from performing the night prayer." He replied: "O Dawud, when you experience any of that [pain], pass your hand over it and say: 'I take refuge in Allah, and seek protection for my self from all that afflicts me, in the Name of Allah, the Mighty, and His Perfect Words, which neither the righteous nor the ungodly can disregard. I seek protection for myself with Allah, the Mighty and Sublime, and with the Messenger of Allah and his family, the pure, the chosen ones. O Allah, by their claim over You, protect me from this suffering of mine.' It will not afflict you again."

Abu Salt al-Harawi narrated from Al-Ridha', peace be upon him, from his father from al-Baqir, peace be upon him, who said; 'Teach our Shi'a to recite the following for a pain in the head: "O Taha, O Dharr, O Tamana, O Tannat". They are Sublime Names and have an authority given by Allah, the Exalted and Sublime. Allah will turn that [pain] away from them.'

'Abd Allah b. Bistam narrated from Ishaq b. Ibrahim from Abu al-Hasan al-'Askari, peace be upon him, that he [Ishaq] said: I was with him [al-'Askari] one day when one of our brothers complained to him, saying: "O son of the Messenger of Allah, my family suffers much from this accursed pain." He asked: "And what is it?" The man replied: "Pains in the head." He said: "Take a cup of water and recite over it:

Have not the unbelievers then beheld that the heavens and the earth were a mass all sewn up, and then We unstitched them and of water fashioned every living thing? Will they not believe? (21:30).

Then drink it and pain will not afflict them, Allah, the Exalted, willing."

Tamim b. Ahmad al-Sayrafi narrated from Muhammad b. Khalid al-Barqi from 'Ali b. al-Nu'man from Dawud b. Farqad and Mu'alla b. Khunays, who both said: Abu 'Abd Allah, peace be upon him, said: "combing the hair on the cheeks strengthens the teeth (*al-adras*); combing the beard dispels infectious diseases (*al-waba'*); combing loose locks of hair dispels anxieties in the breast (*al-sadr*); combing the eyebrows is a safeguard against leprosy (*al-judham*), and combing the head stops phlegm."

A MEDICATION FOR PHLEGM

He said: 'Then he described a medication for phlegm. He said: "Take equal party of Byzantine mastic (*'ilk rumi*), frankincense (*al-kundur*), wild thyme (*sa'tar*), bishop's weed (*al-nankhwah*) and fennel flower (*al-shuniz*). Grind each of them separately into fine powder. Then sift them, put them together, and pound them until they are well mixed. Add honey to the mixture and take the equivalent of a hazelnut (*al-bunduqa*) of it every day and at night before sleeping, It will be beneficial, Allah, the Exalted, willing."'

'Abd Allah b. Mas'ud al-Yamani narrated from at-Taryani from Khalid al-Qammat that 'Ali b. Musa Al-Ridha', peace be upon him, dictated these ingredients for phlegm. He said: 'Take the weight of one *mithqal* of yellow myrobalan (*ihlilaj asfar*), two *mithqal* of mustard (*khardal*) and one *mithqal* of pyrethrum (*'aqir qarha*), Grind them to a fine powder. Brush your teeth with it on an empty stomach (*'ala al-riq*). It will cleanse the phlegm, make the breath fragrant, and strengthen the teeth, Allah, the Exalted, willing.'

AN INVOCATION FOR HEADACHE

Muhammad b. Ja'far al-Bursi narrated from Muhammad b. Yahya al-Armani from Muhammad b. Sinan al-Sinani from Yunus b. Zabyan from al-Mufaddal b. 'Umar from Abu 'Abd Allah al-Sadiq, peace be upon him, who said: This is an invocation revealed by Jibra'il, peace be upon him, to the Prophet, peace be upon him, when the latter was suffering from a headache (*al-suda'*). Jibra'il said: "O Muhammad, take refuge from your headache with this invocation, Allah will relieve you of it." Then he said: "O Muhammad, whosoever takes refuge with this invocation seven times for any pain that afflicts him, Allah will heal him if He wills.

Pass your hand over the painful area and say: 'In the Name of Allah, our Lord, Whose mention is glorified in the heavens, our Lord Whose command in the heavens and the earth is executed and performed. Just as Your command is executed in the heavens, bestow Your Mercy on earth, and forgive us our sins and our faults. O Lord of the good, the pure ones, bestow a cure, and mercy from Your Mercy, on so-and-so, son of so-and-so', and mention his name."

Another invocation for headache: 'O One Who diminishes the great and magnifies the small; O Remover of uncleanliness from Muhammad and his family, and their complete Purifier. Bless Muhammad and his family. Remove what is in me of headache and migraine (*al-shaqiqa*).'

AN INVOCATION FOR MIGRAINE

Muhammad b. Ibrahim al-Sarraj narrated from Ibn Mahbub from Hisham b. Salim from Habib al-Sijistani - he was older than Hariz al-Sijistani, though Hariz was superior in knowledge to Habib - who said: I complained to al-Baqir, peace be upon him, of a migraine that afflicted me once or twice every week. Al-Baqir said: 'Place your hand on the side which pains you and say: "O Apparent, Present, O Hidden, but not absent, answer Your weak servant with Your Gracious Help. Remove from him his pain. Surely You are Compassionate, Loving, All-powerful." Recite this three times and you will be relieved of the pain Allah, the Exalted, willing.'

Another invocation for migraine: Al-Sayyari narrated from Muhammad b. 'Ali from Muhammad b. Muslim from 'Ali b. Abu Hamza from Abu Basir, who said: 'I heard Muhammad b. 'Ali b. al-Husayn, peace be upon him, when visiting one of his followers, mention that he was afflicted with a migraine. He cited an invocation similar to the preceding one.'

Another invocation for migraine: 'Write the following on a paper and attach it to the part which is suffering: "In the Name of Allah, the Merciful, the Compassionate, I bear witness that You are not a god we have invented, nor a lord whose mention has ceased, nor a king with whom people associate partners, nor was there before You a god in whom we took refuge, or sought protection, or prayed to. We pray to You, and no one assists You in our creation or is responsible for You. Glory be to You and Praise! Bless Muhammad and his family. Cure this quickly with your cure."'

AN INVOCATION FOR PAIN IN THE EYE

Ahmad b. Muhammad Abu Ja'far narrated from Ibn Abu 'Umayr from Abu Ayyub al-Khazzaz from Muhammad b. Muslim from Abu 'Abd Allah al-Sadiq, peace be upon him, from al-Baqir from 'Ali b. al-Husayn from his father, who said that 'Ali b. Abu Talib, peace be upon him, said: 'When the Messenger of Allah, blessings of Allah be on him and his family, called me on the day of Khaybar, he was told: "O Messenger of Allah, he has inflammation (*al-ramad*) of the eyes." The Messenger of Allah said: "Bring him to me." So I went to him and said: "O Messenger of Allah, I have inflammation of the eyes and cannot see anything." The Messenger of Allah said:

"Approach me, O 'Ali." I approached him and he passed his hand over my eyes and recited: "In the Name of Allah, and by Allah, and peace be on the Messenger of Allah. O Allah, protect him from the heat and the cold, and preserve him from harm and affliction." 'Ali peace be upon him, said: I recovered, and by Him Who honoured him with Prophethood, bestowed on him the Message, and chose him over His servants, I felt neither heat nor cold nor pain in my eyes after that.'

He said: 'Sometimes 'Ali, peace be upon him, would go out on a bitterly cold winter's day with a torn shirt. It would be said: "O Amir al-Mu'minin, are you not affected by the cold?" He would reply: "Neither heat nor cold has affected me since the Messenger of Allah, blessings of Allah on him and his family, protected me with the invocation." Sometimes he would come out to us on an extremely hot day in a padded garment, and it would be said to him: "Are you not affected as other people are by this severe heat, so that you wear a padded garment?" He would give them the same reply.'

AN INVOCATION FOR PAIN IN THE EAR

Khirash b. Zuhayr al-Azdi narrated from Muhammad b. Jamhur al-Qummi from Yunus b. Zabyan from Abu 'Abd Allah, peace be upon him, that he [Yunus] said: I complained to him of pain in one of my ears (*al-udhun*). He [Abu 'Abd Allah] said: 'Place your hand over it, and say seven times: "I take refuge in

Allah, in Whom trust that which is on the land and in the sea, in the heavens and the earth; and He is All-hearing, All-knowing." It will be cured, Allah, the Exalted, willing.'

Aslam b. 'Amr al-Nusaybi narrated from 'Ali b. Ibn Rabbayta from Muhammad b. Salman from his father from Abu 'Abd Allah, peace be upon him, that he recited an invocation of protection similar to this, for one of his companions who had an earache.

DESCRIPTION OF A MEDICATION FOR PAIN IN THE EAR

Take a handful of unhusked sesame (*simsim ghayr muqashshar*) and a handful of mustard. Grind each of them separately, then mix them together and extract the oil (*duhn*). Place the oil in a bottle and put an iron seal on it. Whenever you require, put two drops of it in the ear and bind it with a piece of cotton for three days. It will be cured. Allah, the Exalted, willing.

[AN INVOCATION] FOR A PEBBLE IN THE EAR

It was narrated from Bakr from his uncle Sudayr, who said: 'I took a pebble and scratched my ear with it. It became embedded in my ear. I made every effort to remove it, but neither I nor the medical practitioners could do it. When I performed the Hajj and met al-Baqir, peace be upon him, I complained to him of the pain I had experienced. He said to al-Sadiq, peace be upon him: "O Ja'far, take him by the hand out into the light and have a look." Al-Sadiq looked into the ear and said: "I do not see anything." Al-Baqir said: "Approach me." I approached him and he said: "O Allah, remove it as You caused it to enter, without trouble or difficulty." Then he said: "Recite that three times." I recited it. He said: "Put your finger in." I put my finger in and brought out the pebble. Praise be to Allah, Lord of the worlds.'

AN INVOCATION FOR DEAFNESS

Hannan b Jabir al-Filistini narrated from Muhammad b. 'Ali from Ibn Sinan from 'Ammar b. Marwan from al-Munkhal from Jabir from Abu Ja'far Muhammad b. 'Ali, peace be upon him, who said that a man complained to him of deafness (*al-samam*). Abu Ja'far said: 'Pass your hand over him and recite:

If We had sent down this Qur'an upon a mountain thou wouldst have seen it humbled, split asunder out of the fear of God. And We make these examples for men; haply they will reflect He is God; there in god but He. He is the knower of the Unseen and the Visible. He is the All-merciful, the All-compassionate. He is God. There is no god but He. He is the King, the All-holy, the All-peaceable, the All-faithful, the All-preserver, the All-mighty, the All-compeller, the All-sublime. Glory be to God, above that they associate! He is God, the Creator, the Maker, the Shaper. To Him belong the Names Most Beautiful. All that is in the heavens and the earth magnifies Him; He is the All-mighty, the All-wise. (59:21-3).'

AN INVOCATION FOR PAIN AFFLICTING THE MOUTH

Hariz b. Ayyub al-Jurjani narrated from Abu Samina from 'Ali b. Asbat from Abu Hamza from Abu Basir from Abu 'Abd Allah, peace be upon him, that Abu Basir said: One of his [Abu 'Abd Allah's] followers complained to him of pain in his mouth (*al-fam*). Abu 'Abd Allah said: 'When that afflicts you, place your hand over it and say: "In the Name of Allah, the Merciful, the Compassionate, In the Name of Allah, with Whose Name illness causes no harm; I take refuge in the Words of Allah, with Which nothing harms, Most Holy. Most Holy, Most Holy. By Your Name, O Lord, the Pure, the Holy, the Blessed, whoever asks You by it, You grant it to him, and whoever calls on You by it, You answer him. I ask You, O Allah, O Allah, O Allah, to bless Muhammad, the Prophet, and his Ahl al-Bayt, and to heal the suffering in my mouth, my head, my hearing, my sight, my belly, my back, my hand, my foot, and in all my limbs."

Your pain will be relieved. Allah, the Exalted, willing.'

AN INVOCATION FOR PAIN IN THE TEETH

Abu 'Abd Allah al-Husayn b. [Ahmad] Muhammad al-Khawatimi narrated from al-Husayn b. 'Ali b. Yaqtin from Hannan al-Sayqal from Abu Basir from Abu Ja'far al-Baqir, peace be upon him, that Abu Basir said: I complained to him of pain in my teeth, and that it kept me awake at nights. Abu Ja'far said: "O Abu Basir, when you experience that, place your hand over it, and recite the sura *al-Hamd* (1) and the sura *al-Ikhlas* (112), then recite:

And thou shalt see the mountains, that thou supposest fixed, passing by like clouds - God's handiwork, who has created everything very well. He is aware of the things you do. (27:88)

The pain will subside, and will not recur."

Hamdan b. A'yan al-Razi narrated from Abu Talib from Yunus from Abu Hamza from Sama'a b. Mihran from Abu 'Abd Allah, peace be upon him, that he [Abu 'Abd Allah] instructed a man to recite the above invocation and added to it, saying: 'Recite the sura *al-Qadr* (97) once. The pain will subside, and will not recur.'

[Also for pain in the teeth,] from Amir al-Mu'minin, peace be upon him, that he said: 'Whoever complains of pain in the teeth, let him take the object on which he performs his prostration, and rub it on the painful area, and say: "In the Name of Allah, and the Healer, Allah; there is no Might nor Power except in Allah, the Most High, the Mighty."'

It is reported from Abu al-Hasan, peace be upon him, that he said: 'My teeth (*al-asnan*) were hurting me and I applied Cyperus rotundus (*al-su'd*) to them.' He said: 'Wine vinegar (*khall al-khumr*) strengthens the gums (*al-litha*).' He also said: "Take wheat (*al-hinta*), husk it, and extract the oil. If the tooth is decayed and rotten, put two drops of the oil in it. Put some oil on a piece of cotton and place it in the ear near the tooth for three nights. It will stop [the decay], Allah, the Exalted, willing.'

THE CHARM FOR THE TOOTH

Ibrahim b. Khalid narrated from Ibrahim b. 'Abd Rabbihi from Tha'laba from Abu Basir from Abu 'Abd Allah, peace be upon him, who said: 'This is a charm for the teeth. It is beneficial and will never fail, Allah, the Exalted, willing. Praise .,. [*sic*] three leaves of the olive tree (*al-zaytun*), and write on the face of the leaf: "In the Name of Allah. There is no sovereign mightier than Allah, the King, and you are his Khalifa. Ya Haya Sharahiyya, remove the illness and send the cure, and may Allah bless Muhammad and his family."'

Abu 'Abd Allah, peace be upon him, said: '"Ya Haya, Sharahiyya", are two of the Names of Allah, the Exalted, in Hebrew. Write that on the back of the leaf, and tie it in a clean piece of cloth with a thread spun by a maid servant who has not...

[*sic*] and tie seven knots in it and name each knot with the name of one of the prophets— Adam. Nuh, Ibrahim, Musa, Isa, Shuayb - and pray for Muhammad and his family, peace be on him and on them, and attach it to it [the tooth]. It will be cured. Allah, the Exalted, willing.'

Jibra'il al-Husayn b. Ali, peace be upon him [*sic*]: 'How amazing it is that a creature eats the bone (*al-'azm*) and leaves the flesh (*al-lahm*). I make an invocation by Allah, the Mighty and Sublime, the Healer, the All-sufficient. There is no god but Allah, and praise be to Allah, the Lord of the worlds.

And when you killed a living soul, and disputed thereon — and God disclosed what you were hiding - so We said: Smite him with part of it .. (2:72-3).

Place your finger on the tooth, then recite this invocation seven times, on both its sides. It will be cured, Allah, the Exalted, willing.'

A PROVEN INVOCATION FOR THE TEETH

Recite the sura *al-Hamd* (1) the two Suras of taking refuge (*al-Falaq* (113) and *al-Nas* (114)), and the sura *al-Ikhlas* (112). Say 'In the Name of Allah, the Merciful, the Compassionate' with each sura. After the sura *al-Ikhlas* (112), say:

'In the Name of Allah, the Merciful, the Compassionate,

And to Him belongs whatsoever inhabits the night and the day, and He is the All-hearing All-knowing (6:13).

We said: O fire, be cooled and safe for Ibrahim! They desired to outwit him, so We made them the worse losers (21:69-70).

He was called: Blessed is He who is in the fire, and he who is about it. Glory be to God, the Lord of all Being' (27:8).

Then say after that: 'O Allah, O One Who protects from every thing, and nothing protects You. Protect Your servant and the son of your bondmaid (*al-ima'*), from the evil of what he fears and is wary of in this pain of which he complains to You.'

AN INVOCATION FOR COUGHING

'Abd Allah b. Muhammad b. Mihran al-Kufi narrated from Ayyub from 'Amr b. Shimr from Jabir from Abu Ja'far Muhammad b. 'Ali b. al-Husayn, peace be upon him, from al-Husayn [*sic*], who said: Amir al-Mu'minin, peace he upon him, said: 'Whosoever has a complaint of the throat (*al-halq*) and excessive coughing (*al-su'al*) and the desperation of his body increases, let him take refuge with these words, which are called 'the comprehensive' (*al-jami'a*), for all things:

"O Allah, You are my hope, and You are my Trust, my Support, my Succour, my Exalter, my beauty.

You are the Refuge of those who are afraid.

There is no sanctuary for those who flee except in You.

There is no one on whom human beings can rely except You.

There is no wish for those who desire except before You.

There is no helper for the oppressed but You.

There is no object for the needy except You.

There is nothing to be given for the seekers except from You.

There is no place to turn for the repentant except You,

Sustenance and good and deliverance are only in Your Hand.

Tibb al-A'imma

Oppressive matters have grieved me, difficult straits have wearied me,

and painful ailments have encompassed me.

I do not find the opening of the door of deliverance open except by Your Hand.

Thus I stand before You and seek help from You, with prayer, against its closing.

Open, O Lord, to the one who asks for help, and answer the one who calls out.

Dispel the grief, remove the harm, fulfil the need, remove the sorrow, banish the anxieties, and save me from destruction, for I am on the brink of it.

I do not find my salvation from it other than in You.

O Allah, O He who answers the constrained, when he calls

unto Him, and removes the evil (27:62),

have mercy on me and remove what is in me of sorrow and grief and pain and illness.

Lord, if You do not, I do not expect my deliverance from other than You.

Have mercy on me, O Most Merciful of the Merciful.

This is the position of the wretched, the poor.

This is the position of one who is afraid, one seeking refuge.

This is the position of one calling for help.

This is the position of the sorrowful, the hurt.

This is the troubled, the one seeking protection.

This is the position of the servant, apprehensive, dying,

drowning, frightened, fearful.

This is the position of one who has awakened from his sleep, been aroused from his forgetfulness, recovered from his illness and the severity of his pain, and is afraid because of his offences.

He acknowledges his sins, is humble before his Lord, and weeps in fear of Him.

He asks forgiveness, sheds tears, and seeks pardon, by Allah, from his Lord.

He dreads His Power, sheds his tears, and hopes, weeps, and prays and calls:

Lord, affliction has visited me (21:83) so set me right.

You see my position. You hear my words. Yon know my secret thoughts and my public affairs.

You know my need and You know me thoroughly.

Nothing in my affairs, whether open or secret, apparent or concealed in my breast, is hidden from You.

So I ask You, since You have authority over regulating [affairs], accepting pleas, and fixing destinies, with the request of one who has done wrong and confessed, wronged his soul, and committed crimes.

He has repented for what is past and turned to his Lord.

He has regretted and taken refuge in His courtyard, held backand restrained his desire, and devoted himself to the Rcvoker of his lapses, the Acceptor of his repentance, the Forgiver of his sins, the One Who has mercy on his state of exile, the Remover of his distress and the Healer of his illness.

Have mercy on my transgressions and my entreaties to You.

Forgive me all my deviations from Your Book which have been counted in Your record.

Your past knowledge of my sins, faults, and offences in privacy, my immorality, my evil deeds, my lapses, and all that Your recording angels witness and have written down during childhood and after puberty, in old age and youth, by night and day, early morning and evening, late evening and daybreak, forenoon and dawn, and at home and in travels, in solitude and in public. Overlook my evil deeds among the inhabitants of Paradise *the promise of the very truth, which they were promised (46:16).*

O Allah, by the right of Muhammad and his family, remove from me the overwhelming illnesses in my body (*jismi*), my hair (*sha'ri*), my skin (*bashari*), my blood vessels (*'uruqi*), my nerves (*'asabi*), and my limbs, for no one will remove that other than You, O Most Merciful of the Merciful, O Answerer of the call of the distressed.'"

AN INVOCATION FOR ANXIETIES IN THE BREAST

Abu al-Qasim al-Taflisi narrated from Hammad b. 'Isa from Hariz b. 'Abd Allah al-Sijistani from Abu 'Abd Allah al-Sadiq, peace be upon him, that Hariz said: I said "O son of the Messenger of Allah, I experience anxieties (*al-balabil*) in my breast and temptations (*al-wasawis*) in my heart (*al-fu'ad*) so that I sometimes break off my prayer and become confused in my recitation." Abu 'Abd Allah said: "And what about the invocation of Amir al-

Mu'minin, peace be upon him?" I replied: "O son of the Messenger of Allah, teach [it to] me."

He said: "When you experience something of this, place your hand on it and say:

'In the Name of Allah and by Allah. O Allah, You have blessed me with faith, and entrusted me with the Qur'an, and bestowed on me fasting in the month of Ramadan.

Grant me mercy and acceptance and compassion and forgiveness and all that You have conferred on me of blessings and beneficence.

O Compassionate. O Benefactor, O Everlasting, O Merciful, Glory be to You. I have no one but You, Glory be to You. I take refuge in You, after these expressions of esteem, from abasement. I ask You to remove the sorrows from my heart.'

Repeat this three times and you will be cured of it, with the help of Allah, the Exalted. Then bless the Prophet, blessings of Allah upon him, and mercy and blessings upon his family."

AN INVOCATION FOR A PAIN IN THE BELLY

Al-Husayn b. Bistam narrated from Muhammad b. Khalaf from al-Washsha' from 'Abd Allah b. Sinan from Ja'far b. Muhammad, peace be upon him, from his grandfather, peace be upon him, who said: A man complained to the Prophet, blessings and peace be on him and his family, and said: "O Messenger of Allah, I have a brother who has a complaint of the belly." The Prophet replied: "Tell your brother to take a drink of honey with hot water." The man returned to him the next day and said: "O Messenger of Allah, I gave him the drink but he did not benefit from it." The Messenger of Allah said: "Allah has said the truth, and the belly of your brother has lied. Go, and give your brother the drink of honey and invoke for him the sura *al-Fatiha* (1) seven times." When the man left, the Prophet said: "O 'Ali, the brother of this man is a hypocrite. Whosoever is such, the drink will not benefit him."

A man complained to Amir al-Mu'minin, peace be upon him, of pain in the belly. He instructed him to drink hot water and say:

"O Allah, O Allah, O Allah, O Merciful, O Compassionate, O Lord of the lords. O God of the gods, O King of the kings, O Master of the masters. Heal me with Your cures from every disease and illness, for I am Your servant and the son of Your servant; I turn about in Your grasp."

Abu 'Abd Allah al-Khawatimi narrated from Ibn Yaqtin from Hassan al-Sayqal from Abu Basir, who said: A man complained to Abu 'Abd Allah al-Sadiq, peace be upon him, of pain of the navel (*al-surra*). Al-Sadiq told him: "Go, and put your hand on the painful area and say three times:

Surely it is a Book Sublime. Falsehood comes not to it from before it nor from behind it. A revelation from One All-wise, All-laudable (41:41-2).

You will be cured, Allah willing."

Abu 'Abd Allah, peace be upon him, said: "There is not one among the believers who complains of any illness and recites with sincere intention, while passing his hand over the area of the illness:

We send down of the Qu'ran that which is a cure and a mercy to the believers. The unbelievers it increases not except in loss (17:82), but that he is cured of that illness, whatever it may be. The truth of that is confirmed in the verse, where it says, *a cure and a mercy to the believers."*

AN INVOCATION AND MEDICATION FOR PAIN OF THE WAIST

Hariz b. Ayyub narrated from Abu Samina from 'Ali b. Asbat from Abu Hamza from Hamran b. A'yan, who said: A man questioned Muhammad b. 'Ali al-Baqir, peace be upon him, saying: "O son of the Messenger of Allah, I suffer from severe pain in the waist (*al-khasira*) and have treated it with many remedies, but it has not been cured."

Al-Baqir said: "What about the invocation of Amir al-Mu'minin?" The man replied: "And what is that, O son of the Messenger of Allah?" He said: "When you complete your prayers, put your hand on the place of prostration, stroke it, and say:

What, did you think that We created you only for sport, and that you would not be returned to Us? Then high exalted be God, the King, the True! There is no god but He, the Lord of the noble Throne. Whosoever calls upon another god with God, whereof he has no proof, his reckoning is with his Lord. Surely the unbelievers shall not prosper. And say: My Lord, forgive and have mercy, for Thou art the best of the merciful (23:115-18)."

The man said: "I did that and the pain subsided, praise be to Allah, the Exalted."

Muhammad b. Ja' far al-Bursi narrated from Muhammad b. Yahya al-Armani from Muhammad b. Sinan from Abu 'Abd Allah, peace be upon him, who said: 'The Messenger of Allah, blessings on him and his family, said: "Drink lovage (*al-kashim*), for it is good for pain of the waist."'

Also from him from Muhammad b. Yahya from Yunus b. Zabyan from Jabir from Abu Ja'far, peace be upon him, who said Amir al-Mu'minin, peace be upon him, said: "Whoever wishes that food may not harm him, let him not eat until he is hungry and his abdomen (*al-ma'ida*) is cleansed. When he eats, let him take the Name of Allah and chew well and let him stop eating while he still has an appetite for it [food] and wants it."

'Abd Allah b. Bistam narrated from Muhammad b. Razin from Hammad b. 'Isa from Hariz from Abu 'Abd Allah, peace be upon him, from Amir al-Mu'minin, peace be upon him, who said: "Whoever wishes for the eternal life in the next world, and not for permanence in this world, let him wear light clothes, eat early, and have intercourse (*al-mujami'a*) with women less frequently."

AN INVOCATION FOR PAIN OF THE SPLEEN

Muhammad b. 'Abd Allah b. Mihran al-Kufi narrated from Ayyub from Umar b. Shimr from Jabir from Abu Ja'far, peace be upon him, who said: A man from Khurasan came to 'Ali b. al-Husayn, peace be upon him, and said: "O son of the Messenger of Allah, I performed the Hajj and resolved to call on you upon my departure, for I have a pain in the spleen (*al-tihal*). Pray for me to be relieved of it."

'Ali b. al-Husayn replied: "Allah has protected you from that, praise be to Him. When you experience the pain, write this verse with saffron (*al-za'faran*) mixed with the water of [the] Zamzam [spring in Mecca], and drink it. Allah, the Exalted, will drive away that pain from you:

Say: Call upon God, or call upon the Merciful whichsoever you call upon, to Him belong the Names Most Beautiful. And be thou not loud in thy prayer, nor hushed therein, but seek thou for a way between that. And say: Praise belongs to God, who has not taken to Him a son, and who has not any associate in the Kingdom, nor any protector out of humbleness. And magnify Him with repeated magnificats (17:110-11).

Write the following on the parchment of a gazelle (*ghazal*) and attach it to your left arm (*al-'adud*) for seven days and the pain will abate: . . ."

لا س س س ح ح ح دم كرم ل له ومحى حج لله صر ه
ر ححب سى ححجت عشره به هك ان عنها ح حل
يصر س هو بوا اميوا مسعوف

Ahmad b. Yazid narrated from al-Sahhaf al-Kufi from Musa b. Ja'far, peace be upon him, from al-Sadiq, peace be upon him, from al-Baqir, peace be upon him, that he said: 'One of his followers complained to al-Baqir of pain in the spleen. He had treated it with every remedy but its evil increased every day until he was on the threshold of death. Al-Baqir said to him: "Buy a piece of leek (*al-kurrath*) and fry it well in Arab clarified butter (*samn 'arabi*). Give it for three days to the one who has this pain. If that is done, he will be cured, Allah, the Exalted, willing."'

AN INVOCATION FOR PAIN IN THE BLADDER

Muhammad b. Ja'far al-Bursi narrated from Muhammad b. Yahya al-Armani from Muhammad b. Sinan al-Sinani from al-Mufaddal b. 'Umar from Muhammad b. Isma'il from Abu Zaynab, who said: One of our brothers complained to Abu 'Abd Allah al-Sadiq, peace be upon him, of pain in the bladder (*al-mathana*). Al-Sadiq said: "Seek protection for it with these verses three times before you sleep, and once when you awaken, and you will not experience the pain after that:

Knowest thou not that God is powerful over everything? Knowest thou not that to God belongs the kingdom of the heavens and the earth, and that you have none, apart from God, neither protector nor helper?" (2:106-7).

The man said: "I did that and did not experience the pain again."

AN INVOCATION FOR PAIN IN THE BACK

Al-Khidr b Muhammad narrated from al-Hawarini from Faddala from Aban b. 'Uthman from lbn Abu Hamza al-Thumali from Abu Ja'far Muhammad al-Baqir, peace be upon him, who said: 'A man from Hamdan complained to Amir al-Mu'minin, peace be upon him, of a pain in the back and that he had sleepless nights [because of it]. He said: "Put your hand on the area that pains you and recite three times:

It is not given to any soul to die save by the leave of God, at an appointed time. Whoever desires the reward of this world, We will give him of this. Whosoever desires the reward of the other world, We will give him of that. We will recompense the thankful (3:145).

Then recite the sura *al-Qadr* (97) seven times and you will be cured of it, if Allah, the Exalted, wills."'

AN INVOCATION FOR PAIN OF THE THIGHS

Abu 'Abd al-Rahman al-Katib narrated from Muhammad b. 'Abd Allah al-Za'farani from Hammad b. 'Isa from Amir a-Mu'minin, peace be upon him, who said: 'When one of you suffers from pain of the thighs (*al-fakhdhan*), let him sit in a large vessel or basin of heated water and place his hand there [on his thighs] and recite:

Have not the unbelievers then beheld that the heavens and earth were a mass all sewn up, and then We unstitched them and of water fashioned every living thing? Will they not believe? (21:30)'

AN INVOCATION FOR PAIN OF THE GENITALS

With this chain of transmitters (*al-isnad*) from Hariz al-Sijistani, who said: I performed the Hajj and called on Abu 'Abd Allah al-Sadiq, peace be upon him, in Medina, and al-Mu'alla b. Khunays, may Allah have mercy on him, was complaining to him of pain in the genitals (*al-farj*). Al-Sadiq said to him: "You exposed your privy parts (*al- 'aura*) on some occasion and Allah has punished you with this pain. But seek protection for it with the invocation which Amir al-Mu'minin, peace be upon him, gave Abu Wa'ila, after which it [the pain] did not recur." Al-Mu'alla asked; "O son of the Messenger of Allah, what is the invocation?" He replied: "Put your left hand on them and say three times:

'In the name of Allah, and by Allah,

Nay, but whosoever submits his will to God, being a good-doer, his wage is with his Lord, and no fear shall be on them, neither shall they sorrow (2:112).

O Allah, I have submitted myself to You and entrusted my affairs to You. There is no refuge or security from You except in You.'

You will be cured, Allah, the Exalted, willing."

AN INVOCATION FOR PAIN OF THE LEGS

Khaddash b. Sabra narrated from Muhammad b. Jamhur from Safwan Bayya' al-Sabiri from Salim b. Muhammad, who said: I complained to al-Sadiq, peace be upon him, of pain in my legs (*al-saqayn*) and that it had prevented me from pursuing my affairs and earning my living. He said: "Recite an invocation of protection over them." I asked: "With what, O son of the Messenger of Allah?" He said: "With this verse. Recite it seven times and you will be cured, Allah, the Exalted, willing:

Recite what has been revealed to thee of the Book of thy Lord; no man can change His words. Apart from Him, thou wilt find no refuge. (18:27)."

He said: I recited the invocation over them seven times, as he had instructed me, and I never experienced the pain again.

AN INVOCATION AND MEDICATIONS FOR HEMORRHOIDS

Al-Hawarini al-Razi narrated from Safwan b. Yahya al-Sabiri - and he is not Safwan al-Jammal - from Ya'qub b. Shu'ayb from

Aban b. Taghlab from 'Abd al-'Ala' from Abu 'Abd al-Rahman al-Sulami from Amir al-Mu'minin, peace be upon him, who said: 'Whosoever seeks protection from haemorrhoids with this invocation will be protected from its evil, Allah, the Exalted willing. It is:

"O Magnanimous, O Exalted, O Compassionate, O Near, O Responder, O Creator, O Merciful, bless Muhammad and his family, and bestow on me Your blessing, and protect me from my pain."

He will be cured of it, Allah, the Mighty and Sublime, willing.'

Muhammad b. 'Abd Allah b. Mihran al-Kufi narrated from Isma'il b. Yazid from 'Amr b. Yazid al-Sayqal, who said: I called on Abu 'Abd Allah, peace be upon him, and asked him about a man who had severe haemorrhoids. He had been prescribed a bowl of strong wine (*al-nabidh*) and he did not want to take it for the enjoyment of it but as a medication.

Abu 'Abd Allah said: "No, not a mouthful." I asked: "Why?" He replied: "It is forbidden. Allah, the Mighty and Sublime, does not create a medication or cure in anything He has forbidden.

"Take a white leek and cut off its white head. Do not wash it or cut it up into small pieces Take fat from the hump of the camel (*al-sinam*), melt it, and pour it over the leek. Take ten walnuts (*jawzat*) shell them, and grind them with the weight of ten dirhams of Persian cheese (*jibn farsi*). Put the leek on the fire. When it is well cooked, add the walnuts and cheese to it and remove it from the fire. Eat it on an empty stomach with bread, for three days or seven days, and abstain from other food. After it, take a little roasted savin (*abhal*) with bread and shelled walnuts. After the fat of the camel's hump and the leek, take, in the Name of Allah, half an *awqiya* of sesame oil (*shiraj*) on an empty stomach, and an *awqiya* of [the resin of the] male storax [tree] (*kundur dhakar*).

Grind and drink it. After that take another half *awqiya* of sesame oil. Take it for three days and delay your eating until after noon. You will be cured, Allah, the Exalted, willing."

AN INVOCATION FOR PAIN OF THE FEET

Hannan b. Jabir narrated from Muhammad b 'Ali al-Sayrafi from at-Husayn al-Ashqar from 'Amr b. Abu al-Miqdam from Muhammad al-Baqir, peace be upon him, who said: 'I was with al-Husayn b. 'Ali, peace be upon him, when one of our Shi'a from the Bani Umayya came to him and said: "O son of the Messenger of Allah, I was hardly able to walk to you because of the pain in my feet." He said: "What about the invocation of al-Husayn b. 'Ali?" The man said: "O son of the Messenger of Allah, and what is that?" He replied: "The verses are:

Surely We have given thee a manifest victory, that God may forgive thee thy former and thy latter sins, and complete His blessing upon thee, and guide thee on a straight path, and that God may help thee with mighty help.

It is He who sent down the Shechina into the hearts of the believers, that, they might add faith to their faith — to God belong the hosts of the heavens and the earth; God is All-knowing, All-wise — and that He may admit the believers, men and women and women alike, into gardens underneath which rivers flow, therein to dwell forever, and acquit them of their evil deeds.

That is in God's sight a mighty triumph, that He may chastise the hypocrites, men and women alike, and the idolaters, men and women alike, and those who think evil thoughts of God. Against them shall be the evil turn of fortune. God is wroth with them, and has cursed them, and has prepared for them Hell - -an evil homecoming! To God belong the hosts of the heavens and the earth; God is All-mighty, All-wise (48:1-7)."

The man said: "I did as he instructed and did not experience any of the pain after that, with the help of Allah, the Exalted."'

AN INVOCATION FOR THE HAMSTRING AND THE SOLE OF THE FOOT

Abu 'Atab 'Abd Allah b. Bistam narrated from Ibrahim b. Muhammad al-Awdi from Safwan al-Jammal from Ja'far b. Muhammad from his father from 'Ali b. al-Husayn, peace be upon him, who said: A man complained to Abu 'Abd Allah al-Husayn b. 'Ali, peace he upon him, and said: "O son of the Messenger of Allah, I suffer from pain in my hamstring (*al-'urqub*) which prevents me from standing up for prayer." He said: "What prevents you from [reciting] the invocation?" He replied: "I do not know it."

He said: "When you experience the pain, place your hand there and say: 'In the Name of Allah, and by Allah, and peace be upon the Messenger of Allah, blessings of Allah on him and his family.' Then recite over it:

They measure not God with His true measure. The earth altogether shall be His handful on the Day of Resurrection, and the heavens shall he rolled up in His right hand. Glory be to Him! High be He exalted above that they associate! (39:67)"

The man did that and Allah, the Exalted, healed him.

AN INVOCATION FOR SWELLING IN ALL THE JOINTS

Al-Hasan b. Salih al-Mahmudi narrated from Abu 'Amr b. Shimr from Jabir b. Yazid al-Ju'fi from Muhammad b. 'Ali b. al-Husayn, peace be upon him, who said: "O Jabir." I [Jabir] replied: "At your service, O son of the Messenger of Allah." He said: "Recite over every swelling (*al-waram*) the end of the sura *al-Hashr*:

If We had sent down this Qur'an upon a mountain, thou wouldst have seen it humbled, split asunder out of the fear of God. And those similitudes — We strike them for men; haply they will reflect. He is God, there is no god but He. He is the knower of the Unseen and the Visible; He is the All-merciful, the All-compassionate.

He is God; there is no god but He. He is the King, the All-holy, the All-peaceable, the All-faithful, the All-preserver, the All-mighty, the All-compeller, the All-sublime. Glory be to God, above, that they associate!

He is God, the Creator, the Maker, the Shaper. To Him belong the Names Most Beautiful All that is in the heavens and the earth magnifies Him. He is the All-mighty, the All-wise (59:21-4).

"Recite it three times over the swelling, and it will subside, Allah, the Exalted, willing.

"Take a knife and pass it over the swelling and say: 'In the Name of Allah, I charm you from affliction and iron and an affair of recurring grief and from the matted stone and from the root of a barren tree (*'irq al-'aqir*), and from another swelling, and from food and its ganglia (*al-'aqd*), and from drink and its coldness. Pass, with the will of Allah, for a time to humans and cattle, In the Name of Allah I begin, and in the Name of Allah I end.'

Then drive the knife into the earth."

AN INVOCATION TO NEUTRALIZE SPELLS

'Abd Allah b. al-'Ala al-Qazwini narrated from Ibrahim b. Muhammad from Hammad b. 'Isa b. Ya'qub from Imran b.Maytham from Ubaya b Rab'i al-Asadi, that he heard Amir al-Mu'minin, blessings of Allah be on him, instruct one of his companions, when the latter complained of spells (*al-sihr*). He said: 'Write [the following] on the parchment of a gazelle and fasten it to yourself. The spell will not harm you and its strategems will not affect you.

"In the Name of Allah, and by Allah; in the Name of Allah, and what Allah wills. In the Name of Allah, there is neither might nor power except with Allah.

Musa said, What you have brought is spells. God will assuredly bring it to naught. God sets not right the work of those who do corruption (10:81-2).

So the truth came to pass, and false was proved what they were doing. So they were vanquished there, and they turned about, humbled (7:118-19).'"

Muhammad b. Musa al-Rab'i narrated from Muhammad b. Mahbub from 'Abd Allah b. Ghalib from Sa'd b. Zarif from al-Asbagh b. Nubata from Amir al-Mu'minin, peace be upon him, that al-Asbagh said: I took this invocation from him. He said to me: 'O Asbagh, this is an invocation for spells and fear (*al-khauf*) of the ruler (*al-sultan*). Recite it seven times:

"In the Name of Allah, and by Allah. We will strengthen thy arm by means of thy brother, and We shall appoint to you an authority, so that they shall not reach you because of Our signs; you and whoso follows you, shall be the victors (28:35)."

Recite it seven times over water when you have completed the night prayer (*salat al-layl*) and before you begin the morning prayer (*salat al-nahar*). It [spells] will not harm you, Allah, the Exalted, willing.'

AN INVOCATION FOR A WOMAN EXPERIENCING DIFFICULTY IN CHILDBIRTH

Al-Khawatimi narrated from Muhammad b. 'Ali al-Sayrafi from Muhammad b. Aslam from al-Hasan b. Muhammad al-Hashimi from Aban b. Abu al-'Ayyash from Salim b. Qays al-Hilali from Amir al-Mu'minin, peace be upon him, who said: 'I know of two verses in the revealed Book of Allah, prescribed for a woman experiencing difficulty (*al-'usr*) in childbirth (*al-wilada*). Write them on the parchment of a gazelle and fasten it to her groin (*al-haqw*). Write seven times:

"In the Name of Allah, and by Allah, Truly with hardship comes ease, truly with hardship comes ease (94.5-6)."

'Write once: O men, fear your Lord! Surely the earthquake of the Hour is a mighty thing. On the day when you behold it, every suckling woman shall neglect the child she has suckled, and every pregnant woman shall deposit her burden, and thou shalt see mankind drunk, yet they are not drunk, but God's chastisement is terrible (22:1-2).

'Write [the following] on a paper and tie it with an untwisted fibre of flax (*kattan*) and fasten it on to her left thigh. When she has given birth, cut it off at once and do not delay in doing it. Write:

"At the time when Maryam gave birth, Maryam brought forth a living [being]. O living [being], come down to the earth immediately, by the will of Allah, the Exalted."'

AN INVOCATION FOR A CHILD WHO CRIES OFTEN, FOR ONE AFRAID OF THE NIGHT, AND FOR A WOMAN SLEEPLESS FROM PAIN

Then We smote their ears many years in the Cave. Afterwards We raised them up again, that We might know which of the two parties would better calculate the while they had tarried (18:11-12).

Abu al-Mu'izz al-Wasiti narrated from Muhammad b. Sulayman from Marwan b. al-Jahm from Muhammad b. Muslim from Abu Ja'far, peace be upon him, from Amir al-Mu'minin, peace be upon him, that he said that.

AN INVOCATION FOR A STUBBORN BEAST

Hatim b. 'Abd Allah al-Azdi narrated from Abu Ja'far al-Maqri, the Imam of the mosque of al-Kufa, from Jabir b. Rashid from Abu 'Abd Allah al-Sadiq, peace be upon him, that he [Jabir] said: While we were on a journey, al-Sadiq noticed a man looking gloomy and dejected. He asked him: "What is wrong with you?" He replied: "My beast (*al-dabba*) is stubborn (*harun*)." He [al-Sadiq] said: "Woe be to you, recite this verse in her ear:

Have they not seen how that We have created for them of that Our hands wrought of cattle that they own? We have subdued them to them, and some of them they ride, and some they eat (36:71-2)"

AN INVOCATION FOR A JOURNEY

'Ali b. 'Urwa al-Ahwazi narrated from al-Daylami from Dawud al-Raqqi, from Musa b. Ja'far, peace he upon him, who said: "Whoever is on a journey (*al-safar*) and fears thieves (*al-lusus*) and predatory animals (*al-sab'*) let him write on the mane (*al-'urf*) of his beast:

Fearing not overtaking, neither afraid (20:77).

He will be safe, Allah, the Mighty and Sublime, willing."

Dawud al-Raqqi said: I performed the Hajj, and when we were in the desert, a group of Bedouins waylaid the caravan in which I was. I wrote on the mane of my camel (*al-jamal*):

Fearing not overtaking, neither afraid (20:77).

By Him Who sent Muhammad, blessings of Allah on him and his family, with the Prophethood, bestowed on him the Message, and honoured Amir al-Mu'minin with the Imamate, not one of them challenged me and Allah made them blind (*a'ma*) to me.

AN INVOCATION FOR ALL ILLNESSES

'Ali b. Ishaq al-Basri narrated from Zakariya b. Adam al-Maqri, who used to serve Al-Ridha', peace be upon him, in Khurasan. He said: One day Al-Ridha' said to me: 'O Zakariya.' I answered: 'At your service, O son of the Messenger of Allah.' He said: 'Recite for all illnesses: "O Bestower of healing and Remover of illness, send down healing for my ailment."

You will be restored to health, Allah, the Mighty and Sublime, willing.'

AN INVOCATION FOR SCIATICA

Mu'alla b. Ibrahim al-Wasiti narrated from Ibn Mahbub from Muhriz b. Sulayman al-Azraq, from Abu al-Jarud from Abu Ishaq from al-Harith al-A'war al-Hamdani from Amir al-Mu'minin, peace be upon him, that one of his companions had complained to him of sciatica *('irq al-nisa')*. He [Amir al-Mu'minin] replied: 'When yon experience it place your hand on it and say:

"In the Name of the Merciful, the Compassionate. In the Name of Allah, and by Allah, I take refuge in the Name of Allah, the Great, and I take refuge in the Name of Allah, the Mighty, from the evil of every throbbing blood vessel *('irq nuqqar)*, and from the evil of the heat of the fire."

You will be cured, Allah, the Exalted, willing.' The man said: 'I recited that only three times, and Allah removed my suffering and I was cured of it.'

AN INVOCATION FOR CONSUMPTION

Muhammad b. Kathir al-Dimashqi narrated from al-Hasan b. 'Ali b. Yaqtin from Al-Ridha' 'Ali b. Musa, peace be upon him, who said: 'This is an invocation for our Shi'a for consumption (*al-sill*):

"O Allah, O Lord of the lords, O Master of the masters, O God of the gods, O King of the kings, O Omnipotent of the heavens and the earth. Heal me and cure me of this disease of mine, for I am Your servant and the son of Your servant. I turn about in Your grasp and my forelock is in Your Hand."

Say it three times; and Allah, the Mighty and Sublime will protect you with His Might and Power, If He, the Exalted, wills.'

AN INVOCATION FOR PUSTULES

'Ali b. al-'Abbas narrated from Muhammad b. Ibrahim al-'Alawi from 'Ali b Musa from his father from Ja'far b. Muhammad al-Sadiq, peace be upon him, who said: 'When you feel a pustule (*al-bathr*) [appearing] put your index finger (*al-sabbaba*) on it and circle it and say seven times:

"There is no god but Allah, the Clement, the Noble."

The seventh time, strike it and press on it with your finger.'

AN INVOCATION FOR COLIC

Al-Darari narrated from Musa b. 'Umar b. Yazid from Abu 'Umar b. Yazid al-Sayqal from al-Sadiq, peace be upon him, that he [al-Sayqal] said that one of his followers had complained of colic (*al-qawlanj*). He [al-Sadiq] told him:

'Write for him the the sura *al-Fatiha* (1), the sura *al-Ikhlas* (112), and the two suras of seeking protection (*al-Falaq* (113) and *al-Nas* (114)). Then write under that:

"I take refuge in the Face of Allah, the Mighty, and in His Might, which is unceasing, and in His Power, which nothing can resist, from the evil of this pain, and the evil within it".

Then drink it [*sic*] with rainwater (*ma' al-matar*) on an empty stomach. You will be cured of it, Allah, the Exalted, willing.'

AN INVOCATION FOR FEVER AND FOR THE FEVER OF THE MESSENGER OF ALLAH

Ahmad b. Muhammad Abu Ja'far narrated from Abu Muhammad b. Khalid from Bakr b. Khalid from Muhammad b. Sinan from 'Abd Allah b. 'Ammar al-Duhni from his father from 'Amr Dhi Far and Taghlaba al-Jammali who both said: We heard Amir al-Mu'minin, peace be upon him, say: 'The Messenger of Allah, blessings of Allah on him, had a severe fever (*al-humma*). Jibra'il, blessings of Allah on him, came to him and recited an invocation of protection over him. He said:

"In the Name of Allah, I invoke you. In the Name of Allah, I cure you of every illness that troubles, you. In the Name of Allah, and Allah is your Healer. In the Name of Allah, take it and may it be good for you. In the Name of Allah, the Merciful, the Compassionate,

No! I swear by the fallings of the stars, and that is indeed a mighty oath, did you but know it! (56:75-6).

You will surely be restored to health, Allah, the Mighty and Sublime, willing."

The Prophet, blessings be on him, undid his headband and said: "O Jibra'il, this is an eloquent invocation." Jibra'il replied: "It is from the treasury of the seventh heaven."'

Ahmad b. Salama narrated from Muhammad b. 'Isa from Hariz b. 'Abd Allah al-Sijistani from Ahmad b. Hamza from Aban b. 'Uthman from al-Fudayl b. Yasar from Abu Ja'far, peace be upon him, who said: 'When a man falls ill and you wish to invoke protection for him say:

"Out with you, O blood vessel, or O eye of jinn, or O eye of man, or O pain, from so-and-so, son of so-and-so. Out with you, by Allah, Who addressed Musa and spoke to him, and took Ibrahim, blessings of Allah on him, as a friend, the Lord of 'Isa b. Maryam, the spirit of Allah and His Word, the Lord of Muhammad and the family of Muhammad, the guides. I put you out as the fire of Ibrahim, the friend, peace be upon him, was put out.'"

Ahmad b. Abu Ziyad narrated from Faddala b. Ayyub from lsma'il b. Ziyad from Abu 'Abd Allah al-Sadiq, peace be upon him, who said: 'When the Messenger of Allah, blessings be on him, felt sluggish (*al-kasal*), or when the evil eye (*al-'ayn*) fell on him, or when he had a headache, he would stretch out his hands and recite the opening of the Book (the sura *al-Fatiha* {1}) and the two suras of taking refuge (*al-Falaq* (113) and *al-Nas* (114)). Then he would pass his hands over his face (*al-wajh*) and whatever he would be suffering would be removed from him.'

Muhammad b. Ja'far al-Bursi narrated from Muhammad b. Yahya al-Armani from Muhammad b. Sinan from Salama b. Muhriz, who said: 1 heard Abu Ja'far al-Baqir, peace be upon him, say: "Whosoever is not cured by the sura *al-Hamd* (1) and the sura *al-lkhlas* (112) will not be cured by anything. All illnesses are cured by these two Suras."

Muhammad b. Yazid narrated from Ziyad b. Muhammad from his father from Hisham b. Ahmar from Abu 'Abd Allah al-Sadiq, peace be upon him, who said: 'Whoever says: "There is no might nor power except with Allah, the Mighty", Allah will drive away from him seventy-three kinds of affliction, the least of which is madness (*al-junun*).'

'Ali b. Abu Talib, peace be upon him, said: The Messenger of Allah, blessings be on him, said: "O 'Ali, shall I show you one of the treasures of Paradise?" I replied: "Yes indeed, O Messenger of Allah." He said: "There is no power or might except with Allah."

Muhammad b. Ibrahim al-Sarraj narrated from Faddala and al-Qasim both from Aban b. 'Uthman from Abu Hamza al-Thumali from Abu Ja'far al-Baqir, peace be upon him, who said: 'When one of you suffers from something, let him recite:

"In the Name of Allah, and blessings of Allah on the Messenger of Allah and his Ahl al-Bayt, I take refuge in the Might of Allah and His Power over what He wills, from the evil of what I suffer."'

Ahmad b. Salih al-Nisaburi narrated from Jamil b. Salih from Dharih, who said: I heard Abu 'Abd Allah, peace be upon him, invoke protection from wind for one of his followers and say:

"I adjure you, O ailment, with the invocation by which 'Ali b. Abu Talib, peace be upon him, and the Messenger of Allah, blessings on him and his family, called on the jinn of the valley of al-Sabra and they obeyed and answered, that you obey and answer and get out of so-and-so, son of so-and-so, at once, at once, by the will of Allah, the Exalted, by the command of Allah, the Mighty and Sublime, by the Power of Allah, by the Sovereignty of Allah, by the Majesty of Allah, by the Grandeur of Allah, by the Greatness of Allah, by the Face of Allah, by the Beauty of Allah, by the Magnificence of Allah, by the Light of Allah."

It was not long before it was expelled.

THE INVOCATION OF AL-RIDHA' FOR EVERY ILLNESS AND FEAR

Muhammad b. Kathir at-Dimashqi narrated from al-Hasan b. 'Ali b. Yaqtin from Al-Ridha', peace be upon him, that he [al-Hasan] said: I took this invocation from Al-Ridha'. He mentioned that it was a comprehensive preventative and a safeguard and protection from every illness and fear:

"'In the Name of Allah, the Merciful, the Compassionate, In the Name of Allah, *slink you into it, and do not speak to me (23:108). I take refuge in the All-merciful from thee if thou fearest God (19:18)* or do not fear God. I take hold, with the Hearing of Allah and His Sight, over your hearing and sight, and with the Might of Allah over your might. No authority have you over so-and-so, son of so-and-so, or over his progeny, or his wealth, or his family. I draw down between you and him the veil of Prophethood, by which they concealed themselves from the assault of the Pharoahs, with Jibra'il on your right, and Mika'il on your left, and Muhammad, blessings be on him and his Ahl al-Bayt before you, with Allah, the Exalted, overshadowing you. Allah guards him, his progeny, his wealth, and his family from the demons (*al-shayatin*). Whatever Allah has willed, there is no might or power except with Allah, the Most High, the Mighty. O Allah, his clemency will not attain Your patience as long as it does not attain the utmost degree of Your Power. You are the most excellent Master and the most excellent Helper. Allah guard you and your progeny, O so-and-so, by that with which He guarded his friends, blessings of Allah on Mohammad and his Ahl al-Bayt."

'Write the verse of the Throne (2:255) up to: *And He is the Most High, the Mighty*. Then write: "There is no might or power except with Allah, the Most High, the Mighty. There is no refuge from Allah except with him. Sufficient for us is Allah, the most excellent protector."'

AN INVOCATION FOR EVERY ACHE

Muhammad b. Hamid narrated from Khalaf b. Hammad from Khalid al-'Abasi, who said: 'Ali b. Musa, peace be upon him, taught me this invocation and said: 'Teach it to your brothers among the believers, for it is for every ache:

"I seek protection for myself in the Lord of the earth and the Lord of the heavens. I seek protection for myself in Him with Whose Name no disease causes harm. I seek protection for myself in Him Whose Name is a blessing and a healing."'

INVOCATION FOR DAYS OF THE WEEK

From al-Sadiq, peace be upon him.

[INVOCATION FOR] SATURDAY

'In the Name of Allah, the Merciful, the Compassionate, I seek protection for myself — or for so-and-so, son of so-and-so — in Allah. There is no God but Him. *He is the Lord of all Being, the All-merciful, the All-compassionate, the Master of the Day of Doom. Thee only we serve. To Thee alone we pray for succour. Guide us in the straight path, the path of those whom Thou hast blessed, not of those against whom Thou art wrathful, nor of those who are astray (1:2-7).* I seek protection in the Lord of the Daybreak *(113:1)*, and *Lord in the of men, the King of men (114:1-2)*, and the Lord of the dusk when it darkens, *from the evil of what He has created, and from the evil of the women who blow on knots, and from the evil of an envier when he envies (113:2-5),*

Allah, the One, the Refuge, Who has not begotten, and has not been begotten, and equal to Him is not any one (112:3-4), Light of the light and Regulator of affairs, the Light of the heavens and the earth. The likeness of His Light is as a niche wherein is a lamp, the lamp in a glass, the glass as it were a glittering star kindled from a Blessed Tree, an olive that is neither of the East nor of the West, whose, oil wellnigh would shine, even if no fire touched it. Light upon Light. God guides to His Light whom He will. And

God strikes similitudes for men, and God has knowledge of everything (24:35).

It is He who created the heavens and the earth in truth ...His saying is true, and His is the Kingdom the day the Trumpet is blown. He is Knower of the Unseen and the visible. He is the All-wise, the All-aware (6:73). God who created the seven heavens, and of earth their like, between them the Command descending, that you may know that God is powerful over everything and that God encompasses everything in knowledge (65:12) He has numbered everything in numbers (72:28).

'[I seek protection] from the evil of everything possessed of evil, whether openly or secretly, from the evil of jinn and man, and from the evil of what flies at night and rests during the day, and from the evil of the calamities of the night and the day, and from the evil of that which lives in pigeons and wild beasts, ruins, valleys, open country, jungles and trees, and from that which is in rivers.

I seek the protection of Allah. Master of the Kingdom, Thou givest the kingdom to whom Thou wilt, and seizest the Kingdom from whom Thou wilt. Thou exaltest whom Thou wilt, and Thou

abasest whom Thou wilt. In Thy hand is the good. Thou art powerful over everything. Thou makest the night to enter into the day and Thou makest the day to enter into the night. Thou bringest forth the living from the dead and Thou bringest forth the dead from the living, and Thou providest whomsoever Thou wilt without reckoning (3:26-7). Like Him there is nothing. He is the All-hearing, the All-seeing. To Him belong the keys of the heavens and the earth. He stretches out His provision to whom He will. Surely He has knowledge of everything (42:11-12).

I seek the protection for hirn in the One Who created the earth and the high heavens. The All-compassionate sat himself upon the Throne. To Him belongs all that is in the heavens and the earth and all that is between them, and all that is underneath the soil. Be thou loud in thy speech, yet surely He knows the secret and that still more hidden. Allah – there is no god but He. To Him belong the Names Most Beautiful (20:4-8). Verily, His are the creation and the command. Blessed be God, the Lord of all Being. Call on your Lord, humbly and secretly. He loves not the transgressors. Do not corrupt the land after it has been set right. Call on Him fearfully, eagerly. Surely the mercy of God is nigh to those who do good (7:54-6).

I seek protection for him in the Revealer of the Torah, the Gospels (*al-Injil*), the *Zabur*, and the Mighty *Furqan*, from the evil of every tyrant and oppressor, demon, ruler, enchanter (*sahir*), soothsayer (*kahin*), watcher, nocturnal visitor, every thing moving or still, silent, imagined, apparent, changeable, or varying. Glory be to Allah, your Protector and Your Helper and Your Solace. He will defend you. He has no partner. There is no one to elevate the one He abases nor any one to abase the one He elevates. He is the One, the Subduer, and Allah bless Muhammad and his family.

INVOCATION FOR SUNDAY

In the Name of Allah, the Merciful, the Compassionate. Allah is the most Great, Allah is the most Great, Allah is the most Great. The Lord sat on the Throne, and the heavens and the earth were established by His Command. The stars were stilled, and the mountains were fixed firmly by His permission. His Name does not pass by those in the heavens and in the earth. The mountains draw near to Him, obedient, and the bodies are resurrected for Him when they are rotten.

Veil every harmful thing and envious one by the Might of Allah from so-and-so, son of so-and-so, and by the One who placed a partition between the two seas (27:61); and set in heaven constellations, and set among them a lamp, and an illuminating moon (25:61). I seek protection for him in the One who decked them out fair to the beholders, and guarded them from every accursed demon (15:16-17). I seek protection for him in the One who set on the earth firm mountains (21:31) and pegs (78:7), lest evil or indecency or affliction should get to him. Ha Mim. 'Ain Sin Qaf. So reveals to thee, and to those before thee, God, the Allmighty, the All-wise (42:1-3). Ha Mim. A sending down from the Merciful, the Compassionate (41:1-2). The blessings of Allah on Muhammad, the Prophet, and his family.

INVOCATION FOR MONDAY

In the Name of Allah, the Merciful, the Compassionate. I seek protection for the soul of so-and-so, son of so-and-so, in my Lord, the most Great, from the evil of what is hidden and apparent, and from the evil of every female and male, and from the evil of what the sun and the moon behold. Most Holy, Most Holy, Lord of the angels and the Spirit.

I call on you, O jinn, if you are hearing, obedient, and I call you, O mankind, to the Gracious, the All-knowing. I call you, O mankind and jinn, to Him Who is obeyed by all creation stamped with the seal of the Lord of the Worlds, and the seal of Jibra' il, Mika'il, and Israfil, and the seal of Sulayman b. Dawud, and the seal of Muhammad, blessings of Allah on him and his family, the chief of the Prophets, blessings of Allah on Muhammad and his Ahl al-Bayt, the good, the pure.

Remove from so-and-so, son of so-and-so, every female jinn with a rebellious spirit, a jinn or demon or rebellious enchanter, or obstinate ruler or accursed devil. Remove from so-and-so, son of so-and-so, that which is seen and that which is unseen, and that which is seen by an eye, sleeping or awake, by the will of Allah, the Gracious, the All-knowing. There is no way for you over him, nor over what is feared for him. Allah, Allah, Allah, no partner has He, and Allah bless Muhammad and his Ahl al-Bayt.

Tibb al-A'imma

INVOCATION FOR TUESDAY

In the Name of Allah, the Merciful, the Compassionate. I seek protection for myself in Allah, the Great, the Lord of the upright heavens, and in Him Who created them in two days and determined affairs throughout all of heaven, created the earth and determined in it its sustenance, made in it mountains and ***set in it ravines to serve as ways (21:31), produced the heavy clouds (13:12)***, made it subservient, made the ships sail, made subservient the sea, and made in the earth mountains and rivers, from the evil of what is in the night and the day and entangles the hearts, and which the eyes of jinn and mankind see. Allah protect us, Allah protect us, Allah protect us, there is no god but Allah, Muhammad is the Messenger of Allah, blessings of Allah be on him and his family.

INVOCATION FOR WEDNESDAY

In the Name of Allah, the Merciful, the Compassionate, I seek protection for you, O so-and-so, son of so-and-so, in the One, the Refuge, from the evil of what is blown on and knotted, and from the evil of Abu Murra [Satan] and what he has begotten. I seek protection for you in the One, the Most High, from that which the eye sees and does not see. I seek protection for you in the Unequalled, the Great, from the evil of what it intends for you [by the decree of the Sovereign]. Go, O so-and-so, son of so-and-so, to the protection of Allah, the Mighty, the Omnipotent, the King, the Most Holy, the Subduer, the Perfect, the Faithful, the Guardian, the Mighty, the All-forgiving, the Knower of the unseen and the apparent, the Great, the Most High. He is Allah, no partner has He, Muhammad is the Messenger of Allah, blessings and mercy of Allah be on him and his family.

INVOCATION FOR THURSDAY

In the Name of Allah, the Merciful, the Compassionate, I seek protection for myself — or for so-and-so, son of so-and-so — in

Tibb al-A'imma

the Lord of the East and the West, from the evil of every rebellious, standing, sitting envious, and refractory demon, and *We send down on you water from heaven, to purify you thereby, to put away from you the defilement of Satan and to strengthen your hearts, and to make firm your feet (8:11). Stamp thy foot! This is a washing-place cool for drinking (38:42). And We sent down from heaven pure water to revive a dead land, and give to drink of it what We created, many cattle and men (25:48). Now God has lightened it for you (8:66). That is a lightening granted you by your Lord, and a mercy (2:178). God desires to lighten things for you ... (4:28). God will suffice you for them (2:137).* He is the All-hearer and the All-knower. There is no power except with Allah, no conqueror except Allah. *God prevails in His purpose (12:21).* There is no god but Allah, Muhammad is the Messenger of Allah, blessings of Allah be on him and his family.

INVOCATION FOR FRIDAY

In the Name of Allah, the Merciful, the Compassionate. There is no might or power except with Allah, the Most High, the Mighty. Allah, the Lord of the angels and the Spirit, the Prophets and the Messengers, Subduer of those in the heavens and the earth. Creator of all things, and their King. Protect me from their might, and blind their sight and their hearts and make between us and them a guard, and a barrier and a defence. Surely You are our Lord. There is no might nor power except with You. In You we trust, and to You we turn. You are the Mighty, the Wise. Protect so-and-so, son of so-and-so, from the evil of every creature You have taken by the forelock, and from the evil of what inhabits the night and day, and from the evil of every evil thing. Amen, O Lord of the Worlds, and bless Muhammad, the Prophet of mercy and his pure family.

INVOCATION FOR THE ENSNARED AND BEWITCHED

Ahmad b. Badr narrated from Ishaq al-Sahhaf from Musa b. Ja'far, peace be upon him, that he said: 'O Sahhaf.' I replied: 'At your service, O son of the Messenger of Allah'. He said: 'You have been ensnared (*ma'khudh*) from your wife.' I said: 'Yes indeed, O son of the Messenger of Allah, For three years I have used every remedy but, by Allah, they have not benefited me.' He said: 'O Sahhaf, you did not tell me.' I said: 'O son of the Messenger of Allah, by Allah, I know that with you is deliverance from everything but I was ashamed before you.' He said: 'Woe be to you, what is shame in a man bewitched [and] ensnared? I wanted to speak to you about that.

'Say: "In the Name of Allah, the Merciful, the Compassionate, I remove you, O enchanters, from so-and-so, son of so-and-so, with Allah, who said to Satan: *Go thou forth from it, despised and banished (7:18). Get thee down out of it. It is not for thee to wax proud here. So go thou forth. Surely thou art among the humbled (7:13).*

I neutralize your action and drive it back to you and nullify it by the will of Allah, the Most High, the Mightiest, the Most Holy, the Exalted, the All-knowing, the Eternal. Your enchantment is reverted just as *evil devising encompasses only those who do it (35:43),* as the plot of the magicians was neutralized when Allah, the Exalted said: *Cast thy staff. And lo, it forthwith swallowed up their lying invention. So the truth came to pass, and false was proved what they were doing (7:117).* By the will of Allah, the Pharoah's magicians were thwarted.

"I neutralize your action, O magicians, and nullify it by the will of Allah, Who revealed: Be not as those who forgot God, and so He caused them to forget their souls (59:19); and by Him Who said: Had We sent down on thee a Book on parchment and so they touched it with their hands, yet the unbelievers would have said, This is naught but manifest spells. Why has an angel not been sent down on him? Then say: Yet had We sent down an angel, the matter would have been determined, and then no respite would he given them. And had We made him an angel, yet assuredly We would have made him a man, and confused for them the thing which they themselves are confusing (6:7-9); by the will of Allah. Who revealed: So the two of them ate of it, and their shameful parts were revealed to them (20:121). You are confused and not accomplishing any of your affairs. You will never return to it.

"Praise be to Allah, your action has been neutralized, your effort has failed and your plot has weakened, along with the demons who were part of it - *Surely the guile of Satan is ever feeble (4:76).* I have overcome you by the will of Allah, defeated your multitude with the armies of Allah, shattered your strength with the Sovereignty of Allah, and set up over you the decree of Allah. Your sight has been blinded, your strength has been weakened, your ties have been broken, and Satan has absolved himself of you, by the will of Allah, Who revealed: *Like Satan, when he said to man, Disbelieve, then, when he disbelieved, he said, Surely I am free of you. Surely I fear God, the Lord of all Being. Their end is that both are in the Fire, there dwelling forever. That is the recompense, of the evildoers (59:16-17).*

"And He revealed: When those that were followed disown their followers, and they see the chastisement, and their cords are cut asunder, and those that followed say, O if only we might return again and disown them, as they have disowned us! Even so God shall show them their works. O bitter regrets for them! Never shall they issue from the Fire (2:166-7).

"By the will of Allah there is no god but He, the Living, the Everlasting. Slumber seizes Him not, neither sleep; to Him belongs all that is in the heavens and the earth. ... He is the All-high, the

All-glorious (2:255). Surely your God is One, Lord of the heavens and the earth, and of what between them is, and Lord of the Easts. We have adorned the lower heaven with the adornment of the stars and to preserve against every rebel demon. They listen not to the High Council for they are pelted from every side, rejected. Theirs is an everlasting chastisement, except such as snatches a fragment, and he is pursued by a piercing flame (37:4-10).

Surely in the creation of the heavens and earth and in the alternation of the night and day there are signs for men possessed of minds (3:190). And the water God sends down from heaven therewith reviving the earth after it is dead and His scattering abroad in it all manner of crawling thing, and the turning about of the winds and the clouds compelled between heaven and earth—surely there are signs for a people having understanding . . (2:164).

"Surely your Lord is God, who treated the heavens and the earth in six days— then sat Himself upon the Throne, covering the day with the night it pursues urgently — and the sun, and the moon, and the stars subservient, by His command. Verily, His are the creation and the command. Blessed be God, the Lord of all Being (7:54). He is God; there is no god but He. He is the knower of the Unseen and the Visible: He is the All-merciful the All-compassionate. He is God; there is no god but He. He is the King, the All-holy, the All-peaceable, the All-faithful, the All-preserver, the All-mighty, the All-compeller, the All-sublime. Glory be to God, above that they associate! He is God, the Creator, the Maker, the Shaper. To Him belong the Names Most Beautiful. All that is in the heavens and the earth magnifies Him; He is the All-mighty, the All-wise (59:22-4).

"Whoever of the jinn or men or any others wish evil for so-and-so, son of so-and-so, after this invocation, Allah has made him of those about whom He said: *They are those who have purchased error at the price of guidance. Their commerce has not profited them, and they are not right-guided. The likeness of them is as the likeness of a man who kindled a fire, and when it lit all about him Allah took away their light, and left them in darkness, unseeing, deaf, blind— so they shall not return (2:16-18).*

"Allah has made him of those of whom He said: The likeness of those who disbelieve is as the likeness of one who shouts to that which hears nothing, save a call and a cry; deaf and blind — they do not understand (2:171). Allah has made him of those of whom He said: Whosoever associates with Allah anything, it is as though he has fallen from heaven and the birds snatch him away, or the wind sweeps him headlong into a place far away (22:31). Allah has made him of those of whom He said: The likeness of what they expend in this present life is as the likeness of a freezing blast that smites the tillage of a people who wronged themselves, and it destroyed that. Allah wronged them not, but themselves they wronged (3:117).

"Allah has made him of those about whom He said: ..the likeness of a smooth rock on which is soil, and a torrent smites it, and leaves it barren. They have no power over anything that they have earned. Allah guides not the people of the unbelievers (2:264). Allah has made him of those of whom He said: The likeness of a corrupt word is as a corrupt tree— uprooted from the earth, having no stablishment. Allah confirms those who believe with the firm word, in the present life and in the world to come. Allah leads astray the oppressors. Allah does what He will. Hast thou not seen those who exchanged the bounty of Allah with unthankfulness, and caused their people to dwell in the abode of ruin? - Hell, wherein they are roasted: an evil stablishment! (14:26-9).

"Allah has made him of those of whom He said: And as for the unbelievers, their works are as a mirage in a spacious plain, which the thirsty man supposes to be water, until, when he comes to it, he finds it is nothing. There indeed he finds God, and He pays him his account in full and God is swift at the reckoning. Or, they are as shadows upon a sea obscure covered by a billow above which is a billow, above which are clouds, shadows piled one upon another. When he puts forth his hand, wellnigh he cannot see it. To whomsoever God assigns no light, no light has he (24:39-40).

"O Allah, so I ask You by Your Truth and Your Knowledge and the excellence of Your examples, and by the right of Muhammad and his family, for whoever wishes evil on so-and-so, that You revert his plot back on to him, and make him low, and turn him over on his head in a pit. Surely You are Powerful over all things, and that is easy for You; and *that is surely no great matter for Allah (14:20).* There is no god but Allah, Muhammad is the Messenger of Allah, blessings of Allah be on him and his family."

'Then recite the following over the soil (al-tin) of the grave and seal and fasten it on to the enchanted person: He is Allah who has sent His Messenger with the guidance and the religion of truth, that He may uplift it above every religion, though the unbelievers be averse (9:33). And God suffices as a witness (48:28). False was proved what they were doing. So they were vanquished there and they turned about, humbled (7:118-19).'

PERMISSIBLE INVOCATIONS, CHARMS AND SPELLS

Ibrahim b. Ma'mun narrated from Hammad b. 'Isa from Shu'ayb al-Aqrqufi from Abu Basir from Abu 'Abd Allah, peace be upon him, who said: "There is no objection to charms for the evil eye, for fever, for the teeth (*al-daras*), and [for] every serious illness accompanied by a fever. When a person is aware of what he says, nothing unknown enters his invocations."

Muhammad b. Yazid b. Salim al-Kufi narrated from al-Nadr b. Suwayd from 'Abd Allah b. Sinan from Abu 'Abd Allah, peace be upon him, that he ['Abd Allah b. Sinan] said: 'I asked him [Abu 'Abd Allah] about the charm for the scorpion (*al-'aqrab*) and the snake (*al-hayya*), and the spell (*al-nashra*) and charm for the insane (*al-majnun*) and the enchanted who is in torment.

He replied: "O Ibn Sinan, there is no objection to the charm and invocation and spell if they are taken from the Qur'an. Whosoever the Qur'an does not cure, Allah does not cure him. Is there anything more effective in these matters than the Qur'an? Did not Allah, Sublime is His Majesty, say: *We send down, of the Qur'an, that which is a cure and a mercy to the believers? (17:82).* Did He not, Exalted be His Mention and Sublime be His Praise, say: *If We had sent down this Qur'an upon a mountain, thou would at have seen it humbled, split asunder out of the fear of God (59:21).* Ask us, we will teach you and acquaint you with the verses of the Qur'an for every illness."

CERTAIN CHARMS ARE TRAPS

Ahmad b. Muhammad b. Muslim said: I asked Abu Ja'far al-Baqir, peace be upon him, "Should I seek protection by using some of these charms?" He replied: "Only those from the Qur'an, for 'Ali, peace he upon him, would say that many of the charms and amulets (*al-tama'im*) are traps (*al-ashrak*).

Ja'far b. 'Abd Allah b. Maymun al-Sa'di narrated from Nasr b. Yazid from al-Qasim that Abu 'Abd Allah al-Sadiq, peace be upon him, said that many amulets are traps.

PERMISSIBLE INVOCATIONS

Ishaq b. Yusuf al-Makki narrated from Faddala from Aban b. 'Uthman from Zarara b. A'yan, who said: I asked Abu Ja'far al-Baqir, peace be upon him, about a patient — should an invocation or some verses from the Qur'an be fastened to him. He replied: "Yes, there is no objection to it. The verses of the Qur'an are beneficial, so make use of them."

Ishaq b. Yusuf narrated from Faddala from Aban b. 'Uthman from Ishaq b. 'Ammar from Abu 'Abd Allah al-Sadiq, peace be upon him, who was asked regarding a man who might have an illness, and whether it was permissible to write [verses of] the Quran and fasten [them] to him, or to write verses for him, wash them out and give him its water to drink. He [al-Sadiq] said: "There is no objection to all of that."

'Allan b. Muhammad narrated from Safwan b. Yahya from Mansur b. Hazim from 'Anbasa b. Mas'ab from Abu 'Abd Allah, peace be upon him, who said: "There is no objection to an invocation (*al-ta'widh*) being fastened to a child or a woman."

'Umar b. 'Abd Allah narrated from 'Umar al-Tamimi from Hammad b. 'Isa from Shu'ayb al-Aqrqufi from al-Halabi, who said: I asked Ja'far b. Muhammad al-Sadiq, peace be upon him, "O son of the Messenger of Allah, shall we fasten some of the Qur'an and charms on to our children and women?" He replied: "Yes, if it is of leather (*al-adim*), the menstruating woman (*al-ha'id*) can wear it. If it is not of leather, a woman cannot wear it."

Shu'ayb b. Zurayq narrated from Faddala and al-Qasim both from Aban b. 'Uthman from 'Abd al-Rahman b. Abu 'Abd Allah— and he is Ibn Salim— who said: I asked Abu 'Abd Allah, peace be upon him about a patient, and whether some [verses] of the Qur'an or an invocation could be fastened to him. He replied: "There is no objection". I said: "Sometimes we may be in a state of *al-janaba* [impurity due to intercourse]". He replied: "A believer is not impure, but a woman should not wear it unless it is of leather. As for men and children, there is no objection."

Ahmad b. al-Marzuban b. Ahmad narrated from Ahmad b. Khalid al-Ash'ari from 'Abd Allah b. Bukayr, who said: I was with Abu 'Abd Allah, peace be upon him, when he had fever. A bondmaid of his entered and said: "How do you find yourself?" She asked him about his condition. There was on him a threadbare garment he had thrown over his thighs. She said to him: "If you wrap yourself up so that you perspire, your body will drive out the wind." He replied: "O Allah, curse them for opposing Your Prophet, blessings of Allah be on him and his family. The Messenger of Allah, blessings be on him, said: 'Fever is from the severity of the heat of Hell', and sometimes he said: 'from the boiling of Hell, so allay it with cold water'".

Al-Khusayb b. al-Marzuban al-'Attar narrated from Safwan h. Yahya Bayya' al-Sabiri and Faddala b. Ayyub from 'Ala' b. Razin from Muhammad b. Muslim from Abu 'Abd Allah, peace be upon him, who said: "Fever is from the severity (*al-fayah*) of the heat of Hell, so allay it with cold water."

Abu Ghassan 'Abd Allah b. Khalid b. Najih narrated from Hammad b. 'Isa from al-Husayn b. al-Mukhtar from Muhammad b. Muslim from Abu Ja'far, peace be upon him, that when he [Abu Ja'far] had fever, he would moisten two garments and put on one of them. When it dried, he would put on the other.

Muhammad b. Muslim said: I heard Abu 'Abd Allah, peace be upon him, say: "We have not found [a cure] for fever like cold water and prayer."

ON FEVER AND THE MANNER OF ITS TREATMENT

'Awn b. Muhammad b. al-Qasim narrated from Hammad b. 'Isa from al-Husayn b. al-Mukhtar from Usama al-Shahham, who said: 'I heard Abu 'Abd Allah, peace be upon him, say: "Our grandfather, blessings of Allah be on him, did not take anything for fever except ten dirhams weight of sugar (*al-sukkar*) with cold water on an empty stomach."'

'Awn narrated from Abu 'Isa from al-Husayn from Abu Usama, who said: 'I heard al-Sadiq, peace be upon him, say that there is twice as much fever among the descendants of the Prophets, peace he upon them.'

Al-Qasari b. Ahmad b. al-Qasari narrated from Muhammad b. Yahya from Muhammad b. Sinan from Yunus b. Zabyan from Muhammed b. Isma'il b. Abu Zaynab, who said: I heard al-Baqir, peace he upon him, say: "Fever is expelled in three things: vomit, sweat (*al-'araq*) and diarrhea."

Al-Sirri b. Ahmad b. al-Sirri narrated from Muhammad b. Yahya al-Armani from Muhammad b. Sinan from Al-Ridha', peace be upon him, who said: 'Musa b. Ja'far, peace be upon him, was ill and the learned came to him with medications, that is the physicians, and they began prescribing marvelous things. I heard him say: "The idea of it! Confine yourselves to the chief of these medicines— myrobalan (*al-ihlilaj*), fennel (*al-raziyanaj*), and sugar. [Take it] at the beginning of the summer for three mouths, three times a month, and at the beginning of the winter for three months, three days a month, three times. Let the place of the fennel be from near the gum mastic (*mastaka*) and one will not fall ill except for the illness of death."

QUARTAN FEVER AND THE METHOD OF ITS TREATMENT

'Abd Allah b. Bistam narrated from Kamil from Muhammad b. Ibrahim al-Ju'fi from his father that he said: I called on Abu 'Abd Allah, peace be upon him, and he said: "I see you looking pale." I replied: "I have the quartan fever (*humma al-rib'*)." He said: "What about the blessed, the good [remedy]. Grind sugar and add it to water. Drink it on an empty stomach whenever you want a drink of water." He [al-Ju'fi's father] said: I did that and the fever did not recur.

AN INVOCATION FOR QUARTAN FEVER

'Abd Allah narrated from Abu Zakariyya Yahya b. Abu Bakr from al-Hadrami that Abu al-Hasan the first [i.e. Musa al-Kazim], peace be upon him, wrote the following for him when his son was suffering from quartan fever. He instructed him to write: 'In the Name of Allah, Jibra'il', on his right hand; 'In the Name of Allah. Mika'il', on his left hand; 'In the Name of Allah, Israfil', on his right foot; 'In the Name of Allah, *therein they shall see neither sun nor bitter cold (76:13)*', on his left foot; and, 'In the Name of Allah, the Mighty, the Omnipotent', between his shoulders. He [Abu al-Hasan] said: "Whosoever has doubts, it will not benefit him."

ON VARIOUS REMEDIES DESCRIBED BY THE IMAMS, ON THEM BE PEACE

Al-Hasan b. Shadhan narrated from Abu Ja'far from Abu al-Hasan, peace be upon him, who, when asked about tertian fever (*al-humma al-ghabb al-ghaliba*) said: 'Take three spoonfuls of honey and fennel flower and the fever will be uprooted, for they are both blessed. Allah, the Exalted, has said of honey:

Then comes there forth out of their bellies a drink of diverse hues wherein is healing for men (16:69).

The Messenger of Allah, blessings on him, said: "In black cumin (*al-habba a-sauda'*) is a healing from every illness except the poison (*al-samm*)." It was said: "O Messenger of Allah, what is the poison?' He replied: "Death." Then he said: "These two [honey and black cumin] are not predisposed to the heat or the cold, or to natural constituents, but are both a healing wherever they are."

Al-Hasan b. Shadhan narrated from Abu Ja'far from Abu al-Hasan the third [the tenth Imam, 'Ali b. Muhammad al-Hadi (d.

254/ 868)], peace be upon him, who said: "The best thing for quartan fever is to eat sweet flummery (*al-faludhaj*) [made of honey] and a lot of saffron on the day the fever occurs, and not to eat anything else on that day."

WATER FROM THE WELL OF ZAMZAM

Al-Jarud b. Ahmad narrated from Muhammad b. Ja'far al-Ja'fari from Muhammad b. Sinan from Isma'il b. Jabir, who said: I heard Abu 'Abd Allah al-Sadiq, peace be upon him, say: "The water of the Zamzam is a healing for every illness", and I think he said: "whatever it may be, for the Messenger of Allah, blessings and peace be upon him, would recommend the water of the Zamzam whenever he drank it."

ON THE SOIL OF THE GRAVE OF AL-HUSAYN, PEACE BE UPON HIM

Al-Jarud b. Ahmad narrated from al-Ja'fari from Muhammad b. Sinan from al-Mufaddal b. 'Umar al-Ju'fi from Muharnmad b. Isma'il b. Abu Zaynab from Jabir b. Yazid al-Ju'fi, who said:

I heard Abu Ja'far Muhammad b. 'Ali, peace be upon him, say: "The soil of the grave of al-Husayn, peace be upon him, is a healing for every illness and a protection from every fear, when it is taken."

ADHAN AND IQAMA ON THE SHIRT OF ONE SUFFERING FROM FEVER

Muhammad b. Ja'far al-Bursi narrated from Muhammad b. Yahya al-Armani from Muhammad b. Sinan Abu 'Abd Allah al-Sinan from Yunus b. Zabyan from al-Mufaddal b. 'Umar from Ja'far b. Muhammad al-Sadiq, peace be upon him, that one of his clients who was unwell called on him. He [al-Sadiq] said to him: "Why is it that I see your colour has changed?" He replied: "May I be your sacrifice, I have been feeling very unwell for a month. The fever has not subsided and I have treated myself with all the remedies prescribed by the learned, but have not benefited from any of that." Al-Sadiq said to him: "Undo the buttons of your shirt and put your head in it.

Recite the *adhan* [the call to prayer) and the *iqama* [the introduction to prayer], and recite the sura *al-Hamd* (1) seven times." The man said: I did that and recovered as quickly as a camel loosened from its cord.

ON APPLES

Al-Husayn b. Bistam narrated from Muhammad b. Khalaf from al-Washsha' a-Husayn b. 'Ali b. 'Abd Allah b. Sinan that Ja'far b. Muhammad, peace be upon him, said: "If people knew what was in apples (*al-tuffah*), they would treat their illnesses only with them."

Al-Khidr b. Muhammad narrated from al-Hawarini from Muhammad b. al-Abbas from 'Abd Allah b. al-Fadl al-Nawfali that one of the Imams, peace be upon him, said: "I have not read the sura *al-Hamd* (1) seventy times without [the illness] abating. So try it and you will not suffer."

ON SCATTERING WHEAT FOR FEVER

Al-Fayd b. al-Mubarak al-Asadi narrated from 'Abd al-Aziz from Yunus from Dawud al-Raqqi, who said: I was severely ill in Medina and news of that reached Abu 'Abd Allah, peace be upon him. He wrote to me: 'News of your illness has reached me. Buy [the measure of] a *sa'* of wheat (*al-burr*), lie down on your back (*al-qafa'*), and scatter it in any way whatever on your chest and say: "O Allah, I ask You by Your Name by Which, if the distressed asks You, his trouble is removed, and You have established him on the earth and made him Your vicegerent over Your creation, to bless Muhammad and his family and to cure me of this illness of mine." Then sit up, gather the wheat from around you, and recite the same prayer. Then divide the wheat, giving [the measure of] a *madd* to each beggar and recite the name prayer again.' Dawud said: I did as he instructed and recovered as quickly as a camel loosened from its cord. More than one person used this remedy and benefited from it.

AN EFFECTIVE AND TRIED CHARM FOR QUARTAN FEVER

Abu Ghassan 'Abd Allah b. Khalid h. Najih narrated from Ibn Mas'ud Muhammad b. 'Abd Allah b. Abu Ahmad from 'Abd al-Rahman Abu Najran from Yunus b Ya'qub that he said: I was with Abu 'Abd Allah, peace be upon him, while he was teaching one of his followers the charm for fever, so I copied it from the man.

He said: 'Recite the opening of the Book (*al-Fatiha* (1)), the sura *al-Ikhlas* (112), the sura *al-Qadr* (97), and the verse of the Throne (2:255). Then write with your index finger on the feverish side: "O Allah, spare his tender skin (*al-jild*) and fragile bones from the violence of the fire. O Umm Muladdim, if you believe in

Allah and the Day of Judgement, then do not eat the flesh, or drink the blood, or weaken the body, or cause aches in the head. Depart from so-and-so, son of so-and-so, to one who ascribes other gods with Allah. There is no god but Allah, Exalted is Allah over those who associated partners with Him, Sublime, Great."

ON CAUTERIZATION AND CLYSTERS

Muhammad b. Ibrahim al-'Alawi al-Musawi narrated from Ibrahim b. Muhammad [that is, his father] from Abu al-Hasan al-'Askari, peace be upon him, who said: I heard Al-Ridha', peace be upon him, speak of his father. He said: 'Yunus b. Ya'qub, a follower of al-Sadiq, peace be upon him, said: "O son of the Messenger of Allah, a man is cauterized with fire and sometimes is killed and sometimes survives." He [al-Sadiq] said: "One of the companions of the Messenger of Allah was cauterized during the time of the Messenger of Allah, blessings be on him, while the latter was standing at his head."'

Ja'far b. 'Abd al-Wahid narrated from al-Nadr b. Suwayd from 'Asim b. Hamid from Muhammad b. Muslim, who said: I asked Abu Ja'far, peace be upon him: "Can cauterization be used as a treatment?' He replied: "Yes. Allah, the Exalted, made in the remedy a blessing and a cure and much good. What if someone is treated in this way? There is no objection to it."

Ibn Masha'Allah Abu 'Abd Allah narrated from al-Mubarak b. Hammad from Zur'a from Sama'a, who said: I heard Abu 'Abd Allah, peace be upon him, say; "The clyster is one of the remedies. They claim it strengthens the belly. Righteous people used it."

CUPPING, INHALING [MEDICATIONS], STEAM BATHS, AND CLYSTERS

Hafs b. 'Umar narrated from al-Qasim b. Muhammad from Isma'il b. Abu al-Hasan from Hafs b. 'Umar — and he is Bayya' al-Sabiri— who said: Abu 'Abd Allah, peace be upon him, said: "The best ways in which you treat yourselves are through cupping, inhaling medications, steam baths, and clysters."

Al-Mundhir b. 'Abd Allah narrated from Hammad b. 'Isa from Hariz b. 'Abd Allah al-Sijistani from Ja'far b Muhammad, peace be upon him, who said: "The medications are of four kinds: cupping, daubing (*al-taly*) [of oil, tar, clay, mud, etc.] vomiting, and clysters."

Ibrahim b. 'Abd al-Rahman narrated from Ishaq b. Hassan from 'Isa b. Bashir al-Wasiti from Ibn Muskan and Zarara, who both said: Abu Ja'far, peace be upon him, said: "The medicine of the Arabs is of three kinds: cupping, clysters, and, the final remedy, cauterization."

From Abu 'Abd Allah, peace be upon him, who said: "The medicine of the Arabs is of five kinds: cupping, clysters, inhaling medications, vomiting, steam baths, and the final remedy is cauterization."

From Abu Ja'far al-Baqir, peace be upon him, "The medicine of the Arabs is of seven kinds: cupping, clysters, steam baths, inhaling medications, vomiting, taking honey. The final remedy is cauterization, and sometimes added to that is [the application of] lime."

ON SIGNS OF DISTURBANCE IN THE BLOOD

'Abd Allah b. 'Ubayda narrated from Muhammad b. 'Isa from Maysar from Ibn Sinan, who said: Al-Sadiq, peace be upon him, said: "Disturbance (*al-hayajan*) in the blood has three signs: [emitting an] odour (*al-nashr*), itching (*al-hakka*), and the [sensation of] crawling creatures (*dabib al-dawabb*)."

AN INVOCATION DURING CUPPING

Muhammad b. al-Qasim b. Munjib narrated from Khalaf b. Hammad from 'Abd Allah b. Muskan from Jabir b. Yazid al-Ju' fi, who said: Abu Ja'far al-Baqir, peace be upon him, said to one of his companions: 'When you wish to perform cupping and the blood comes out into your cupping-glass, recite before you finish and while the blood is still flowing:

"In the Name of Allah, the Merciful, the Compassionate, I take refuge in Allah, the Noble, from the evil eye in the blood and from every evil in this cupping of mine."'

Then he said: 'Did you know that when you say this, you have combined together [the following]: Allah, the Mighty and Sublime, says in His Book: ***Had I knowledge of the Unseen I would have acquired much good, and evil would not have touched me (7:188),*** that is, poverty.

Then He, Sublime be His Majesty, said: For she desired him, and he would have taken her, but that he saw the proof of his Lord. So was it that We might turn away from him evil and abomination (12:24). Evil here means adultery.

He, the Mighty and Sublime, said in the story of Musa, peace be upon him: ***Thrust thy hand in thy bosom and it will come forth white without evil (27:12)*** — that is, without illness. Combine together all this in your cupping and the blood will flow with this aforementioned invocation.'

CHOOOSING DAYS FOR CUPPING

Muhammad b. Yahya al- Bursi narrated from Muhammad b Yahya al-Armani from Muhammad b. Sinan from al-Mufaddal b. 'Umar al-Ju'fi, who said: Talha b. Zayd asked Abu 'Abd Allah, peace be upon him, about cupping on Saturday and Wednesday. He mentioned the hadith narrated by the Sunnis from the Messenger of Allah, blessings of Allah on him and his family. He [Abu 'Abd Allah] rejected it and said: 'The authentic report on the authority of the Messenger of Allah, blessings and peace be upon him, is: "When the blood is inflamed in one of you then perform the cupping; it will not be fatal."' Then he said: 'I do not know any of my Ahl al-Bayt who had any objection to it.'

It is also related from Abu 'Abd Allah, peace be upon him: "Cupping on the first Tuesday of the Greek month of Azar [March] promotes health for a year, Allah, the Exalted, willing."

It is also related from the Imams, peace be upon them: "Cupping on Tuesday up to the 17th of the lunar month promotes health for a year."

Al-Sijistani narrated from Ja'far b. Muhammad, peace be upon him, who said: "Travel any day you wish and give alms (*al-sadaqa*)."

THE BENEFITS OF CUPPING

Muhammad b. al-Husayn narrated from Faddala b. Ayyub from Isma'il from Abu 'Abd Allah, peace be upon him, from al-Baqir, peace be upon him, who said; "The Messenger of Allah, blessings and peace be on him, never complained of any pain without taking recourse to cupping." Abu Tiba said: 'I cupped the Messenger of Allah, blessings be on him, and he gave me a dinar. I drank his blood. The Messenger of Allah asked: "Did you drink it?" I replied: "Yes." He said: "And what made you do that?" I replied: "I am blessed by it." He said: "You have taken protection from pains and illnesses, poverty and want. By Allah, Hell will never touch you.'"

Al-Zubayr b. Bakkar narrated from Muhammad b. 'Abd al-'Aziz, from Muhammad b. Ishaq from Ammar from al-Fadl al-Rassan, who said: "Abu 'Abd Allah, peace be upon him, said: "Among the medical treatments of the Prophets are cupping, lime and inhaling medications."

THE VARIOUS TIMES FOR CUPPING

Ahmad b. 'Abd Allah b. Zurayq said Ja'far b. Muhammad, peace be upon him, passed by some people performing cupping. He said: "Where was the harm if you had delayed it until Sunday evening, for he would have been cured of the illness."

The Messenger of Allah, blessings and peace be upon him, said: "Perform the cupping when there is a disturbance of the blood in you. Sometimes it becomes inflamed in a person and kills him."

From al-Baqir, peace be upon him, "The best remedies you treat yourselves with are clysters, inhaling medications, cupping, and steam baths."

CUPPING IN VARIOUS PARTS OF THE BODY

Ahmad b. Muhammad narrated from Abu Muhammad b. Khalld from 'Abd Allah b. Bukayr from Zarara b. A'yan who said: I heard Abu Ja'far al-Baqir, peace be upon him, say: 'The Messenger of Allah, blessings of Allah on him and his family, said: "Cupping in the head is a healing for every illness except the poison."'

Al-Hadr b. Muhammad narrated from al-Hawarini from Abu Muhammad al-Bardha'i from Safwan from Abu 'Abd Allah, peace be upon him, who said: "The Messenger of Allah, blessings of Allah on him and his family, would be cupped in three places: one of them in the head, which he called the *al-mutaqaddima*; one between the shoulders, called *al-nafi'a*; and one between the hips, called *al-mu'ayyana*."

LOOKING AT THE FLOW OF BLOOD

'Abd Allah b. Musa al-Tabari narrated from Ishaq b. Abu al-Hasan from his mother Umm Muhammad, who said: My master, peace be upon him, said: "Whoever looks at the first cupping-glass of his blood will be safe from *al-wahiya* until his next cupping." I asked my master: "What is *al-wahiya*?" He replied: "Pain of the neck (*al-'unq*)."

Ibrahim b. 'Abd Allah al-Khuzami narrated from al-Husayn b. Yusuf b. 'Urnar from his brother from 'Umar b. Shimr from Jabir b. Yazid al-Ju'fi from Abu Ja'far Muhammad b. 'Ali, peace be upon him, who said: "Whoever is cupped and looks at the first of his blood will be protected from inflammation until his next cupping."

Abu Zakariyya Yahya b. Adam narrated from Safwan b. Yahya al-Sabiri from 'Abd Allah b. Bukayr from Shu'ayb al-'Aqrqufi from Abu Ishaq al-Azdi from Abu Ishaq al-Sabi'i from one who said to him that Amir al-Mu'minin, peace be upon him, used to bathe himself after the cupping and steam bath. Shu'ayb said: I mentioned this to Abu 'Abd Allah, peace be upon him, who said: "When the Prophet, blessings of Allah on him and his family, would be cupped, blood would be stirred up and inflamed, so he would bathe in cold water to abate the heat of the blood. When Amir al-Mu'minin, peace be upon him, entered the steam bath, the heat of the blood would rise in him and he would pour cold water on himself to cool it down."

CUPPING AT THE BASE OF THE NECK

Al-Harith, the son of al-Harith al-A'war al-Hamdani, narrated from Sa'id b. Muhammad from Abu Basir, who said: Abu 'Abd Allah, peace he upon him, said: "The Prophet, blessings on him, would be cupped in the lateral parts of the neck (*al-akhda'an*) so Jibra'il, peace be upon him, brought him [the message] from Allah, the Blessed and Exalted, regarding cupping at the base of the neck (*al-kahil*)."

Dawud b. Sulayman al-Basri al-Jawhari narrated from Ahmad b. Muhammad b. Abu Nasr from his father from Abu Basir, who said: "I asked al-Sadiq, peace be upon him, about cupping on Wednesday. He disagreed with the people who regard it as an evil omen [and said that] it was a cure from every disease and protection from every calamity."

Ibrahim b. Sinan narrated from Ahmad b. Muhammad al-Darimi from Zarara b. A'yan from Abu 'Abd Allah Ja'far al-Sadiq, peace be upon him, that he was cupped and said: "O maid, bring three darnel grasses (*sakkarat*). After cupping, it will bring out pure blood and will put an end to the heat."

From Abu al-Hasan al-Askari, peace be upon him, "After cupping, eat a sweet pomegranate (*al-rumman*), for it calms the blood and purifies it in the chest (*jawf*)."

ON ABSTAINING FROM CERTAIN FOODS

Ishaq b. Yusuf narrated from Muhammad b. al-'Ays that he said to Abu 'Abd Allah, peace be upon him: "May I be your sacrifice, someone among us is ill and the medical practitioners instruct him to abstain from certain foods." He [Abu 'Abd Allah] said: "We Ahl al-Bayt do not abstain except from dates (*al-tamr*) and we cure ourselves with apples and cold water." He [Muhammad] said: "Why do you abstain from dates?" He said: "Because the Prophet, blessings on him, made 'Ali peace be upon him abstain from eating them when he was ill."

And he said: "The patient is not harmed by the food from which he abstains."

Ahmad b. Muhammad narrated from al-Hasan b. Mahbub from 'Ali b. Ri'ab from al-Halabi who said: I heard Abu 'Abd Allah, peace be upon him, say: "Abstaining from food is not beneficial after seven days."

Al-Hasan b. Raja' narrated from Ya'qub b. Yazid from one of his associates from Abu 'Abd Allah, peace be upon him, who said: "Abstaining from food is for eleven mornings, then there is no abstaining [from it]."

ON INDIGESTION

Muhammad b. 'Abd Allah al-Asqalani narrated from al-Nadr b. Suwayd from 'Ali b. Abu Salb, the son of my brother Shihab, [that he said:] I complained to Abu 'Abd Allah, peace be upon him, of pains and indigestion [*al-tukham*]. He said to me: "Eat the morning meal and the evening meal, and do not eat anything in between, for in it is corruption of the body. Did you not hear Allah, the Exalted, say: ***There they shall have their provision at dawn and evening (19:62)?***"

ON PRONOUNCING ALLAH'S NAME OVER FOOD

Muhammad b. Bukayr al-Musaffi narrated from Faddala b. Ayyub from Dawud b. Farqad from one who mentioned it from Amir al-Mu'minin, peace be upon him, [that] he said: "I fully guarantee that one who eats food and says Allah, the Exalted's, Name, will not be harmed by it." A man from among the people stood up and said: "O Amir al-Mu'minin, I ate food yesterday and pronounced Allah's name over it, but it harmed me." He replied: "You ate various kinds [of food] and pronounced Allah's Name over some and did not do so over others." The man laughed and said: "You have spoken truly, Amir al-Mu'minin." He said: 'That [harm] is only from [the food] over which you did not pronounce Allah's Name, foolish man."

FOR PAIN IN THE WAIST

Muhammad b. Ja'far al-Bursi narrated from Muhammad b. Yahya al-Armani from Muhammad b. Sinan from Abu 'Abd Allah, peace be upon him, that the Messenger of Allah, blessings and peace be upon him, said: "Drink lovage, for it is good for pain of the waist."

Al-Bursi [narrated] from Muhammad b. Yahya from Sinan from Yunus b. Zabyan from Ja'far from Jabir from Abu Ja'far, peace be upon him, who said that Amir al-Mu'minin, peace be upon him, said: 'Whosoever wishes that food not harm him should not eat until he is hungry. When he eats, let him say: "In the Name of Allah, and by Allah". Let him chew his food well and stop eating while he still has an appetite for it and desires it.'

'Abd Allah b. Bistam narrated from Muhammad b. Zurayq from Hammad b. 'Isa from Hariz from Abu 'Abd Allah from al-Husayn b. 'Ali, peace be upon him, who said that Amir al-Mu'minin, peace be upon him, said: "Whoever wishes for the eternal life and not for permanence [in this world], let him wear light clothes, eat early, and have less frequent sexual intercourse with women."

Salih b. Muhammad al-'Anbari narrated from al-Nadr b. Suwayd from 'Abd Allah b. Sinan from 'Awn b 'Abd Allah that Abu 'Abd Allah, peace be upon him, said: 'Pass your hand over the warts (*al-thu'alil*) and say: "In the Name of Allah, the Merciful, the Compassionate. In the Name of Allah, and by Allah, Muhammad is the Messenger of Allah, blessings of Allah on him and his family. There is no power nor might except with Allah, the Most High, the Mighty, O Allah, remove from me my suffering." Pass your right hand [over it] and repeat the invocation three times.'

DESCRIPTION OF A DRINK

'Abd Allah b. Bistam narrated from Muhammad b. Isma'il b. Hatim at-Tamimi from 'Umar b. Abu Khalid from Ishaq b.'Ammar, who complained to Ja'far b. Muhammad al-Sadiq, peace be upon him, of a pain and said to him that a physician had suggested for him a drink and said that it was beneficial for this illness. Al-Sadiq said: 'And what did the physician suggest for you?' He said; 'Take raisins (*al-zabib*) and pour water over them. Then pour honey over it and cook it until two-thirds of it evaporates and one-third is left.' He [al-Sadiq] said: 'Is it sweet?' He replied: 'Yes indeed, O son of the Messenger of Allah.' He said: 'Drink the sweet when you experience it [the pain] and when you are afflicted with it.' He did not tell [Ishaq] any more than this.

DISAPPROVAL OF TAKING MEDICATIONS EXCEPT WHEN REQUIRED

Al-Muzaffar b. 'Abd Allah al-Yamani narrated from Muhammad b. Yazid al-Ashhali from Salim b. Abu Khaythama from al-Sadiq, peace be upon him, who said: 'He whose good health overcomes his illness and then drinks medications has helped [his health to work] against itself.'

Ayyub b. Hariz narrated from Abu Hariz b. Abu al-Ward from Zur'a from Muhammad al-Hadrami and from Sama'a b. Mihran, who said: Abu 'Abd Allah al-Sadiq, peace be upon him, said to me concerning a man who had an illness and was instructed to drink urine (*al-bawl*). 'He should not drink it.' I said: 'He is compelled to drink it.' He [al-Sadiq] replied: 'If he is compelled to drink it and finds no medicine for his illness, then let him drink his urine. As for the urine of others, no.'

WINE USED IN MEDICATIONS

Hatim b. Isma'il narrated from al-Nadr b. Suwayd from al-Husayn b. 'Abd Allah al-Arjani from Malik b. Musamma' al-Musamma'i from Qa'id b. Talha, who said: I asked Abu 'Abd Allah, peace be upon him, about wine used in medications. He said: "It is not proper for anyone to seek a cure in what is forbidden."

Ibrahim b. Muhammad narrated from Faddala b. Ayyub from Isma'il b, Muhammad from Ja'far b. Muhammad, peace be upon him, who said: "The Messenger of Allah, blessings of Allah on him and his family, forbad that one should be treated with impure (*khabitha*) medications."

From 'Abd al-Hamid b. 'Umar b. al-Hurr who said: I called on Abu 'Abd Allah al-Sadiq, peace be upon him, when he arrived from Iraq. He said: "Go to [my son] Isma'il b Ja'far, for he is ill. See what ails him." He said: I left al-Sadiq, peace be upon him, and went to him [Isma'il] and asked him about the pain which he suffered. He told me of it and I described for him a medication which contained wine. He told me: "O Isma'il b. Hurr [*sic*], wine is forbidden and we Ahl al-Bayt do not seek a cure in the forbidden."

MEDICATIONS PREPARED WITH WINE AND PIG FAT

'Abd Allah b. Ja'far narrated from Safwan b. Yahya al-Bayya' from 'Abd Allah b. Muskan from al-Halabi, who said: I asked Abu 'Abd Allah, peace be upon him, about a medication prepared with wine (*al-khamr*). It could not be prepared without it and was only a necessity. He said: "No, by Allah, it is not permissible for a Muslim to look at it, so how can he be treated with it? It is merely the same as the fat (*shahm*) of a pig (*al-khinzir*) used in such-and-such a medication which is not complete without it. Allah does not heal anyone with a medication of wine and the fat of a pig."

ON THE URINE OF CATTLE AND SHEEP

Ahmad b. al-Fadl al-Damighani narrated from Muhammad from Isma'il b. 'Abd Allah from Zur'a from Sama'a b. Mihran, who said: I asked Abu 'Abd Allah, peace be upon him, about a person drinking the urine of camels, cattle, and sheep, suggested to him for pain, and if it were permissible to drink it. He replied: "Yes, there is no objection to it."

Ibrahim b. Riyah narrated from Faddala b. Ayyub from al-'Ala' b. Abu. Ya'qub, who said: I asked Abu 'Abd Allah, peace be upon him, about a person drinking the milk (*alban*) of she-asses (*al-utun*) as a medication. He replied: "There is no objection to it."

ON THE MEDICATIONS OF JEWS, CHRISTIANS, AND MAGIANS

Marzuq b. Muhammad al-Ta'i narrated from Faddala b. Ayyub from al-'Ala' from Muhammad b. Muslim from Abu Ja'far al-Baqir, peace be upon him, about a man being treated by Christians and Jews and taking medications frum them. He [al-Baqir] replied: "There is no objection to that. Healing is only in the Hand of Allah, the Exalted."

Ibrahim b. Muslim narrated from 'Abd al-Rahman b. Abu Najran from Yunus b. Ya'qub, who said: I asked Abu 'Abd Allah, peace be upon hirn, about a man taking medications which sometimes kill and sometimes cure, those who are cured being more numerous. He replied: "Allah has sent down the illness and the cure. He has not created an illness without making a cure for it. So take it, and take the Name of Allah, the Exalted."

ON THERIACA

Muhammad b. 'Abd Allah al-Ajlah narrated from Safwan b. Yahya al-Bayya' from 'Abd al-Rahman b. al-Hajjaj, who said: A man asked Abu al-Hasan, peace be upon him, about theriaca (*al-tiryaq*). He replied: "There is no objection to it." He said: "O son of the Messenger of Allah, it contains the flesh of vipers (*al-afa'i*)." He [Abu al-Hasan] replied: "It has no power over us."

ON APPLES

Ibrahim b. Muhammad narrated from Zur'a from Sama'a, who said: I asked Abu 'Abd Allah al-Sadiq, peace be upon him, about a patient who craved apples but was forbidden to eat them.

He replied: "Give apples to those among you who have fever, for there is nothing more beneficial."

ON THE CONTINUOUS FLOWING OF BLOOD

Al-Mas'udi narrated from al-Hasan b. Khalid, who said: A woman wrote to Al-Ridha', peace be upon him, complaining of a continuous flow of blood (*dawam al-dam*). He wrote to her: "Take, Allah willing, one handful of coriander (*kuzbara*) and one of sumac (*summaq*), and soak them for a night outdoors. Then boil them in a clay pot and drink a saucer of it. It will stop the blood flow except during the time of menstruation."

ON THE WEAKNESS OF THE BODY

Muhammad b. Musa al-Sudayfi narrated from Ibn Mahbub and Harun b. Abu al-Jahm from Isma'il b. Muslim al-Sakuni from Abu 'Abd Allah from Muhammad b. 'Ali al-Baqir, peace be upon him, that the Messenger of Allah, blessings of Allah on him and his family, said: 'Nuh, peace be upon him, complained to his Lord, the Mighty and Sublime, of weakness (*al-du'f*) of his body, Allah, the Exalted, revealed to him: "Cook meat (*al-lahm*) with milk and eat it, for I have created strength and blessing in both."'

Ibrahim b. Hizam al-Hariz narrated from Muhammad b. Abu Nasr from Taghlaba from 'Abd al-Rahman b. 'Abd al-Majid al-Qusayr from Ja'far b. Muhammad al-Sadiq, peace be upon him, who said: 'Whosoever is afflicted with weakness in his heart or his body, let him eat mutton (*lahm al-da'n*) with milk. It will expel from his limbs every illness and danger, and will strengthen his body and harden his gums.

Let him say: "There is no god but Allah, the One. No partner has He. He gives life, and makes to die (7:158), and makes die and gives life. He is the Living, the Undying."

Repeat it ten times before sleep, glorify Allah with the *tasbih* of Fatima, peace be upon her. And recite the verse of the Throne (2:255) and the sura *al-Ikhlas* (112).'

ON THE COMMON COLD

Sa'id b. Mansur narrated from Zakariyya b, Yahya al-Muzni from Ibrahim b. Abu Yahya from Abu 'Abd Allah, peace be upon him, that Ibrahim said: I complained to him of a common cold (*al-zukam*). He said: "[It is] one of the workings of Allah and one of the armies of Allah. Allah has sent it to an illness in your body to remove it. When it has been removed, you must take one *daniq* weight of fennel flower, and half a *daniq* weight of sneeze wort (*kundus*). Grind it and inhale it all. It will get rid of the cold. If it possible that you not treat it with something else, then do that, for it [the cold] has many benefits."

FOR *AL-KHAM*, COLD IN THE BELLY, AND COLIC

Harun b. Shu'ayb narrated from Dawud b. 'Abd Allah from Ibrahim b. Abu Yahya from Muhammad b. Isma'il b. Abu Zaynab from al-Ju'fi from Jabir from Abu Ja'far Muhammad b. 'Ali, peace be upon him, [that Jabir] said: A man complained to him [Abu Ja'far] of *al-kham*, cold in the belly, and wind of colic. He [Abu Ja'far] said: 'As for the colic, write for it the first sura of the Qur'an (*al-Fatiha* (1)), the two suras of taking refuge (*al-Falaq* (113) and *al-Nas* (114)), and the sura *al-Ikhlas* (112). Write below that:

"I take refuge in the Face of Allah, the Mighty, and in His Strength, which is unceasing, and in His Power, which nothing can resist, from the evil of this pain, and the evil of what is in it, and the evil of what I fear from it."

Write this on a shoulder-blade (*al-katif*), tablet, or cup, with musk (*misk*) and saffron. Then wash it out with rainwater and drink it before breakfast (*'ala al-riq*) or before bed.'

Al-Hasan b. 'Abd Allah narrated from Faddala b. Ayyub from Muhammad b. Muslim b. Yazid al-Sakuni from Abu 'Abd Allah from his father from 'Ali b. Abu Taib, peace be upon him, "Whosoever eats *'ajwa* [a variety of dates from Medina] seven times before sleeping will kill the worms (*al-dud*) in his belly."

From him, that he said: "Give him wine vinegar to drink, for it kills the creatures in the belly (*dawwab al-butn*)."

From Amir al-Mu'minin, peace be upon him: "Eat *'ajwa*, for the dried date of the *'ajwa* will cause them to die – and eat it on an empty stomach."

ON LOOSENESS OF THE BOWELS

Bishr b. 'Abd al-Hamid al-Ansari narrated from al-Washsha' from Muhammad b. Fudayl from Abu Hamza b. al-Thumali from Abu Ja'far Muhammad b. 'Ali al-Baqir, peace he upon him, that a man complained to him of looseness of the bowels (*al-zahir*). He [al-Baqir] said to him: "Take some Armenian clay (*al-tin al-Armani*). Turn it over on a low fire, then eat some of it. It will cease."

From him, peace be upon him, that he said concerning looseness of the bowels: "Take one part of white clay (*khazaf abyad*) one part of fleawort (*bizr qutuniya*) seeds, one part of gum

Arabic (*samgh 'arabi*), and one part of Armenian clay. Boil over a low fire and eat of it."

ON PHLEGM AND ITS TREATMENT

Hariz b. Ayyub al-Jurjani narrated from Muhammad b. Abu Nusayr from Muhammad b. Ishaq from 'Ammar al-Nawfali from Abu 'Abd Allah, peace be upon him, who attributed it to Amir al-Mu'minin, peace be upon him, who said: "Recitation of the Qur'an, *al-siwak* [twig of a particular tree used for cleansing of teeth], and storax (*al-luban*) are purifiers of phlegm."

From al-Sadiq, peace be upon him, that he said: "Whoever enters a steam bath on an empty stomach purifies the phlegm. Whoever enters it after eating, purifies the bile. If you wish to put on weight, enter the bath when you are full: and if you wish to lose weight, enter it on an empty stomach."

ON DAMPNESS

Salim b. Ibrahim narrated from al-Daylami from Dawud al-Raqqi, who said: 'A man complained to Musa b. Ja'far, peace be upon him, of dampness (*al-rutuba*). He instructed him to eat *barni* dates on an empty stomach and not to drink water. He did that and the dampness left him and he became excessively dry (*al-yubs*). So he complained of that to Musa b. Ja'far, who instructed him to eat *barni* dates on an empty stomach and to drink water after it. He did that and his balance was restored.'

Muhammad b. al-Sirraj narrated from Faddala b. Isma'il from Abu 'Abd Allah al-Sadiq from his father from 'Ali b. Abu Talib, peace be upon him, that he said: "Three things take away the phlegm, reciting the Qur'an, storax, and honey."

From Abu Ja'far al-Baqir, peace be upon him, that he said: "Much carding (*al-tumushshut*) takes away the phlegm, and combing the head (*tasrih al-ra's*) cuts the phlegm and takes it away at its root."

THE EXCELLENCE OF LUMP SUGAR

Hamdan b. A'yan al-Razi narrated from Safwan b. Yahya from Jamil b. Darraj from Zarara, who said: I related to Abu Ja'far, peare be upon him, the statement of Amir al-Mu'minin, peace be upon him, "I am the divider of the fire (*qasim al-nar*) for me and for you." He said: "Yes, Amir al-Mu'minin said that before the people."

From Abu Ja'far al-Baqir, peace be upon him, who said: "Woe be to you, O Zarara, what makes people heedless of the excellence of lump sugar (*al-sukkar al-tabarzad*) when it is beneficial for seventy illnesses and it devours phlegm completely and uproots it?"

ON DRINKING *SAWIQ*

Salih b. Ibrahim al-Misri narrated from Faddala b. Abu Bakr from Abu Ya'fur, from Abu 'Abd Allah al-Sadiq, peace be upon him, who said: "When dry *sawiq* [meal of parched barley] is taken on an empty stomach, it allays the heat and calms the bile; when it is crushed and then drunk, it does not do that."

From Abu Ja'far al-Baqir, peace be upon him, who said: "How great is the blessing of *sawiq*. If a person drinks it when he is full, it is wholesome for him and digests the food. If he drinks it when he is hungry, it fills him. The most excellent provision on a journey and at home is *sawiq*."

ON VOMITING

Ja'far b. Mansur al-Wida'i narrated from al-Husayn b. 'Ali b. Yaqtin from Muhammad b. Fadl from Hamza al-Thumali from Abu Ja'far al-Baqir, peace be upon him, who said: "Whoever is made to vomit before he vomits, it is better for him than seventy kinds of medications. In this way vomit expels every disease and illness."

ON WILD RUE

Ibrahim b. Khalid narrated from Abu Ishaq b. Ibrahim b. 'Abd Rabbihi from 'Abd al-Wahid b. Maymun from Abu Khalid al-Wasiti from Zayd b. 'Ali [Zayn al-'Abidin, the fourth Imam (d.122/740)] who attributed it to his forefathers, peace be upon them, that [one of them] said: 'The Messenger of Allah, blessings of Allah on him and his family, said: "The wild rue (*al-harmal*) does not grow a tree, or a leaf, or a fruit, but that it has an angel in charge of it until it reaches the one who comes to it, or until it becomes debris. In its root and branches is a secret, and in its seed is healing from seventy-two illnesses. So treat yourselves with it and with frankincense."'

From Abu 'Abd Allah al-Sadiq, peace be upon him, that he was asked about wild rue and storax. He said: "As for wild rue, neither its root in the earth nor its branch in the sky is shaken without there being an angel in charge of it until it becomes debris and becomes what it becomes. For Satan avoids seventy houses before the house in which it is, and it is a healing for seventy illnesses, the least of which is leprosy. So do not be heedless of it."

ON FENNEL FLOWER (*AL-SHUNIZ*) AND ITS BENEFITS

Al-Qasim b. Ahmad b. Ja'far narrated from al-Qasim b. Muhammad from Abu Ja'far from Muhammad b. Ya'la Abu 'Amr from Dharih, who said: I said to Abu 'Abd Allah, peace be upon him. "I suffer from rumbling (*al-qaraqir*) and pain in my belly." He replied: "What prevents you from [taking] black cumin? It is a cure for every illness except the poison."

From Abu Ja'far al-Baqir, peace be upon him, who said: 'The Messenger of Allah, blessings of Allah on him and his family, said concerning this black cumin that in it is a cure for every illness except the poison. It was said: "O Messenger of Allah, what is the poison?" He replied: "Death."'

From Zarara b. A'yan, who said: I heard Abu Ja'far al-Baqir, peace be upon him, when asked about the statement of the Messenger of Allah, blessings of Allah on him and his family, about black cumin, say: 'Yes, the Messenger of Allah said that and made an exception in it, for he said: "except the poison". But shall I show you what is more effective than it, and about which the Prophet, blessings on him and his family, has not made an exception?' I said: 'Yes indeed, O son of the Messenger of Allah.' He said: 'Prayer repels destiny (*al-qada'*) and that has been decided conclusively, and alms extinguish anger,' and he brought his fingers together.

ON DRIPPING URINE

Muhammad b. Ibrahim al-'Alawi narrated from Faddala from Muhammad b. Abu Basir from his father, who said: Amr al-Afraq complained to al-Baqir, peace be upon him, of dripping urine (*taqtir al-bawl*). He [al-Baqir] said: "Take wild rue and wash it six times in cold water and once in hot water. Then dry it in the shade and mix it with pure and clear oil. Eat it on an empty stomach and it will stop the dripping, Allah, the Exalted, willing."

GRIPES

Hamid b. 'Abd Allah al-Madani narrated from Ishaq b. Muhammad, companion of Abu al-Hasan, from 'Ali b. Sindi from Sa'd b. Sa'd from Musa b. Ja'far, peace he upon him, who said to one of his companions who was complaining of gripes (*al-alwa'*): 'Take water and read over it this invocation three times, and do not pour oil over it. "Allah wishes for you ease, and He does not wish for you hardship". Then recite:

Have not the unbelievers then beheld that the heavens and the earth were a mass all sewn up, and then We unstitched them and of water fashioned every living thing? Will they not believe? (21:30).

Then drink it and pass your hand over your belly and you will be cured. Allah, the Exalted, willing.'

FOR SEVERE LABOUR PAINS AND DIFFICULTY IN CHILDBIRTH

Salih b. Ibrahim al-Misri narrated from Ibn Faddala from Muhammad b. al-Jahm from al-Munkhal from Jabir b. Yazid al-Ju'fi that a man came to Abu Ja'far al-Baqir, peace be upon him, and said: "O son of the Messenger of Allah, help me!" He [al-Baqir] said: "What is it?" He replied: "My wife in on the threshold of death from the severity of labour pains (*al-talq*)." He said: "Go and read over her:

And the birthpangs surprised her by the trunk of the palm tree (al-nakhla). She said. Would 1 had died ere this, and became a thing forgotten! But the one that was below her called to her: Nay, do not sorrow. See, thy Lord has set below thee a rivulet. Shake also to thee, the palm trunk, and there shall come tumbling upon thee dates fresh and ripe (19:23-5).

Then raise your voice with this verse:

And it is God who brought you forth from your mother's abdomen not knowing anything. He appointed for you hearing, and sight, and hearts, that haply so you will be thankful (16:78). Thus come out, O labour pains, Allah, the Exalted, willing.

She will recover immediately, with Allah the Exalted's help."

ON BLOOD VESSELS THROBBING IN THE JOINTS

Muhammad b. Ja'far al-Bursi narrated from Muhammad b. Yahya al-Armani from Yuuus b. Zabyan from Abu Zaynab, who said: While 1 was with Ja'far b. Muhammad, peace be upon him, there came to him Sinan b. Sulama looking pale-faced. He [Ja'far b Muhammad] asked him: 'What is the matter with you?' He described to him the severe throbbing (*al-darban*) that he suffered from in his joints (*al-mafasil*). He [Ja'far b. Muhammad] said to him: 'Woe be to you, say: "O Allah, I ask You by Your Names and Your Blessings, and the call of Your noble, blessed Prophet, who has influence with You, and by his right and the right of his daughter Fatima, the

blessed, and by the right of his trustee (*wasi*), Amir al-Mu'minin, and the right of the Chiefs of the Youth of the people of Paradise [al-Hasan and al-Husayn], to remove from me the evil of what I suffer; by their right, by their right, by their right. By Your

Right, O God of all the worlds.'" By Allah, he had not risen from his seat when his suffering abated.

ON PENETRATING WINDS

Ja'far b. Jabir al-Ta'i narrated from Musa b. Imran b. Yazid al-Sayqal from 'Umar b. Yazid, who said Jabir b. Hassan al-Sufi wrote to Abu 'Abd Allah, peace be upon him: 'O son of the Messenger of Allah, I have been detained by a wind penetrating (*rih shabika*) me from my head to my feet, so pray to Allah for me.' Abu 'Abd Allah, peace be upon him, prayed for him and wrote to him: 'Inhale ambergris (*al-'anbar*) and mercury (*al-zaybaq*) on an empty stomach and you will be cured of it, Allah, the Exalted, willing.' He did that and recovered as quickly as a camel loosed from its cord.

ON THE EVIL WIND WHICH STRIKES THE FACE

Ahmad b. Ibrahim b. Riyah narrated from al-Sabbah b. Muharib, who said: I was with Abu Ja'far b. Al-Ridha', peace be upon him. He mentioned that Shabib b. Jabir was struck by the evil wind (*al-rih al-khabitha*), which had pulled down his face and eyes [to one side]. He [Abu Ja'far] said: "Take five *mithqal* of cloves (*al-qaranful*) and put it in a dry bottle. Close the lid tightly and coat it with clay and place it in the sun for one day in the summer or two days in the winter. Then take out the cloves and grind it until fine. Mix it with rainwater until it becomes a thick liquid. Let him lie on his back and coat the ground clove on the side of the face that is pulled down. Let him remain lying down until the clove mixture dries. When it dries, Allah will remove it from him and restore him to his best condition, Allah, the Exalted, willing."

He [al-Sabbah] said: Our companions hastened to him and gave him the good news of that. He treated himself as the Imam, peace be upon him, had instructed, and was restored to the best condition, with the help of Allah, the Exalted.

ON LEPROSY AND VITILIGO

'Abd Allah and al-Husayn, the sons of Bistam, narrated from Muhammad b. Khalaf from Muhammad al-Washsha' from 'Abd Allah b. Sinan that he said; A man complained to Abu

'Abd Allah, peace be upon him, of vitiligo (*al-wadah*) and leprosy (*al-bahaq*). He [Abu 'Abd Allah] said: "Enter the steam hath and mix henna (*al-hinna'*) with lime and coat your body with it. You will not be cured by anything else after that." The man said; "By Allah, I did that only once and Allah cured me, and it did not recur after that."

ON A PAIN IN THE HEAD

Salim b. Ibrahim narrated from al-Daylami from Dawud al-Raqqi, who said: I was with Abu 'Abd Allah al-Sadiq, peace be upon him, when a man from Khurasan who had performed the Hajj entered. He greeted him and questioned him on some point of religion. Al-Sadiq, peace be upon him, began to explain it to him. Then the man said to him: "O son of the Messenger of Allah, since I left my house I have been suffering from a pain in the head." He [al-Sadiq] said to him: "Go at once, enter the steam bath and do not do anything until you pour over your head seven handfuls of hot water. Say Allah's Name each time, and you will not suffer [from it] after that, Allah, the Exalted, wiling."

FOR PAIN, COLD, AND WEAKNESS IN THE ABDOMEN

He said: "Take the quantity of one *ratl* of Cassia fistula (*khiyar shanbar*) and clean it. Pound it and steep it in a *ratl* of water for a day and a night. Then strain it and throw away the residue.

Mix with the clear liquid one *ratl* of honey, two *ratl* of the juice (*afshuraj*) of quince (*al-safarjal*) and forty *mithqal* of the oil of roses (*duhn al-ward*). Cook on a low fire until it thickens. Then take the pan off the fire and leave it until cool. When it cools, add three *mithqal* each of Cassia tona (*al-qilqil*), long pepper (*dar filfil*), cinnamon (*qirfa al-qaranfal*), cardamom (*qaqula*), ginger (*zanjabil*), Chinese cinnamon (*dar sini*) and nutmeg (*juzbawwa*), all ground and sieved. Mix these well and put the mixture in a green earthenware jar. Drink two *mithqal* of it on an empty stomach at one time. It will warm the abdomen, digest the food and expel the wind from all the joints, if Allah, the Exalted, wills."

ON STONES IN THE WAIST

Al-Khidr b Muhammad narrated from al-Kharrazi that he said: I called on one of them [the Imams, peace be upon him]. I greeted him and asked him to pray for my brother, who was suffering from stones (*al-hasah*) and could not sleep. He said to me: "Return and take some black myrohalan (*al-ihlilaj al-aswad*), beleric myrobalan (*al-balilaj*), and emblic myrobalan (*al-amlaj*). Take equal parts of blue bdellium (*al-kur*), pepper (*al-filfil*), long pepper, Chinese cinnamon, ginger, secacul (*shaqaqul*), sweet flag (*wajj*), anise (*anisun*), and galanga (*khulanjan*). Grind and sieve them and mix with the clarified butter from a cow (*samn baqr*). Then mix all of that with twice its weight of honey which has had its froth (*al-rughwa*) removed. Drink of it the equivalent of a hazelnut or a gallnut (*afsa'*)."

THE MEDICATION FOR JAUNDICE

Hammad b. Mihran al-Balkhi said: We frequently visited Al-Ridha', peace be upon him, in Khurasan. One day a youth among us complained of jaundice (*al-yaraqan*). He [Al-Ridha'] said: "Take cucumber (*khiyar*) and peel it. Cook the peel in water and drink one *ratl* of it every day for three days, on an empty stomach." The youth informed us later that he treated a friend of his twice with the remedy and he recovered, by the will of Allah, the Exalted.

AN INVOCATION FOR ONE WHO HAS A BURNING IN THE HEAD

Hatim b. 'Abd Allah narrated from Ibrahim b. 'Abd Allah al-Sai'gh from Hammad b. Zayd al-Shahham from Abu Usama, who said: Abu 'Abd Allah, peace be upon him, said: 'Do the following for every pain and burning in the head.

Draw a square and write in it:

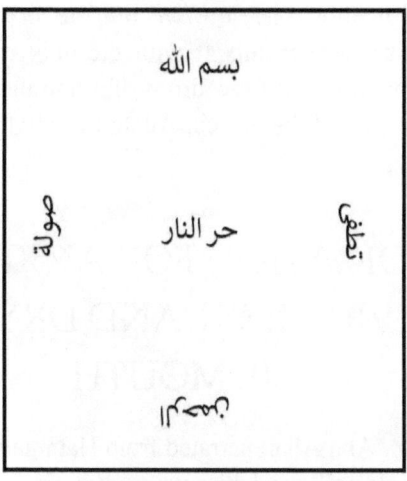

Burn this drawing in the fire, then say: "In the Name of Allah, and blessings of Allah and peace be on the Prophet and his family." Write the *adhan* and the *iqama* on a piece of paper and tie it to the person. The burning and the pain will subside immediately, Allah, the Mighty and Exalted, willing.'

AN EXCELLENT AND TRIED MEDICATION FOR A THROBBING EAR

Take rue (*al-sadhab*) and cook it with olive oil (*al-zayt*). Put a few drops into the ear and it [the pain] will subside, Allah, the Mighty and Sublime, willing.

'Abd Allah b. al-Ajlah narrated from Ibrahim b. Muhammad al-Mutatabbib that he said: One of the followers complained to one of them [the Imams, peace be upon him] of a pain in the ear and of blood and pus (*al-qaih*) coming out of his ear. He [the Imam] said to him: "Take matured cheese (*jibn 'atiq*) as mature as possible, and grind it finely. Then mix it with the milk of a woman and warm it on a low fire. Put a few drops of it into the ear from which the blond flows. It will be healed, Allah, the Mighty and Sublime, willing."

MEDICATION FOR ANXIETY, EXCESSIVE THIRST AND DRYNESS OF THE MOUTH

Ibrahim b. 'Abd Allah narrated from Hammad b. 'Isa from al-Mukhtar from Isma'il b. Jabir, who said: One of our brothers complained to Abu 'Abd Allah, peace be upon him, of excessive thirst (*al-'atash*) and of dryness of the mouth and saliva (*al-riq*). He [Abu 'Abd Allah] instructed him to take two *mithqal* each of scammony (*soghmuniya*), cardamom, Indian nard (*sunbula*), secacul, the branches and seed of balm (*al-balasan*), Cassia spuria (*narmishk*) cinnamon (*silikha*) with its bark removed, Byzantine mastic, pyrethrum, and Chinese cinnamon. Grind and sieve them all except the scammony which is ground separately and not sieved. Then mix them together. Take eighty-five *mithqal* of *Sajzi fanidh* [sweet made of sugar candy and starch], and melt it in two pans on a low fire. Pour it over the rest of the ingredients, then mix it all with honey which has had its froth removed. Put it in a bottle or green earthenware jar. Whenever required, take two *mithqal* of it with whatever drink you wish, before breakfast or before bed.

ON THE EVIL EYE AND AILMENTS OF THE BELLY

'Abd Allah b. Musa al-Tabari narrated from Muhammad b. Isma'il b. Muhammad b. Khalid al-Barqi from Muhammad b. Sinan al-Sinani from al-Mufaddal b. 'Umar, who said: One of our brothers complained to Abu 'Abd Allah, peace be upon him, of his wife who was afflicted with the evil eye (*al-nazar wa al-'ayn*), ailments of the belly and navel, pain in the head, and migraine. The man said: 'O son of the Messenger of Allah, she is still sleepless, and cries out all night. I am in distress from her crying and shrieking, so favour us and her with an invocation.' Al-Sadiq, peace be upon him, said: 'When you have performed the obligatory prayer, stretch out your hands together to the heavens and say humbly and submissively:

"I take refuge in Your Sublimity, Your Power, Your Magnificence, and Your Sovereignty, from what I suffer. O my Succour, O Allah, O my succour, O Messenger of Allah, O my succour, O Amir al-Mu'minin, O my succour, O Fatima, daughter of the Messenger of Allah, help me."

Then pass your right hand over your head (*al-hama*) and say: "O He in Whose trust is what is in the heavens and what is in the earth, calm what is in me by Your Strength and Your Power; bless Muhammad arid his family and calm what is in me."'

ON HEADACHES

Muhammad b. Isma'il narrated from Muhammad b. Khalid from Ya'qub al-Zayyat from Mu'awiya from 'Ammar al-Duhni, who said: I complained to Abu 'Abd Allah, peace be upon him, of that [headache] and he said: 'When you complete your obligatory prayer, place your right index finger on your eyes and say seven times while passing your finger over your right eyebrow (*al-hajib*): "O Compassionate, heal me." Then pass it seven times over your left eyebrow and say: "O Bountiful, heal me." Then place your right palm (*al-raha*) on your head and say: "O He in Whose trust is what is in the heavens and what is in the earth, bless Muhammad and his family and calm what is in me." Then rise for the supererogatory prayer.'

AN INVOCATION FOR ALL ILLNESSES

Mohammad b. Isma'il narrated from Muhammad b. Khalid Abu 'Abd Allah from Sa'dan b. Muslim from Sa'd al-Mawla, who said: Abu 'Abd Allah, peace be upon him, dictated to us the invocation called 'the comprehensive'.

[It is] "In the Name of Allah, the Merciful, the Compassionate. In the Name of Allah with Whose Name nothing in the earth or in the heavens causes harm. O Allah, I ask you by Your Pure, Chaste, Immaculate, Holy, Perfect, Preserving, Protective, and Blessed Name, by Which whoever asks, You grant him, and by Which whoever calls You, You answer him, to bless Muhammad and the family of Muhammad and to cure me of what I suffer in my hearing and my sight, my hand and my foot, my hair and my skin (*al-bashari*), and my belly. Surely You are Gracious to whomsoever You will, and You are Powerful over all things."

MEDICATIONS FOR THE AFOREMENTIONED ILLNESSES

'Abd Allah and al-Husayn, the sons of Bistam, narrated from Ahmad b. Ribah al-Mutabbib, who cited these medications and said that they were shown to the Imam, peace be upon him, and he approved of them. He [Ahmad] said: 'They will be beneficial, if Allah, the Exalted, wills, for black and for yellow bile, for phlegm, pain in the belly, vomiting, fever, pleurisy (*al-birsam*), chapping of hands and feet, suppression of urine (*al-'usr*), looseness of the bowels, pain in the belly and in the liver, and heat in the head. It is necessary to abstain from dried dates, fish, vinegar (*khall*) and legumes (*al-baql*), and the person who drinks it should eat *zirabaja* [a dish of sugar, almonds, and vinegar] with sesame oil. He should drink it for three days, two *mithqal* a day. I would give him one *mithqal* to drink but the Imam, peace be upon him, said: "Two mithqal", and said that the Prophets had apportioned it for our Prophet, blessings be on him and his family.'

'Take one *ratl* of cleansed Cassia fistula and steep it in a *ratl* of water for a day and a night. Then strain it, taking the clear liquid and throwing away the residue. Add to the clear liquid one *ratl* of honey, one *ratl* of the juice of quince, and forty *mithqal* of the oil of roses. Cook it on a low fire until it thickens. Then remove it from the fire and leave to cool. When cooled, add three *mithqal* each of pepper, long pepper, cinnamon, clove, cardamom, ginger, Chinese cinnamon, and nutmeg, all ground and sieved. Mix it well and put in a green earthenware jar or in a bottle. Drink two *mithqal* of it on an empty stomach and it will be beneficial, Allah, the Mighty and Sublime, willing. It is beneficial for what has been mentioned, and for jaundice and severe, continuous fever from which there is a fear of the person getting pleurisy, and for a high temperature.'

PAIN OF THE BLADDER AND URETHRA

He said: "Take cucumber and peel it. Cook its peel in water with the roots of endive (*al-hindiba'*). Then strain it and pour lump sugar over it. Drink one *ratl* of it every day before breakfast for three days. It is good, tried, and beneficial, Allah, the Exalted, willing."

ON PAIN IN THE WAIST

He said: "Take four *mithqal* of pepper, and a similar quantity of ginger, long pepper, rice (*birinj*), mace (*basbasa*), and Chinese cinnamon, each of them the same quantity, that is, four *mithqal*. Take forty-five *mithqal* of good, pure, fresh butter (*al-zibd*), and forty-six *mithqal* of white sugar. Grind them all and sieve them in a cloth or fine sieve. Add twice its total weight of honey which has had its foam removed. Whoever drinks it for the waist, let him take the weight of three *mithqal*; whoever drinks it as a laxative (*al-mashw*), let him take the weight of seven *mithqal* or eight with tepid water. It will remove every illness, Allah, the Exalted, willing, and with this medication there is no need for any other. It compensates and is a substitute for all medication. When it is taken as a laxative and the bowels have stopped moving, then let it be taken with honey, for it is good and tried."

THE MEDICATION FOR SCIATICA

He said: "Take the nail parings (*qulama zufur*) of one who has sciatica and tie them on to the place of the vessel, for it is beneficial, Allah, the Exalted, willing. If it overcomes the person and his throbbing increases in severity, take two pillows and tie them on to the thigh which is affected by sciatica from the hip (*al-wark*) to the foot (*al-qadam*) as tightly as possible until he almost faints. Do that while he is standing, then press on the arch of the foot (*batin hadr al-qadam*) which is painful and squeeze it hard. It will bring out black blood. Then apply salt (*milh*) and olive oil and it will be cured, Allah, the Mighty and Sublime, willing."

MEDICATIONS FOR Heart FLUTTER, STRENGTHENING THE ABDOMEN, PAIN IN THE WAIST, INCREASING BRIGHTNESS OF THE FACE, AND REMOVING THE YELLOWNESS

Take seventy-two *mithqal* of dry ginger, forty of long pepper, and four each of heelweed (*shina*), cinnamon leaves (*sadhaj*), pepper, black myrobalan, preserved cardamom (*qaqula murabban*), walnut, bishop's weed, sweet-pomegranate (*al-rumman al-hulw*) seeds, fennel flower and *Kirmani* cumin (*kammun*). Grind and sieve them all. Then take six hundred *mithqal* of good *fanidh* and put it into a clay vessel and pour some water over it. Light a low fire under it so the *fanidh* melts. Then put it in a clean container and add to it the ground ingredients. Mix them well, then put it away in a bottle or green jar. Drink of it the equivalent of a walnut and it will not disagree [with you], Allah, the Exalted, willing.

A MARVELLOUS REMEDY FOR SWELLING OF THE BELLY, PAIN OF THE ABDOMEN, STOPPING PHLEGM, MELTING STONES IN THE BLADDER, AND FOR PAINS IN THE WAIST

Take equal parts ol black myrobalan, beleric myrobalan, emblic myrobalan, blue bdellium, pepper, long pepper, Chinese cinnamon, ginger, seeacul, *wash*, *asarawan*, and galanga. Grind and sieve them and add the clarified butter from a cow. Mix all that with twice its weight of honey which has had its froth removed, or with good quality *fanidh*. Drink the equivalent of a hazelnut or gallnut.

A MEDICINE TO INCREASE INTERCOURSE, ETC.

He said: "This is a marvellous [remedy]. It warms the kidneys (*al-kulyatan*) increases intercourse (*al-jima'*) for the person who takes it, and removes *al-barun* [sic] from all the joints. It is beneficial for pains of the waist and the belly, for wind (*al-riyah*) in the belly and in the joints, for one who experiences difficulty in passing urine, for one not able to control his urine, for heart palpitations (*darban al-fu'ad*), difficulty in breathing, flatulence (*al-nifkha*), indigestion, and worms in the belly. It clears the heart, arouses an appetite for food, allays pain in the breast, yellowness of the eyes (*sufra al-'ayn*) and yellowness of the colour, jaundice, and excessive thirst. It is for one who complains of his eyes, for pain in the head, deficiency in the brain (*al-dimagh*) degenerative fever, and for every illness, old and new. It is good, has been tried, and will never disagree. Drink two *mithqal* of it — it was one *mithqal* among us, but the Imam, peace be upon him, changed it.

"Take six *mithqal* each of black myrobalan, yellow myrobalan and scammony; four *mithqal* each of pepper, long pepper, dry ginger, bishop's weed, red-poppy seeds (*khishkhash ahmar*), and Indian salt (*milh hindi*), two *mithqal* each of Cassia spuria, cardamom, Indian nard, secacul, balm branches, balm seeds, cinnamon (*silikha*) with its bark removed, Byzantine mastic, pyrethrum, and Chinese cinnamon. Grind all these ingredients and mix after having sieved them all, except the scammony, which is ground separately and not sieved. Mix them all together and take eighty-five *mithqal* of good quality *Sajzi fanidh*, and melt it in two pans on a low fire Add the other ingredients to it and mix all that with honey which has had its froth removed. Put it away in a bottle or green earthenware jar. Whenever required, take two *mithqal* of it before breakfast, and before sleeping, with whatever drink you wish. It is marvellous for all that we have described, Allah, the Exalted, willing."

A MEDICATION FOR PAIN OF THE BELLY AND THE BACK

Take ten *mithqal* each of dry storax and the roots of sweet asa (*al-anjudan*) and two *mithqal* of dodder (*al-afitimun*). Grind each of them separately and sieve them in a piece of silk or a fine cloth, all except the dodder, which does not need to be sieved but only ground finely. Mix them all with honey which has had its froth removed, and drink two *mithqal* of it with tepid water when you go to bed.

Muhammad b. 'Abd Allah, of the family of al-Mu'alla b. Khunays, narrated from Ya'qub b. Abu Ya'qub al-Zayyat from Muhammad b. Ibrahim from al-Husayn b. Mukhtar from al-

Mu'alla b. Abu 'Abd Allah from Abu 'Abd Allah al-Sadiq, peace be upon him, that he [al-Mu'alla] said: We were with him on a journey, and Isma'il b. al-Sadiq was with him. He complained to him [al-Sadiq] of pain in his belly and his back. He [al-Sadiq] dismounted and made him lie down and said:

"In the Name of Allah, and by Allah, and by **the handiwork of God, who has created everything very well. He is aware of the things you do (27:88).** Subside, O wind, by Him in Whose trust is what is in the night and the day, and He is All-hearing, All-knowing."

ON THE SEVERE AGONY OF DEATH

Al-Khidr b. Muhammad narrated from al-'Abbas b. Muhammad from Hammad b. 'Isa from Hariz al-Sijistani, who said: We were with Abu 'Abd Allah, peace be upon him, when a man came to him and said: "O son of the Messenger of Allah, my brother has been suffering from the agony of death (*al-naz'*) for three days and it has increased in severity, so pray to Allah." He [Abu 'Abd Allah] said: "O Allah, ease for him the agonies of death." Then he told the man: "Move his mattress to the place in which he prayed, and his suffering will be eased for him, if there is a delay in his appointed time of death. If his time has come, then it will be made easy for him. Allah, the Exalted, willing."

ON INSTRUCTIONS FOR THE DYING

Muhammad b. Ja'far al-Bursi narrated from Muhammad b. Yahya al-Armani from Muhammad b. Sinan al-Zahiri al-Sinani from al-Mufaddal b. 'Umar and Fadl Allah from Muhammad b. Abu Zaynab, who said: Abu 'Abd Allah, peace be upon him, said: "When you are present before a dying person, instruct him on this matter, that is [recitation of] the declaration of unity (*kalima al-tawhid*) of Allah. It strikes terror into their hearts. If he has adhered to the truth, he will be saved."

Muhammad b. Ja'far al-Massisi narrated from al-Qaddah from Ja'far b. Muhammad from his father, peace be upon him, who said: When 'Ali b. Abu Talib was with any member of his family at their death, he would say to him: 'Say: "There is no god but Allah, the Most High, the Mighty. There is no god but Allah the Clement, the Noble. Glory be to Allah, the Lord of the seven heavens and the Lord of the seven earths, and what is between the two, and what is in them, and what is between them, and what is under them, and the Lord of the Mighty Throne. Praise be to Allah, the Lord of the Worlds."' When the patient had said that, he ['Ali] would say: "Go, there is no fear for you."

Ahmad b. Yusuf narrated from al-Nadr b. Suwayd from Abu al-Ash'ath al-Khuza'i from Jabir from Abu Ja'far from his grandfather, peace be upon him, that the Messenger of Allah, blessings be on him, was with a man who was in the agony of death and said: 'Say: "O Allah, forgive me the greatness of my disobedience to You, and accept from me the insignificance of my obedience to You."'

THE CONDITION OF A DYING PERSON

Muhammad b. al-Ash'ath, one of the offspring of al-Ash'ath b. Qays al-Kindi, narrated from 'Ali b. al-Hakam from 'Abd Allah b. Bukayr from Zarara b A'yan, who said: A son of Ja'far b. Muhammad al-Sadiq, peace be upon him, was ill during the lifetime of Abu Ja'far, peace be upon him. Ja'far was sitting in a corner of the room and the boy was in the agony of death. Whenever anyone came close to him [the boy], he said: "Do not touch him, for his weakness will increase. A patient is at his weakest when he is in this condition, so whoever touches him makes him weaker." When the boy died, he gave instructions about bim and the boy's eyes were closed. Then he said to us: "Sadness and distress and grief are only as long as Allah's command has not been revealed. When Allah's command is revealed, then there is nothing but submission and acceptance."

Then he called for oil and anointed himself and applied *al-kuhl* around his eyes. He called for food, and he and those with him ate together. Then he said: "This is the ***sweet patience (12:18)*** in which we were promised excellence. Allah, the Exalted, has said: ***Upon those rest blessings and mercy from their Lord, and those— they are the truly guided (2:157).*** Then he gave orders concerning him (the boy] and he was bathed. He [al-Sadiq] dressed in his finest clothes and went out to pray over him."

From Abu 'Abd Allah al-Sadiq, peace be upon him, that he said; 'There is not one who is about to die but that Satan assigns to him one of his demons to call him to disbelief and make him doubt his charge and his religion until his soul departs. He [the demon] will not have any power over whoever is an enlightened believer, declaring the unity of Allah. He will make whoever is weak in his religion doubt his condition and his religion. So, when you are present with those about to die instruct them to recite the declaration of sincerity, and it is: "There is no god but Allah, the Most High, the Mighty. There is no god but Allah, the Clement, the Noble. Glory be to Allah, the Lord of the seven heavens and the Lord of the seven earths, and what is in them, and what is between them, and what is under them, and the Lord of the Mighty Throne. Praise be to Allah, the Lord of the Worlds.'"

He said: Al-Mu'alla narrated from Ahmad b. 'Isa from Ibrahim b Muhammad from Ahmad b. Yusof from Abu 'Abd Allah al-Sadiq, peace be upon him, that he said: 'When a believer who is a stranger is about to die, he turns to the right and the left and, seeing no one, raises his head to the heavens. Then Allah, the Mighty and Sublime, says, "My servant and my friend, to whom do you turn? Do you seek a friend or a relative closer to you than Me? By My Power and My Majesty, if I loosen your bond, I will surely cause you to worship Me, and if I hold you to Me, I will surely bring you to my Magnanimity and into the proximity of your friends and loved ones."'

ON A CHANGE IN COLOUR

Ahmad b. Ishaq narrated from 'Abd Allah b. 'Abd al-Rahman b. Abu Najran from Abu Muhammad al-Thumali from Ishaq al-Jariri, who said: 'Al-Baqir, peace be upon him, said: "O Jariri, I see you have become pale. Do you have haemorrhoids?" I replied: "Yes, O son of the Messenger of Allah, and I ask Allah, the Mighty and Sublime not to deny me the reward." He said: "Shall I suggest a medication for you?" I replied: "O son of the Messenger of Allah, by Allah, I have treated it with more than a thousand remedies, but have not benefited from any and my hemorrhoids are bleeding." He said; "Woe be to you, Jariri. I am the physician of physicians, the leader of the scholars and the sages, the treasure-house of the religious scholars, and the chief of the progeny of the Prophets on the earth." I said: "It is so, my lord and master."

He said: "Your haemorrhoids are female (*inath*), they pour out blood." I said: "You are right, O son of the Messenger of Allah." He said: "You must take beeswax (*sham'*), the oil of jasmine (*duhn zanbaq*), storax (*lubna 'asal*), sumac, *sar* and flax. Put them together on a ladle over the fire. When they are mixed together, take a quantity equal to a chick-pea and smear it on your buttocks (*al-maq'ad*). You will be cured, Allah, the Exalted, willing".'

Al-Jariri said: 'By Allah, there is no god but Him, I did that only once and I was cured of what was in me I did not experience any bleeding or pain after that.'

Al-Jariri said: 'I waylaid him [al-Baqir] the next time and he said to me: "O Abu Ishaq, you have been cured, praise be to Allah." I replied: "May I be your sacrifice [blank in the original]." Then he said: "As for Shu'ayb b. Ishaq, his hemorrhoids are not as they were with you. They are masculine (*dhukran*)." Then he said: "Tell him to take *abradhar* and divide it into three parts. Let him dig a hole, then pierce a baked brick, and make a hole in it. Then put that *abradhar* on the fire, place the brick over it, and sit on it. Let the hole on the brick be opposite the buttocks. When the fumes rise from it, its heat will reach him. Let him prolong [his sitting] as long as possible, perhaps five to seven *nathalil* [*sic*]. If it is successful let him remove it and throw it away. If not, let him put the second third of *abradhar* on it and it will remove it completely.

Then let him apply the ointment (*al-marham*) of beeswax, oil of jasmine, storax, *sar*, and flax." He said; This is for the masculine hemorrhoids, so let him prepare it as I have prescribed and coat the buttocks with it with only a single coating". I returned and prescribed that to him [Shu'ayb]. He did it and was cured, by the will of Allah, the Exalted.

'When I performed the Hajj next time, he [al-Baqir] said to me: "O Abu Ishaq, tell rne the news of Shu'ayb." I said to him: "O son of the Messenger of Allah, by Him Who chose you over mankind and made you a proof (*hujja*) on earth, he only applied one coating of it."'

EXCESSIVE DIRT

Ibn Jariri narrated from Muhammad b. Isma'il from al-Walid b. Aban from al-Nu'man b. Ya'la from Jabir al-Ju'fi, who said: I complained to Abu Ja'far, peace be upon him, of excessive dirt (*wasakh kathir*) making my garment filthy. He said: "Grind myrtle and extract its water. Whisk it vigorously with the best wine vinegar available until it becomes foamy. Then wash your head and beard with it as vigorously as possible; after that, oil it with fresh sesame oil. It will remove it [the dirt], Allah, the Exalted, willing".

ON TRUFFLES, MANNA, AND 'AJWA DATES

Ahmad b. Muhammad narrated from his father from Muhammad b. Sinan from Yunus b. Zabyan from Jabir b. Yazid al-Ju' fi from Muhammad b. 'Ali b. al-Husayn, peace be upon him, from his grandfather, that the Messenger of Allah, blessings be on him, said: "Truffles (*al-kama'*) are from manna (*al-mann*) and manna is from Paradise. Its water is a healing for the eyes. The *'ajwa* dates are from Paradise arid in them is a healing from poison (*al-samm*)."

ANTIMONY

Jabir b. Ayyub al-Jurjani narrated from Muhammad b. 'Isa from Ibn al-Mufaddal from 'Abd al-Rahman b. Yazid from Abu 'Abd Allah, peace be upon him, who said: A Bedouin called Fulayt came to the Prophet, blessings of Allah on him and his family, and he had watery eyes (*ratb al-'ayn*). The Messenger of Allah, blessings of Allah on him and his family, said to him: "I see your eyes are watery, O Fulayt." He replied: "Yes, O Messenger of Allah, as you see they are weak." He [the Prophet] said: "You must use antimony (*al-ithmid*) for it is manure (*al-sirjin*) for the eyes."

Mansur b. Muhammad narrated from his father from Abu Salih al-Ahwal from 'Ali b. Musa Al-Ridha', peace be upon him, who said: "Whoever is afflicted with weakness in his sight should apply seven strokes of antimony before sleeping."

AN INVOCATION FOR INFLAMMATION OF THE EYES

From Abu 'Abd Allah al-Sadiq, peace be upon him, that he [the narrator] said: A man complained about his eyes. He [al-Sadiq] said: "What about the three ingredients?" The man said to him: "O son of the Messenger of Allah, what are the three ingredients, may my father and mother be your sacrifice?" He replied: "Aloe (*al-sabir*), myrrh (*al-murr*), and camphor (*al-kafur*)."

Muhammad b. al-Muthanna narrated from Muhammad b. 'Isa from 'Amr b. Abu al-Miqdam from Jabir from al-Baqir, peace be upon him, who said: 'When the Prophet, blessings of Allah on him and his family, or one of his family, or one of his companions suffered from inflammation of the eyes, he prayed this prayer: "O Allah, grant me my hearing and my sight and make them my heirs, and help me against the one who oppresses me, and give me my revenge of him."'

From Abu 'Abd Allah al-Sadiq, peace be upon him, that he said: "[Applying] kohl (*al-kuhl*) at night makes the mouth fragrant."

From Jabir b. Khaddash from 'Abd Allah b. Maymun al-Qaddah from Abu 'Abd Allah from his father, peace be upon him, who said: "The Prophet, blessings of Allah on him and his family, had a container of kohl, and he would apply three strokes of kohl from it on each eye every night before sleeping."

ON FISH

Ahmad b. al-Jarud al-'Abdi narrated from the son of al-Hakam b. al-Mundhir from 'Uthman b. 'Isa from Maysar al-Halabi from Abu 'Abd Allah, peace be upon him, who said: "Fish liquifies the fat of the eye."

From him, peace be upon him, that he said: 'Al-Baqir, peace be upon him, said: "This fish damages the covering of the eye (*ghiswa al-'ayn*). Fresh flesh produces flesh."

Al-Husayn b. Bistam narrated from 'Abd Allah b. Musa from al-Mutallib b. Ziyad al-Radi'i from al-Halabi from Abu 'Abd Allah, peace be upon him, who said: "*Al-haff* [sic] is beneficial for the sight."

ON CLIPPING THE NAILS

Ahmad b. 'Abd Allah narrated from Muhammad b. 'Isa from Muhammad b. Abu al-Hasan from Abu 'Abd Allah, peace be upon him, who said: "Whoever clips his nails every Thursday will never have inflammation of the eyes. Whoever clips them on Friday removes from under each nail an illness." He said: "Kohl increases the light of the eyes and causes eyelashes (*al-ashfar*) to grow.'

From him, that he would clip his nails every Thursday beginning with the right little finger (*al-khinsir*), then beginning with the left. He said: "Whoever does that has taken protection from inflammation of the eyes."

AN INVOCATION FOR INFLAMMATION OF THE EYES

Muhammad b. 'Abd Allah al-Za'farani narrated from 'Umar b. 'Abd al-Aziz from 'Isa b. Sulayman, who said: I went to Abu 'Abd Allah, peace be upon him, one day and saw him with his eyes somewhat inflamed and I was grieved for him. I visited him the next day and he no longer had any inflammation. I asked him about that and he said: 'I treated it with something. It is an invocation I have, in which I took refuge.' He ['Isa] said: He informed me of it and this is the copy of it:

"I take refuge in the Might of Allah. I take refuge in the Power of Allah. I take refuge in the Exaltedness of Allah. I take refuge in the Majesty of Allah. I take refuge in the Beauty of Allah. I take refuge in the Magnificence of Allah. I take refuge in the Forgiveness of Allah. I take refuge in the Clemency of Allah. I take refuge in the remembrance of Allah. I take refuge in the Messenger of Allah. I take refuge in the family of the Messenger of Allah, blessings of Allah on him and on them, from what I am wary of and fear for my eyes, and the pain that I suffer in my eyes and what I fear from it and am wary of. O Allah, Lord of the Good, remove that from me by Your Might and Your Power."

FOR INFLAMMATION OF THE EYES

Ahmad b. Bashir narrated from Ja'far b. Muhammad b. 'Abd Allah al-Jammal attributing the *hadith* to Amir al-Mu'minin, peace be upon him, that he said: 'Salman and Abu Dharr, may Allah be pleased with them, complained of an ailment of the eyes. The Prophet, blessings of Allah on him and his family, came to visit them. When he saw them, he said to each one: "Do not sleep on your left side as long as your eyes are suffering, and avoid dates until Allah, the Mighty and Sublime, cures you.'"

ON CONSUMPTION

Ja'far b. Muhammad b. Ibrahim narrated from Ahmad b. Bashara that he said: When I went to perform the Hajj, I went to Medina. I entered the mosque of the Messenger of Allah, blessings be on him, and there was Abu Ibrahim sitting by the side of the *minbar*. I approached him and kissed his head and hands and greeted him. He returned my greeting and said: "How is your illness?" I replied: "I am still suffering from it." I had consumption. He said: "Take this medication in Medina before you leave for Mecca and you will be restored to health, Allah, the Exalted, willing."

I brought out an ink-well and paper and he dictated to us: "Take equal parts of Indian nard, cardamom, saffron, pyrethrum, henbane (*al-banj*), white hellebore (*kharbaq abyad*), and two parts of *abarfiyun*. Grind and sieve them in a piece of silk, and mix with honey which has had its froth removed. Give the person afflicted with consumption the equivalent of a chick-pea with warm water to take before sleeping. You will not drink that for three nights without being cured, Allah, the Exalted, willing." I did that and Allah removed it from me and I was cured by the will of Allah, the Exalted.

ON COUGHING

Ahmad b. Salih narrated from Muhammad b. 'Abd al-Salam, who said: I visited Al-Ridha', peace be upon him, with a group of people from Khurasan. We greeted him and he responded. He asked each of us our request and fulfilled it. Then he looked at me and said: "And you, make your request." I said: "O son of the Messenger of Allah, blessings of Allah on him and his family, I complain to you of a severe coughing." He asked: "Is it recent (*hadith*) or chronic (*'atiq*)?" I replied: "Both." He said: "Take one part of white pepper (*al-filfil al-abyad*), two parts of *abarfiyun*, and one part each of white hellebore, Indian nard, cardamom, saffron, and henbane. Sieve with a piece of silk and mix with an equal weight of honey which has had its froth removed. Take one grain (*habba*) with fennel water before sleeping, for chronic and recent coughs. Let the water be tepid and not cold. It will remove it [the cough] completely."

JASMINE OIL

Ahmad b. Talib al-Hamdani narrated from 'Urnar b. Ishaq from Muhammad b. Salih b. 'Abd Allah b. Ziyad from al-Dahhak from Ibn 'Abbas, who said: 'The Messenger of Allah, blessings be on him, said: "There is nothing better for the body than *al-raziqi*." I asked: "And what is *al-raziqi*?" He replied: "Jasmine (*al-zanbaq*)."

Al-Hasan b. al-Fadl narrated from Hammad b. 'Isa from Hariz from Abu 'Abd Allah al-Sadiq, peace be upon him, who said: "Jasmine (*al-raziqi*) is the most excellent thing with which you oil your body."

MYROBALAN

From al-Musayyib b. Wadih, who served al-'Askari, peace be upon him, from his father from his grandfather from Ja'far b. Muhammad from his father from al-Husayn b. 'Ali b. Abu Talib, peace be upon him, who said: "If people knew what was in yellow rnyrobalan (*al-halilaj al-asfar*), they would buy it by its weight in gold." He said to one of his companions: "Take one grain of yellow rnyrobalan and seven grains of pepper. Grind and sieve them and use as *kuhl* around the eyes."

FOR WHITENESS IN THE EYES AND PAIN IN THE TEETH

Abu 'Atab and al-Husayn, the sons of Bistam, narrated from Muhammad b. Khalaf from 'Umar b. Thuwayh from his father from al-Sadiq, peace be upon him, that a man complained to him [al-Sadiq] of whiteness in the eyes (*bayad al-'ayn*), pain in his teeth, and wind in his joints. He instructed him to take the weight of two dirhams each of white pepper and long pepper and the weight of one dirham of good, pure salammoniac (*nushadir*). Grind and sieve them, and apply three strokes around the edges of each eye. Keep it on for an hour. It will put an end to the whiteness, purify the white of the eye, and ease the pain, Allah, the Exalted, willing. Then wash the eyes with cold water and apply antimony.

Ahmad h. Habib narrated from al -Nadr b. Suwayd from Jamil b. Salih from Dharih, who said: A man complained to Abu Ja'far al-Baqir, peace be upon him, of whiteness in the eyes. He [al-Baqir] said: "Take one part each of impure oxide of zinc, (*tutiya hindi*), scoria of gold (*iqlimiya al-dhahab*), good quality antimony, yellow myrobalan, and *andarani* salt [salt evaporated from sea water]. Grind each one separately with rainwater. Then grind them together and apply around the eyes. It will put an end to the whiteness, clear the white of the eye, and purify it of every illness, Allah, the Mighty and Sublime, willing."

Al-Hasan b. Aruma narrated from 'Abd Allah b. al-Mughira from Buzigh al-Mu'adhdhin, who said: I said to Abu 'Abd Allah, peace be upon him, "I wish to remove my cataract." He said: "Ask Allah and do it." I said: "They claim that the person should sleep on his back in such-and-such a way, and should not pray sitting down." He said: "Do that."

ON COLD IN THE HEAD

'Ali b. al-Husayn al-Hannat narrated from 'Ali b. Yaqtin that he said: I wrote to Abu al-Hasan, Al-Ridha', peace be upon him, "I suffer from severe cold in my head so that when the wind blows I almost faint." He wrote to me: "You must inhale ambergris and jasmine (*al-zanbaq*) after eating. You will be cured of it, Allah, the Sublime and Majestic, willing."

FLATULENCE

'Abd Allah b. Zuhayr al-'Abid, one of the Shi'a ascetics, narrated from 'Abd Allah al-Mufaddal al-Nawfali, from his father, who said: "A man complained to Abu 'Abd Allah al-Sadiq, peace be upon him, and said: "I have a son who is sometimes seized by the winds of flatulence *(rih umm al-sibyan)*, and I give up all hope for him because of the severity of what seizes him. If you think it proper, O son of the Messenger of Allah, blessings on him and his family, pray to Allah, the Mighty and Sublime, that he be cured." He [the narrator] said: He [al-Sadiq] prayed for him and said: "Write the sura *al-Hamd* (1) for him in saffron and musk seven times. Then wash it out with water and let him drink of it for one month. He will be cured of it." He [the man] said: We did that for one night and it did not recur. He was calm and we rested."

From him [al-Sadiq, peace be upon him], that he said: "The sura *al-Hamd* (1) is not read over any pain seventy times without it subsiding, Allah, the Exalted, willing."

FOR THE NEWBORN BABY SUFFERING FROM MOISTURE AND WEAKNESS

Ahmad b. Ghayath narrated from Muhammad b. 'Isa from al-Qasim b. Muhammad from Bukayr b. Muhammad, who said: I was with Abu 'Abd Allah al-Sadiq, peace be upon him, when a man said to him: "O son of the Messenger of Allah, a child has been born with moisture (*al-billa*) and weakness." He [al-Sadiq] said: "What prevents you from [giving him] *sawiq*. Make him drink it, and tell your wife to take it, for it produces flesh and strengthens the bones and you will beget only strong children."

FOR THE STING OF A SCORPION

Ahmad b. al-'Abbas b. al-Mufaddal narrated from his brother 'Abd Allah b. al-'Abbas b. al-Mufaddal that he said: A scorpion stung me and when it struck me its pincers nearly entered my belly from the severity of its sting. Abu al-Hasan al-'Askari, peace be upon him, was our neighbour, so I went to him. He [my father] said: "My son 'Abd Allah has been stung by a scorpion and there is fear for him." He [al-Askari] said: "Give him 'the comprehensive medication' (*al-dawa' al-jami'*) to drink, for it is the medicine of Al-Ridha', peace be upon him." I said: "What is it?" He replied: "It is a well known medicine." I said: "My lord, I do not know it."

He said: "Take Indian nard, saffron, cardamom, pyrethrum, white hellebore, henbane, and white pepper, all in equal measures, and two parts of *abarfiyun*. Grind them finely and sieve in a piece of silk. Mix with honey which has had its froth removed. Give one grain of it to drink with asafetida water (*al-hiltit*) for the bite (*al-lasa'*) of the snake and scorpion, and he will be cured immediately." He said: We treated him with it and gave it to him to drink, and he was restored to health at once. We use it and give it to people until this day.

THE MEDICINE FOR PUFFINESS AROUND THE EYES

Ibrahim b. Muhammad b. Ibrahim narrated from al-Fadl b. Maymun al-Azdi from Abu Ja'far b. 'Ali b. Musa, peace be upon him, that he [al-Azdi] said: "O son of the Messenger of Allah, I experience severe pain from this puffiness around the eyes (*al-shausa*)." He replied: "Take one gram of the medicine of Al-Ridha', peace be upon him, with some saffron and apply it around the [affected] area." He asked: 'And what is the medicine of your father?" He replied: "The 'comprehensive medication', and it is well known among such-and-such [people]." He said: "I went to one of them and took from him one grain and applied it around the area with saffron water, as he had mentioned, and I was cured of it."

FOR SEMI-PARALYSIS AND FACIAL PARALYSIS

Ahmad b. al-Musayyib b. al-Musta'in narrated from Salih b. Abd al-Rahman that he said: I complained to Al-Ridha', peace be upon him, of my wife's being afflicted with semi-paralysis (*al-falij*) and facial paralysis (*al-laqwa*). He said: "What about the medicine of my father?" I asked: "And what is it?" He replied: "The 'comprehensive medication'. Take one grain of it in marjoram (*al-marzanjush*) water and make her inhale it. She will be cured, Allah, the Exalted, willing."

FOR PAIN OF THE THROAT

Al-Kalabi al-Basri narrated from 'Umar b. 'Uthman al-Bazzaz from al-Nadr b. Suwayd from Muhammad b. Khalid from al-Halabi, who said: Abu 'Abd Allah, peace be upon him, said: "We have not found anything similar to milk soup (*hasw al-laban*) for pain of the thoat."

ON COLDNESS OF THE ABDOMEN AND FLUTTERING OF THE HEART

Muhammad b. 'Ali b. Ranjawayh al-Mutatabbib narrated from 'Abd Allah b. 'Uthman that he said: "I complained to Abu Ja'far Muhammad b. 'Ali b. Musa, peace be upon him, of coldness in my abdomen and of fluttering (*al-khafaqan*) in my heart. He said: "What about the medication of my father, the 'comprehensive medication'?" I replied: "O son of the Messenger of Allah, what is it?" He said: "It is well known among the Shi'a." I said: "My lord and master, I am one of them, so describe it to me so that I may use it as treatment and give it to people."

He replied: "Take equal measures of saffron, pyrethrum, Indian nard, cardamom, henbane, white hellebore, and white pepper, and two parts of *abarfiyun*. Grind them all finely, sieve in a piece of silk, and mix with twice its weight of honey which has had its froth removed. Give the one suffering from heart-fluttering and coldness in the abdomen one grain to drink with a decoction of cumin water. He will be cured, Allah, the Exalted, willing."

A MEDICATION FOR PAIN OF THE SPLEEN

'Abd al-Rahman Sahl b. Mukhlid narrated from his father, who said: I went to 'Ali Al-Ridha', peace be upon him, and complained to him of a pain in my spleen, the severity of which kept me sleepless at night and confined to bed during the day. He said: "What about the 'comprehensive medication'?" that is the previously mentioned ingredients. He said: "Take a grain of it with cold water and vinegar soup." I did as he instructed me and what was in me abated, praise be to Allah, the Exalted.

FOR PAIN IN THE SIDE

Muhammad b. Kathir al-Bazwadi narrated from Muhammad b. Sulayman, who studied the teachings of the Ahl al-Bayt from Al-Ridha', peace be upon him, that he said: I complained to 'Ali b. Musa Al-Ridha' peace be upon him, of a pain on my right and left side (*janb*). He said: "What about the 'comprehensive medication', for it is a well-known medication" — meaning by it the medicine previously mentioned. He said: "As for the right side, take one grain of it with a decoction of cumin. For the left side, take it with a decoction of celery root (*usul al-karafs*)." I said: "O son of the Messenger of Allah, shall I take one or two *mithqal* of it?" He replied: "No, rather take the weight of one grain and you will recover, Allah, the Exalted, willing."

THE MEDICATION FOR THE BELLY

Muhammad b. 'Abd Allah al-Katib narrated from Ahmad b. Ishaq, who said: I would often sit with Al-Ridha', peace be upon him. I said to him: "O son of the Messenger of Allah, my father has been suffering from an ailment of the belly for three nights and he cannot control it." He said: "What about the 'comprehensive medication'?" I replied: "I do not know it." He said: "Ahmad b. Ibrahim al-Tammar knows it. Take one grain of it and give it to your father to drink with a decoction of myrtle. He will recover at once." He [Ahmad b. Ishaq] said: I went to him [al-Tammar] and took from him a large amount. I gave my father one grain of it and he found relief immediately.

ON STONES

Muhammad b. Hakim narrated from Muhammad b. al-Nadr, a teacher of the child of Abu Ja'far Muhammad b. 'Ali b. Musa, peace be upon him, that he said: I complained to him [Abu Ja'far] of my suffering from stones. He said: "Woe be to you, what about the 'comprehensive medication' of my father?" I said: "My lord and master, describe it for me." He said: "We have it. Girl, bring out the green container." He [Muhammad b. al-Nadr] said: She brought it out and he took out a grain of it and said: "Drink this grain with rue water or a decoction of radish (*al-fujl*) and you will be cured of it." He [al-Nadr] said: I took the grain with rue water and, by Allah. I have not felt its pain until this day.

A BENEFICIAL INVOCATION FOR A YOUNG BOY

Ishaq b. Hassan al-'Allaf al-'Arif narrated from al-Husayn b. Mahbub from Jamil b. Salih from Dharih al-Muharibi, who said: I called on Abu 'Abd Allah, peace be upon him, and he was seeking protection for a young boy of his, saying: "In the Name of Allah, I adjure you, O pain and O wind, wherever it may be, with the invocation with which the Messenger of Allah, blessings be on him, and 'Ali b. Abu Talib, peace be upon him, conjured the jinn of the valley of al-Sabra, and they answered and obeyed, that you answer and obey and get out of so-and-so, son of so-and-so, at once, at once." He said that three times.

FOR PERSISTENT PAIN

Al-Hasan b. al-Husayn al-Damighani narrated from al-Hasan 'Ali b. Faddal from Ibrahim b. Abu al-Bilad, who attributed it to Musa b. Ja'far al-Kazim, peace be upon him, that he [Ibrahim] said: The governor of Medina complained to him [Musa b. Ja'far] of his son's persistent pain. He [Musa b. Ja'far] said: 'Write for him this invocation on parchment, put it in a silver container, and fasten it on to the boy. Allah will remove every illness through it:

"In the Name of Allah, I take refuge in Your Exalted Face, and Your Might, which is unceasing, and Your Power, which nothing can resist, from the evil of what I fear in the night and the day, from all the pains, and from the evil of this world and the next and from every illness, pain, sorrow, sickness, affliction, or tribulation, or that which Allah knows he created me for and which I do not know myself. Protect me, O Lord, from the evil of all of that in my night until it is morning, and in my day until it is evening, by the Perfect Words of Allah, which neither the righteous nor the ungodly can pass over, and from the evil of what comes down from the heavens, and what ascends it, and what enters into the earth and what comes out of it. Peace be upon the Messengers and praise be to Allah, the Lord of the Worlds.

"I ask you, O Lord, by that with which Muhammad, blessings of Allah on him and his Ahl al-Bayt, asked You.

God is enough for me; there is no god but He. In Him I have put my trust. He is the Lord of the Mighty Throne (9:129).

Put a seal on that from You, O Good, O Compassionate, with Your Name, O Allah, the Single, the One, the Refuge. Allah bless Muhammad and his family and repel from me the evil that I suffer, by Your Power."'

AN INVOCATION FOR SOMEONE AFFLICTED WITH THE FALLING SICKNESS

Ibrahim b. al-Mundhir al-Khuza'i narrated from Ahmad b. Muhammad b. Abu Bishr from Abu 'Abd Allah, peace be upon him, who said: 'Invoke protection for the individual afflicted with the falling sickness (*al-masru'*) and say: "I call on you, O possessing one, with an invocation with which 'Ali b. Abu Talib, peace be upon him, and the Messenger of Allah, blessings be on him, called on the jinn of the valley of al-Sabra, and they answered and obeyed, that you answer and obey and get out of so-and-so, son of so-and-so, at once."'

Al-Husayn b. Mukhtar al-Hanzali narrated from 'Abd al-Rahman b. Abu Hashim from Abu al-Jarud from Abu Ja'far Muhammad b. 'Ali, peace be upon him, that he recited this invocation for every pain: 'Place your hand on your mouth once and say: "In the Name of Allah, the Merciful, the Compassionate" three times; "By the Majesty of Allah", three times; "By the Perfect Words of Allah", three times. Then place your hand on the painful area and say three times: "I take refuge in the Might of Allah and His Power over what He wills, from the evil that is under my hand." It will subside, Allah, the Exalted, willing.'

Ibrahim b. al-Hasan narrated from Ibn Mahbub from 'Abd Allah b. Sinan from Abu Hamza from Abu Ja'far al-Baqir, peace be upon him, who said: "Oil [applied] at night passes into the blood vessels and nourishes the skin."

OIL OF VIOLETS

Hisam b. Muhammad narrated from Sa'd b. Junab from Muhammad b. Abu 'Umayr from Hisham b. al-Hakam, who said: Abu 'Abd Allah, peace be upon him, said: "The oil of violets (*al-banafsaj*) is the chief oil."

From him, peace be upon him, that he said: "The most excellent oil is violet. Anoint yourselves with it, for its excellence over the rest of the oils is like our excellence over men."

From him, peace be upon him, that he said: "Oil of violets among the oils is as the believer among men." Then he said: "It is hot in the winter and cold in the summer. The rest of the oils do not have this merit."

He also said: "The violet is hot in the winter and cold in the summer, gentle for our Shi'a, and dry for our enemies. If people knew what is in the violet, it would be valued in dinars."

From him, peace be upon him, that he said: 'The Messenger of Allah, blessings of Allah on him and his family, said: "Use oil of violets, for the excellence of violet over all the oils is as the excellence of the Ahl al-Bayt over people."'

THE OIL OF BEN

Yahya b. al-Hajjaj narrated from Muhammad b. 'Isa from Khalid b. 'Uthman from Abu al-'Ays, who said: I mentioned the oils in the presence of Abu 'Abd Allah, peace be upon him, until I came to mention the oil of the ben tree (*al-ban*). Al-Baqir, peace be upon him, said: "A male oil (*duhn dhakar*) and an excellent oil, the oil of ben." Then he said: "*Al-khaluq* [a perfume] appeals to me."

From Yahya b. al-Husayb from Hamza b. 'Isa from Hariz b. 'Abd Allah al-Sijistani from Zarara from Abu Ja'far, peace be upon him, who said: 'The Messenger of Allah, blessings of Allah on him and his family, said: "Whoever anoints himself with the oil of ben," then he said: "Before Satan he will not be harmed, Allah, the Exalted, willing.'"

Amir al-Mu'minin, peace be upon him, said: "The best oil is the oil of ben. It is a protection and it is masculine, a security from every affliction. So anoint yourselves with it, for the Prophets, blessings of Allah be on them, used to use it."

THE OIL OF JASMINE

Al-'Abbas b. 'Asim al-Mu'adhdhin narrated from Ibrahim b. al-Mufaddal from Hammad b. 'Isa from Hariz b. 'Abd Allah al-Sijistani from Abu Hamza from Abu Ja'far Muhammad al-Baqir, peace be upon him, who said: 'The Messenger of Allah, blessings on him, said: "There is no oil more beneficial for the body than oil of jasmine (*al-zanbaq*). In it are numerous benefits and healing for seventy illnesses."

From Abu 'Abd Allah, peace be upon him, who said: "Use *al-kays* and anoint yourselves with it, for in it is a healing for seventy illnesses." We said: "O son of the Messenger of Allah, what is *al-kays*?" He replied "Jasmine (*al-zanbaq*), that is the *al-raziqi* variety."

THE PAINS OF THE BODY

Muhammad b. Ja'far al-Bursi narrated from Muhammad b. Yahya al-Armani from Muhammad b. Sinan al-Zahiri from al-Mufaddal b. 'Umar al-Ju'fi from Muhammad b. Isma'il b. Abu Ri'ab from Jabir b. Yazid al-Ju'fi from al-Baqir, peace be upon him, from his father 'Ali b. al-Husayn b. Abu Talib, peace be upon him, who attributed it to Amir al-Mu'minin, peace be upon him, that he said: " If anyone of you has pains in his body and is overcome by fever, he must [practise] *al-firash*." It was said to al-Baqir, peace be upon him, "O son of the Messenger of Allah, what is the meaning of *al-firash*?" He replied: "Intercourse (*hashayan*) with women, for it will calm and allay it."

AN INVOCATION FOR DIFFICULTY IN CHILDBIRTH

'Abd al-Wahhab b. Mahdi narrated from Muhammad b. 'Isa from Ibn Himmam from Muhammad b. Sa'id from Abu Hamza from Abu Ja'far, peace be upon him, who said: "If a woman experiences difficulty during childbirth, write these verses for her in a vessel cleaned with musk and saffron. Then wash it out with spring water (*ma' al-bi'r*) and have the woman drink from it and sprinkle her belly and genitals (*al-farj*). She will give birth at once. Write:

It shall be as if, on the day they see it, they have but tarried for an evening, or its forenoon (79:46). It shall be as if, on the day they see that they are promised, they had not tarried but for an hour of a single day. A Message to be delivered! And shall any be destroyed but the people of the ungodly? (46:35). In their stories is surely a lesson to men possessed of minds; it is not a tale forged, hut a confirmation of what is before it, and a distinguishing of everything, and a guidance, and a mercy to a people who believe (12:111)

AN INVOCATION FOR CHILDBIRTH

'Isa b. Dawud narrated from Musa b. al-Qasim from al-Mufaddal b. ' Umar from Abu al-Zabyan from al-Sadiq, peace be upon him, who said: "Write these verses on paper for the pregnant woman when she has entered her month [for delivery]. She will not be afflicted with labour pains or difficulty at childbirth. Wrap a strip [of paper] lightly around the paper and do not tie it. Write:

Have not the unbelievers then beheld that the heavens and the earth were a mass all sewn up and then We unstitched them and of water fashioned every living thing? Will they not believe? (21:30).

And a sign for them is the night; We strip it of the day and lo, they are in darkness. And the sun — it runs to a fixed resting-place; that is the ordaining of the All-mighty, the All-knowing. And the moon — We have determined it by stations, till it returns like an aged palm-bough, it behoves not the sun to overtake the moon, neither does the night outstrip the day, each swimming in a sky. And a sign for them is that We carried their seed in the laden ship, and We have created for them the like of it whereon they ride, and if We will, We drown them, then none have they to cry to, neither are they delivered, save as a mercy from Us, and enjoyment for a while (36:37-44).

And the Trumpet shall be blown; then behold, they are sliding down from their tombs unto their Lord (36:51).

"Write on the back of the paper these verses:

It shall be as if on the day they see that they are promised, they had not tarried but for an hour of a single day. A Message to be delivered! And shall any be destroyed but the people of the ungodly? (46:35). It shall be as if, on the day they see it, they have but tarried for an evening, or its forenoon (79:46).

"Fasten the paper on her middle and when her child is born do not leave it on for an instant."

WHAT IS WRITTEN FOR THE NEWBORN CHILD AT BIRTH

Sa'd b. Mihran narrated from Muhammad b. Sadaqa from Muhammad b. Sinan al-Zahiri from Yunus b. Zabyan from Muhammad b. Isma'il from Jabir b. Yazid al-Ju'fi, who said: A man from the Bani Umayya came to Abu Ja'far, peace be upon him. He was a believer from the family of Fir'awn, attached to the family uf Muhammad. He said: "O son of the Messenger of Allah, my bondmaid has entered her month [of childbirth] and I have no child, so pray to Allah to grant me a son." He [Abu Ja'far] said: "Allah, grant him a healthy male child." Then he said: "When she enters her month [of childbirth] write for her the sura *al-Qadr* (97), and protect her and what is in her belly with this invocation [written] with musk and saffron. Wash it out and make her drink its water and sprinkle her genitals [with it]."

The invocation is this:

'I seek protection for my newborn child in the Name of Allah, in the Name of Allah.

We stretched towards heaven, but we found it filled with terrible guards and meteors. We would sit there on seats to hear, but any listening now finds a meteor in wait for him (72:8-9).'

Then say: 'In the Name of Allah, in the Name of Allah, I take refuge in Allah, the All-hearing, the All-knowing, from the accursed Satan, I and you and the house and those in it, and the dwelling and those in it. We, all of us, are in the refuge of Allah, and the protection of Allah, and the preserve of Allah, and the safekeeping of Allah, secure and safeguarded.'

"Then recite the two Suras of taking protection [*al-Falaq* (113) and *al-Nas* (114)], and begin with the sura *al-Fatiha* (1) and the sura *al-Ikhlas* (112). Then recite:

What, did you think that We created you only for sport, and that you would not be returned to Us? Then high exalted be God, the King, the True! There is no god but Allah, the Lord of the noble Throne. Whosoever calls upon another god with God, whereof he has no proof, his reckoning is with his Lord. Surely the unbelievers shall not prosper. And say: My Lord, forgive, and have mercy, for Thou art the best of the merciful (23:115-18). If We had sent this Qur'an down upon a mountain, thou wouldst have seen it humbled, split asunder out of the fear of God (59:21), to the end of the Sura.

"'Then say: 'Banished are they who contend with Allah and His Messenger. I adjure you, O house and those in you, by the seven names and the seven angels who come and go between

the heavens and the earth, veiled from this woman and what is in her belly, every possession by a jinn and stealing, or touch, or shining apparition touched by man or jinn.'

When he has finished this statement and this invocation, he should say: 'I mean by this statement and this invocation so-and-so, his wife and child, his dwelling, his house and his wife and child.' Then let him name himself and his dwelling and his house and his wife and his child, and let him utter it and say:

'The wife of so-and-so, son of so-and-so; and his son – so-and-so, son of so-and-so.' It is wiser for him and better, and I guarantee that his wife and child will not be afflicted with trial, mental disorder (*al-khabl*), or madness, Allah, the Exalted, willing."

AN INVOCATION FOR ONE WHO DOES NOT WISH SATAN TO TRIFLE WITH HIS WIFE

Al-Walid b. Bayyina, the *mu'adhdhin* of the Kufa mosque, narrated from Abu al-Hasan al-Askari, peace be upon him, from his fathers from Muhammad al-Baqir, peace be upon him, who said. "Whoever wishes that Satan should not trifle with his wife during her confinement (*al-nifas*), let him write this invocation in musk and saffron with pure rainwater, let him squeeze it out on to a new garment, not previously worn, and put it on his wife and child. Let him sprinkle the place and the house in which the woman is. His wife will not be afflicted as long as she is in her confinement, and his child will not be afflicted with insanity (*al-khubat*) or madness or panic (*al-faz'*) or the evil eye (*al-nazara*), Allah, the Exalted, willing.

'In the Name of Allah, the Merciful, the Compassionate; In the Name of Allah, in the Name of Allah, in the Name of Allah, and peace be on the Messenger of Allah, and peace be on the family of the Messenger of Allah, and blessings and the mercy of Allah be on them. In the Name of Allah and by Allah, depart by the will of Allah, depart by the will of Allah;

out of the earth We brought you, and We shall restore you into it, and bring you forth from it a second time (20:55). So, if they turn their backs, say: God is enough for me. There is no god but He. In Him I have put my trust. He is the Lord of the Mighty Throne (9:129)

Tibb al-A'imma

In the Name of Allah, and by Allah, I expel you by Allah, I expel you by the Messenger of Allah.'"

FOR A MARE AT THE TIME OF ITS DELIVERY

Al-Khidr b. Muhammad narrated from al-Haradini from al-Hasan b. 'Ali b. Faddala from Muhammad b. Harun from Ibn Ri'ab from Ibn Sinan from al-Mufaddal from Jabir from Abu Ja'far, peace be upon him; also from 'Ali b. Asbat from Ibn Bakayr from Zarara b. A'yan from Abu Ja'far, peace be upon him, that he said: "Write this invocation for an old and noble mare (*al-faras*) at its time of delivery (*al-wad'*) on the parchment of a gazelle and fasten it to her at her groin:

'O Allah, Dispeller of grief, and Remover of sorrow, the Merciful and the Compassionate of this world and the next, have mercy on so-and-so, son of so-and-so, the owner of the mare, with a mercy which will make him free of mercy from other than you. Dispel his grief and sorrow, relieve his anxiety (*al-hamm*), keep his mare from harm, and make easy for us its delivery.'"

'Isa b. Maryam and Yahya b. Zakariyya, blessings be on our Prophet and his family and on them be peace, came out among creation. We heard the sound of a female wild animal (*wahshiya*). The Messiah, 'Isa b. Maryam, peace be upon him, said: "How strange! What is this sound?" Yahya replied: "This is the sound of a wild animal giving birth." 'Isa b. Maryam, peace be upon him, said: "Come forth with ease, with ease, by the will of Allah, the Exalted."

AN INVOCATION FOR PREGNANT WOMEN AND ANIMALS

Abu Yazid al-Qannad narrated from Muhammad b. Muslim from Abu al-Hasan Al-Ridha', peace be upon him, who said: "Write this invocation on a paper or parchment for pregnant animals:

'In the Name of Allah, the Merciful, the Compassionate, in the Name of Allah, in the Name of Allah, in the Name of Allah, truly with hardship comes ease.

Truly with hardship comes ease (94:5-6).

God desires ease for you, and desires not hardship for you, and that you fulfil the number and magnify God that He has guided you, and haply you will be thankful. And when My servants question thee concerning Me — I am near to answer the call of the caller, when he calls to Me. So let them respond to Me, and let them believe in Me. Haply they will go aright (2:185-6).

And He will furnish you with a gentle issue of your affair (18:16).

He will provide you with guidance in your affair. God's it is to show the way ... If He willed, He would have guided you all together (16:9).

Then the way eased for him (80:20). Have not the unbelievers then beheld that the heavens and the earth were a mass all sewn up, and then We unstitched them and of water fashioned every living thing? Will they not believe? (21:30).

..and [she] withdrew with him to a distant place. And the birthpangs surprised her by the trunk of the palm tree. She said, Would I had had died ere this, and become a thing forgotten. But the one that was below her called to her, Nay, do not sorrow. See, thy Lord has set below thee a rivulet. Shake also to thee the palm trunk, and there shall come tumbling upon thee dates fresh and ripe. Eat therefore, and drink, and be comforted. And if thou shouldst see any mortal, say, I have vowed to the All-merciful a fast, and today I will not speak to any man. Then she brought the child to her folk, carrying him; and they said, Maryam, thou hast surely committed a monstrous thing! Sister of Harun, thy father was not a wicked man, nor was thy mother a woman unchaste.

Maryam pointed to the child then; but they said, How shall we speak to one who is still in the cradle, a little child? He said. Lo, I am God's servant; God has given me the Book, and made me a Prophet. Blessed He has made me, wherever I may be; and He has enjoined me to pray, and to give the alms, so long as I live, and likewise to cherish my mother. He has not made me arrogant, unprosperous. Peace be upon me, the day 1 was born, and the day I died, and the day I am raised up alive! That is 'Isa, son of Maryam (19:22-34).

'And it is God who brought you forth from your mothers' abdomens not knowing anything, He appointed for you hearing, and sight, and hearts, that haply so you will be thankful. Have they not regarded the birds, that are subjected in the air of heaven? Naught holds them but God, surely in that are signs for a people who believe (16:78-9).

Thus, O newborn child, come forth healthy, by the will of Allah, the Mighty and Sublime.'

"Then fasten it to her and when she gives birth, remove it from her. Take care that you do not leave out any part of the verse or stop after [writing] part of it, and that you complete it. It is the statement of Allah, the Exalted:

God who brought you forth from your mothers' wombs not knowing anything. If you stop here, the child will be born dumb (akhras).

If you do not recite: and appointed for you hearing, and sight, and hearts, that haply so you will be thankful, the child will not be born healthy."

ON THINNESS

Isma'il b. al-Qasim al-Mutatabbib al-Kufi narrated from Muhammad b. 'Isa from Muhammad b. Ishaq b. al-Fayd who said: I was with al-Sadiq, peace be upon him, when a man from the Shi'a came and said to him: "O son of the Messenger of Allah, my daughter is wasting away and her body has become thin (*nahal*). Her illness has been protracted and she has a loose belly."

Al-Sadiq, peace be upon him, replied: "What keeps you from eating this rice (*al-aruzz*) with the blessed fat. Allah only made fat unlawful for the Banu Isra'il because of its great blessing in eating it, until Allah removed what was in it. Perhaps you think it will be harmful because of the amount of treatment she has had?" He [the man] said: "O son of the Prophet of Allah, how shall I prepare it?"

He replied: "Take four stones and place them under the fire. Put the rice in a pot and cook it until it is done. Then take the fresh fat of two kidneys and put it in a bowl. When the rice is cooked, take the four stones and throw them into the bowl which contains the fat and turn over it another bowl. Shake it violently and do not let its steam escape. When the fat melts, add it to the rice and let her sip it, neither hot nor cold. She will be cured, Allah, the Mighty and Sublime, willing." The man said: "By Allah, there is no god but Him, she ate it only once and recovered."

ON LOOSENESS OF BOWELS

Abu Ya'qub Yusuf b. Ya'qub al-Za'farani narrated from 'Ali b. al-Hakam from Yunus b. Ya'qub, who said: Abu 'Abd Allah, peace be upon him, told me while I was serving him when he was in pain from looseness of the bowels: "Woe be to you, O Yunus, you know that I was inspired in my illness to eat rice, and was commanded to eat it. So wash and dry it, then roast, crush, and cook it, for I eat it with fat and Allah will remove the pain from rne."

FOR AILMENTS OF THE BELLY AND THE PRAYER FOR IT

Ahmad b. 'Abd al-Rahman b. Jamila narrated from al-Hasan b. Khalid, who said: I wrote to Abu al-Hasan, peace be upon him, complaining of an ailment in my belly and asking for a prayer.

He wrote: "In the Name of Allah, the Merciful, the Compassionate." He wrote the first sura of the Qur'an, the two suras of taking refuge *al-Falaq* (113) and *al-Nas* (114), and the sura *al-Ikhlas* (112). Then he wrote under that:

"I take refuge in the Face of Allah, the Magnificient, and His Might, which is unceasing, and His Power, which nothing can resist, from the evil of this pain and the evil of what is in it and what I fear."

[He said:] "Write that on a tablet or a shoulder-blade, then wash it out with rainwater and drink it before breakfast and before bed. Write below that: 'He made it a healing from every illness.'"

FOR RUMBLING IN THE BELLY

Ahmad b. Muharib al-Sudani narrated from Safwan b.Yahya al-Bayya' from 'Abd al-Rahman b. al-Jahm that Dharih al-Muharibi complained to Abu 'Abd Allah, peace be upon him, of rumbling in his belly. He [Abu 'Abd Allah] asked: "Does it pain you?" He replied: "Yes." He [Abu 'Abd Allah] said: "What prevents you from taking black cumin and honey for it?"

Salama b. Muhammad al-Ash'ari narrated fmm 'Uthman b. 'Isa who said: A man complained to Abu al-Hasan, the first [Musa al-Kazim], peace be upon him, and said: "I have a rumbling, it never subsides and I am ashamed of talking to people for they will hear the sound of that rumbling. So pray for me to be cured of it." He [Abu al-Hasan] replied: "When you finish your night prayer, say: 'O Allah, whatever I know of good, it is from You, there is no praise for me in it. Whatever I know of evil, You have warned me of it, so I have no excuse in it. O Allah, I take refuge in You from relying on that in which there is no praise for me, or trusting in that for which I have no excuse.'"

ON STOPPING FLOWING BLOOD

Al-Sabbah b. Muhammad al-Azdi narrated from al-Husayn b. Khalid, who said: A woman wrote to Al-Ridha', peace be upon him, complaining of a continuous flow of blood. He [Al-Ridha'] wrote to her: "Take one handful of coriander and one of sumac and soak it for one night in the open air. Then put it on the fire and sieve it. Drink a saucer of it and the blood will cease, Allah, the Exalted, willing."

GRIPES

Ayyub b. 'Umar narrated from Muhammad b. 'Isa from Kamil from Muhammad b. Ibrahim al-Ju'fi who said: A man complained to Abu al-Hasan al-Rida, peace be upon him, of gripes (al-maghs), the pains of which almost kiiled him. He asked him to pray to Allah, the Mighty and Sublime, for him, since the many medications he had taken for it had wearied him and had not benefited him. On the contrary, the severity [of the pain] had increased. He [Al-Ridha'] smiled and said: "Woe be to you, our prayer to Allah has weight, and I ask Allah to ease it for you with His Power and His Strength. When the affair [i.e. the pain] intensifies and you are in agony from it, take a walnut and throw it on the fire until you know that its kernel has been roasted and the fire has altered all of its shell. It [the pain] will subside at once." He [the man] said: "By Allah, I only did that once and the gripes subsided, by the will of Allah, the Mighty and Sublime."

HEMORRHOIDS

Abu al-Fawaris b. Ghalib b. Muhammad b. Faris narrated from Ahmad b. Hammad al-Basri from the son of Nasr b. Sayyar from Mu'ammar b. Khallad, who said: "Abu al-Hasan Al-Ridha', peace be upon him, would often instruct me to take this medication and would say that there are many benefits in it. I have tried it for wind and hemorrhoids and by Allah, it did not disagree with me.

Take equal parts of black myrobalan, beleric myrobalan, and emblic myrobalan. Grind them, then sieve through silk. Take a similar measure of blue almonds (*lauz azraq*), called blue *muql* among the Iraqis. Soak the almonds in leek water for thirty days until it becomes soft and dissolves. Then add these ingredients to it and knead them together vigorously until mixed. Form them into pellets like lentils (*al-'adas*), and oil your hand with violet oil or the oil of the yellow gilliflower (*khiri*) or sesame oil, so that it does not stick. Then dry it in the shade. If it is summer, take one *mithqal* of it, and if it is winter, take two *mithqal*. Abstain from fish, vinegar, and legumes, for it has been proved by experience."

VITILIGO AND WHITENESS OF THE EYES

'Abd al-Aziz b. 'Abd al-Jabbar narrated from Dawud b. 'Abd al-Rahman from Yunus, who said: I was afflicted with whiteness in my eyes, so I went to Abu 'Abd Allah, peace be upon him, and complained of that to him. He said: "Purify yourself and pray two *rak'as* and say: 'O Allah, O Merciful, O Compassionate, O All-hearing, O Hearer of supplications, O Bestower of blessings. Grant me the good of this world and the next, and protect me from the evil of this world and the evil of the next world, and remove from me my suffering, for the affair has vexed me and grieved me.'"

Yunus said: I did as he instructed me and Allah removed that from me, praise be to Him.

From him, blessings of Allah on him and his family, that he said: "Place your hand on it and say: 'O Bestower of healing and Remover of illness, bestow a cure on the illness that is in in me.'

THE MILK OF MILCH CAMELS

Al-Jarud b. Muhammad narrated from Muhammad b. 'Isa from Kamil who said: I heard Musa b. 'Abd Allah, the son of al-Husayn say: I heard the shaykhs say: "The milk of milch camels (*alban al-liqah*) is a cure for every illness in the body."

From Abu 'Abd Allah, peace be upon him, that he said the same, except that he added: "In it is a cure for every illness and disease in the body. It purifies the body, removes its impurity, and cleanses it completely."

SHORTNESS OF BREATH

Abu Ja'far Ahmad b. Muhammad narrated from Abu Muhammad b. Khalid from Muhammad b. Sinan al-Sinani from al-Mufaddal b. 'Umar, who said: I asked Abu 'Abd Allah, peace be upon him, "O son of the Messenger of Allah, severe shortness of breath (*al-rabw*) afflicts me when I walk so that I sometimes have lo rest twice between my house and yours." He replied: "O Mufaddal, drink the urine of milch camels." He [al-Mufaddal] said: I drank that and Allah removed my illness.

Ibrahim b. Sirhan al-Mutatabbib narrated from 'Ali b. Asbat from Hakim b. Miskin from Ishaq b. Isma'il and Bishr b. 'Ammar, both of whom said: We came to Abu 'Abd Allah, peace be upon him, and Yunus had been afflicted with 'the evil disease' (*al-da' al-khabith*). We sat before him and said: "'May Allah be good to you, we have been afflicted with a misfortune, the like of which has never afflicted us before." He [Abu 'Abd Allah] asked: "And what is that?" So we acquainted him with the story. He said to Yunus: "Rise and purify yourself. Pray two *rak'as*, then praise Allah and extol Him, and bless Muhammad and his Ahl al-Bayt.

Then say: 'O Allah, O Allah, O Allah; O Merciful, O Merciful, O Merciful; O Compassionate, O Compassionate, O Compassionate; O Single, O Single, O Single; O One, O One, O One; O Refuge, O Refuge, O Refuge; O Most Merciful of the merciful, O Most Merciful of the merciful O Most Merciful of the merciful; O Most Powerful of the powerful, O Most Powerful of the powerful, O Most Powerful of the powerful; O Lord of the Worlds, O Lord of the Worlds, O Lord of the Worlds; O Hearer of supplications, O Revealer of blessings, O Bestower of favours, bless Muhammad and his family and grant me the good of this world and the good of the next, and avert from me the evil of this world and the evil of the next. Remove what is in me, for the matter has vexed me and grieved me.'"

He said: I did what al-Sadiq, peace be upon him, instructed, and by Allah, we had not left Medina when it was removed from me.

HABBABA AL-WALIBIYYA AND THE 'EVIL DISEASE'

Ahmad b. al-Mundhir narrated from 'Umar b. 'Abd al-Aziz from Dawud al-Raqqi, who said: I was with Abu 'Abd Allah al-Sadiq, peace be upon him, when Habbaba al-Walibiyya entered. She was a righteous woman. She asked him questions dealing with the lawful and the unlawful, and we marveled at the beauty of those questions. He [al-Sadiq] said to us: "Have you seen questions better than those of Habbaba al-Walibiyya?" We replied: "May we be your sacrifice, it has left an impression on our eyes and our hearts." Then her tears flowed. Al-Sadiq, peace be upon him, asked: "Why is it I see your tears streaming?"

She replied: "O son of the Messenger of Allah, one of the evil diseases that would afflict the Prophets and the friends has afflicted me. My relatives and the people of my family say: 'The "evil disease" has afflicted her, and if her master is as she says, it is incumbent that he pray for her, so Allah, the Exalted, will remove it from her.' By Allah, I was pleased with that and knew it was a purification and an expiation, and that it is the illness of the righteous." Al-Sadiq, peace be upon him, said to her: "Is your affliction chronic?" She replied: "Yes, O son of the Messenger of Allah."

He [Dawud al-Raqqi] said: Al-Sadiq, peace be upon him, moved his lips with some prayer I did not know and said: "Go into the womens' quarters so that you may look at your body." He [al-Raqqi] said: She went in and removed her clothing, then rose. Nothing remained on her chest or her body. He [al-Sadiq] said:

"Go now to them and tell them: This is the one who, by his Imamate, seeks nearness to Allah, the Exalted."

From Abu al-Hasan, the first [Musa al-Kazim], "Whoever eats the broth of meat (*maraq bi-lahm*), Allah, the Exalted, removes from him vitiligo (*al-baras*) and leprosy."

THE 'EVIL DISEASE'

Al-Hasan b. al-Khalil narrated from Ahmad b. Zayd from Shadhan b. al-Khalil from Dhari', who said: A man came to Abu 'Abd Allah, peace be upon him, and complained to him that one of his clients was afflicted with the 'evil disease'. He instructed him to take gypsum (*tin al-jir*) with rainwater and drink it. He [Dhari'] said: "He did that and was cured."

From him, peace be upon him, that he said: "There is nothing more beneficial for the 'evil disease' than the clay (*al-tin*) of al-Jarir." 1 said: "O son of the Messenger of Allah, how do you take it?" He said: "Drink it with rainwater and daub it over the affected area, for it is beneficial and has been proven, Allah, the Exalted, willing.'"

PROTECTION FROM LEPROSY

Ibrahim narrated from al-Husayn b. 'Ali b. Faddal and al-Husayn b. 'Ali b. Yaqtin from Sa'dan b. Muslim from Ishaq b. 'Ammar from Abu 'Abd Allah al-Sadiq, peace be upon him, who said: "Amplitude of the side and [the profusion of] hair in the nose (*al-anf*) are a protection from leprosy."

From Salama b. 'Umar al-Hamdani. who said: I entered Medina and went to Abu 'Abd Allah, peace be upon him, and said: "O son of the Messenger of Allah, I brought the people of my house for the Hajj, and I have come to you to seek refuge for them from an illness which has afflicted me - it is the 'evil disease'." He [Abu 'Abd Allah] said: "Stand by the side of [the tomb of] the Messenger of Allah, blessings be on him, and in his sanctuary and protection. Write the sura *al-An'am* (6) with honey and drink it. It will be removed from you."

From him, peace be upon him, that he said: "The soil (*al-turba*) of al-Medina, the city of the Messenger of Allah, blessings of Allah on him and his family, removes leprosy.

ON TURNIPS (AL-SALJAM)

Abu Bakr Muhammad b. al-Huraysh narrated from Muhammad b. 'Isa from 'Ali b. Musayyib from al-'Abd al-Salih [Musa al-Kazim], peace be upon him, that he said: "Eat turnips (*al-lift*), that is *al-saljam*, for there is not one who has a strain of leprosy (*'irq al-min al-judham*) but that the eating of turnips (*al-saljam*) dissolves it." He ['Ali b. Musayyib] asked: "Raw or cooked?" He replied: "Both".

From Abu Ja'far, peace be upon him, that he said: "There is no creature who has in him a strain of leprosy but that it is dissolved by [eating] turnips (*al-saljam*)."

ON GANGLIA

Muhammad b. Ja'far al-Bursi narrated from Muhammad b. Yahya al-Armani from Muhammad b. Sinan from al-Mufaddal b. 'Umar al-Ju'fi from Abu 'Abd Allah al-Sadiq, peace be upon him, from his forefathers from Amir al-Mu'minin, peace be upon him, that he said: 'The Messenger of Allah, blessings on him and his family, said: "Beware of eating ganglia (*al-ghadad*), for it stirs up leprosy."' He said: "The Jews were restored to health because of their avoiding the eating of ganglia." He said: "When you see those afflicted with leprosy, ask your Lord for good health and do not be unmindful of Him."

ON LOOKING AT THE AFFLICTED

Muhammad b. Sinan al-Sinani from Ja'far b. Muhammad, peace be upon him, from his father, who said: 'The Messenger of Allah, blessings on him, said: "Do not stare at the afflicted (*ahl al-bala'*) and those with leprosy, for that grieves them."'

From Abu 'Abd Allah al-Sadiq, peace be upon him, from his fathers, who said: 'The Messenger of Allah, blessings and peace be upon him, said: "Do not look much at the afflicted and do not visit them. When, you pass by them, quicken the pace so that what has afflicted them may not befall you."'

CLIPPING THE MOUSTACHE AND THE HAIR IN THE NOSE

Ahmad b. Basir narrated from Ziyad b. Marwan al-'Abdi from Muhammad b. Sinan, from Abu 'Abd Allah, peace be upon him, who said: 'Amir al-Mu'minin, peace be upon him, said: "Clipping the moustache (*al-sharib*) every Friday is a protection against leprosy. Hair in the nose is aiso a protection from it."'

ON FLIES

Sahl b. Ahmad narrated from Muhammad b. Aruma from Salih b. Muhammad from 'Umar b. Shimr from Jabir from Abu Ja'far al-Baqir, peace be upon him, who said: 'The Messenger of Allah, blessings on him, said: "If a fly (*al-dhubab*) falls into one of your vessels, let it be immersed in it, for in one of its wings (*al-janah*) is a healing and in the other a poison. It dips its poisonous wing into the liquid and does not dip the wing in which is healing. Therefore immerse it, so that it may not harm you.'"

He [al-Baqir] said: "Were it not for flies which fall into people's food from whence they know not, leprosy would have spread rapidly among them."

From Muhammad b. 'Ali al-Baqir, peace be upon him, who said: "Were it not that people eat flies from whence they know not, they would be afflicted with leprosy", or he said: "they would all be afflicted with leprosy."

ON THE THE COMMON COLD

'Ali b. al-Khalil narrated from 'Abd al-Aziz b. al-Hassan from Hammad b. 'Isa from Hariz b. 'Abd Allah al-Sijistani from Abu 'Abd Allah, peace be upon him, who said to his children's teacher: "If any of my children are affected with a cold, inform me." The teacher would inform him, but he said nothing in response. So the teacher said: "You instructed me to inform you of this. I have informed you, but you did not answer me with anything." He replied: "It [the cold] is not from anything but a strain of leprosy in him. When it stirs up, Allah repels it with a cold."

ON EATING FRANCOLIN

Marwan b. Muhammad narrated from 'Ali b. al-Nu'man from 'Ali b. al-Hasan b Musa, peace be upon him, from his forefathers from Amir al-Mu'minin, peace be upon him, who said: 'I heard the Messenger of Allah, blessings on him, say: "Whoever wishes to lessen his anger, let him eat francolin (*al-durraj*).'"

From him, blessings on him and his family, he said: "Whoever complains of his heart and has many sorrows, let him eat francolin."

AN INVOCATION FOR MENTAL DISORDER

'Uthman b. Sa'id al-Qattan narrated from Sa'dan b. Muslim related from Muhammad b. Ibrahim, who said: A man came to Abu 'Abd Allah, peace be upon him, and a mental disorder had afflicted him. Abu 'Abd Allah, peace be upon him, said: 'Recite this prayer when you go to bed: "In the Name of Allah, and by Allah. I believe in Allah, and disbelieve in the idols. O Allah, protect me in my sleep and my wakening. I take refuge in the Might of Allah and His Magnificence from that which I suffer and fear."'

The man said: "I did it and was cured, by the will of Allah, the Exalted."

From him, peace be upon him, that he said: "Whoever is afflicted with a mental disorder, let him seek protection on Thursday night with this healing, beneficial invocation." Then he mentioned the like of the previous hadith and said: "It will not recur. Recite that at dawn after seeking forgiveness from Allah, and after completing the night prayer."

FOR PANIC

Ja'far b. Hannan at-Ta'i narrated from Muhammad b. 'Abd Allah b. Mas'ud from Muhammad b. Muskan al-Halabi, who said: Abu 'Abd Allah, peace be upon him, said to one of his followers when the man had asked him: "O son of the Messenger of Allah, I have a daughter, and I am sorry and anxious for her since she is in a panic night and day. If you think it proper, pray to Allah for her well-being." He [al-Halabi] said: He prayed for her, then said: "Instruct her to open a blood vessel (*al-fasd*), for she will benefit by that."

From Abu Ja'far Muhammad al-Baqir, peace be upon him, that a believer complained to him and said: "O son of the Messenger of Allah, 1 have a bondmaid who is afflicted by winds." He replied: "Seek protection for her in the opening of the Book (the sura *al-Fatiha* (1)) and the two suras of taking refuge (*al-Falaq* (113) and *al-Nas* (114)) ten times. Then write it for her in a vessel in musk and saffron and give her to drink of it. Use it for her drinking, her ablution, and her washing, Do that for three days and Allah will remove it from her."

FOR EXCESSIVELY HEATED BLOOD

'Ali b. Muhammad b. Hilal narrated from 'Ali b. Mihran from Hammad b. 'Isa from Hariz b. 'Abd Allah from Abu 'Abd Allah al-Sadiq, peace be upon him, who said: 'Most of these abscesses (*al-damamil*) and sores (*al-quruh*) are from this excessively heated blood (*al-dam al-muhtariq*) which a person does not take out at its time. Whoever is overcome by something of that, let him say when he goes to bed: "I take refuge in the Face of Allah, the Mighty, and Bis Perfect Words, which neither the righteous nor the ungodly pass by, from the evil of everything possessed of evil." When he has said that, none of the jinn will harm him and he will be restored to health by it, Allah, the Exalted, willing.

'Finally, write on a paper and make the person suffering from abscesses swallow it:

لا الآء إلا آلاؤك يا الله

Tibb al-A'imma

علمك به محيط علمك

به كهلسون

ON WARTS

Sa'dawayh b. 'Abd Allah narrated from 'Ali b. al-Nu'man from Abu al-Hasan Al-Ridha', peace be upon him, from [one of his] forefathers, that he [al-Nu'man] said: I said to him [Al-Ridha']: "May I be your sacrifice, I have a much-wanted son who is not able to mix with people because of the numerous warts he has. I ask you, O son of the Messenger of Allah, to teach me something that will benefit him." He replied: "For each wart, take seven barleycorns (*sha'irat*) and recite over each one seven times:

When the Terror descends... until the verse: and become a dust scattered (56:1-6). They will question thee concerning the mountains. Say: My Lord will scatter them as ashes. Then He will leave them a level hollow wherein thou wilt see no crookedness neither any curving (20:105-7).

"Then take a barleycorn and rub the centre of the wart with it. Tie it in a new piece of cloth and fasten a stone on to it and throw it into a toilet (*kanif*)." He ['Ali b. al-Nu'man] said: I did that and looked at him. By Allah, on the seventh and eighth day he was like the palm of my hand and more clear!

'Some of them say that it should be treated at the time of the *muhaq* of the month [from the 28th to the 30th of the month], that is, when the moon is hidden and cannot be seen. It is the most effective and beneficial time for treatment.'

ON THE CYST

Muhammad b. 'Amir narrated from Muhammad b. 'Alim al-Thaqafi from 'Ammar b. 'Isa al-Kilabi from 'Abd Allah b. Sinan on the authority of Abu 'Abd Allah, peace be upon him, that he [Ibn Sinan] said: A man from the Shi'a complained to him [Abu 'Abd Allah] of a cyst (*sil'a*) that had appeared on him. Abu 'Abd Allah, peace be upon him, told him: 'Fast for three days, then bathe on the fourth day at noon and go out into the open plain to your Lord. Take with you a clean, patched, and ragged garment. Read four *rak'as* of prayer and recite in it whatever is easy of the Qur'an, and be submissive in your endeavour. When you finish your prayer, cast off your clothes and put on the ragged garment, and put your right cheek on the earth.

'Then say in supplication, humbly, and submissively: "O Single, O One, O Noble, O Compassionate, O Omnipotent, O Near, O Responder, O Most Merciful of the merciful, bless

Muhammad and the family of Muhammad, and remove what is in me of illness, and clothe me with well-being, sufficient and healing, in this world and the next. Bestow on me all the blessings and remove what is in me for it has troubled and distressed me."

Then Abu 'Abd Allah, peace be upon him, said to him: 'Know that it will not benefit you until there is no conflict against it in your heart, and you know that it will benefit you.' He [Ibn Sinan] said: The man did as Ja'far al-Sadiq, peace be upon him, instructed him, and he was cured of it.

FOR A SWELLING IN THE BODY

Muhammad b. Ishaq al-Walid narrated from his cousin Ahmad b. Ibrahim b. al-Walid from 'Ali b, Asbat from al-Hakam b. Sulayman from Maysar from Abu 'Abd Allah al-Sadiq, peace be upon him, who said: "This verse is for every swelling m the body for which a man is afraid to resort to anything [else]. When you recite it, do so when you are in a state of purity. When you have performed the ablution for the obligatory prayer, seek protection with it [the verse] from your swelling before the prayer and meditate on it. The verse is:

If We had sent down this Qur an upon a mountain, thou wouidst have seen it humbled, split asunder out of the fear of God . . . until the end of the sura (59:21-4).

If you do that according to what has been mentioned to you, the swelling will subside."

FOR PANIC DURING SLEEP

Abu 'Ubayda b. Muhammad b. 'Ubayd narrated from Abu Muhammad b. 'Ubayd from al-Nadr b. Suwayd from Maysar from Abu 'Abd Allah al-Sadiq, peace he upon him, that a man said to him: "O son of the Messenger of Allah, I have a bondmaid who is often in a panic during sleep. Sometimes the condition becomes more severe so that she does not calm down. An amulet (*al-hirz*) has been fastened to her arm and someone has seen her to cure her and said that she has been touched by the jinn and it is not possible to treat her." He [al-Sadiq] said: "Instruct her to open a blood vessel and give her dill water (*al-shabath*) cooked with honey to drink for three days. Allah, the Exalted, will restore her to health." He [the man] said: I did that and she was cured, by the will of Allah, the Mighty and Sublime.

FOR WINDS

Muhammad b. Bukayr narrated from Safwan b. Yahya from al-Mundhir b. Haman from Muhammad b. Muslim and Sa'd al-

Mawla, who both said: Abu 'Abd Allah al-Sadiq, peace be upon him, said: "All these winds are from the predominant bile (*al-mirra al-ghaliba*) or excessively heated blood or predominant phlegm. So a person should take care of himself before any of these natural constituents overcome and destroy him."'

ON TREATMENT FOR SOMEONE AFFLICTED WITH FALLING SICKNESS

From Abu al-Hasan Al-Ridha', peace be upon him, that he saw someone afflicted with falling sickness and called for a tumbler of water for him. Then he recited the sura *al-Hamd* (1) and the two suras of taking refuge (*al-Falaq* (113) and *al-Nas* (114)) over it and ordered the water to he poured over his head and face. The man rose and he [Al-Ridha'] said to him: "It will never recur again."

ON PIGEONS

'Ali b. Sa'id narrated from Muhammad b Karama, who said: I saw a pair of pigeons (*hamam*) in the house of Musa b. Ja'far, peace be upon him. The male was green, with something of brown on it, and the female was black. I saw him [Musa b. Ja'far] crumbling up bread for them while he was at the table, saying: "They move about at night and keep me company. There is not a single tremor they are shaken with at night but that Allah repels by it the spirits that have entered the house."

KILLING PIGEONS

'Ali b. Sa'id narrated from Muhammad b. Karama from Abu Hamza al-Thumali, who said: My grandson had pigeons and I slaughtered them in anger. Then I went to Mecca and called on

Abu Ja'far al-Baqir, peace be upon him, before sunrise. When the sun rose, I saw many pigeons in the house. I asked him [al-Baqir] questions and wrote down his answers to me.

My heart was preoccupied with what I had done in Kufa and my slaughtering the pigeons meaninglessly. I said to myself: Had there been no good in pigeons, he would not have kept them. Abu Ja'far, peace be upon him, said to me: "What is the matter with you, O Abu Hamza?" I said: "O son of the Messenger of Allah, I am well." He said: "Your heart is elsewhere." I said: "Yes, by Allah", and narrated the story to him, mentioning that I had slaughtered them, and that now I was surprised at the number of pigeons that he had. Al-Baqir, peace be upon him, said: "Evil is what you have done, O Abu Hamza. Did you not know that when the jinn play with our children, the harm is driven away from them by the fluttering of the pigeons, and that they perform the call to prayer at the end of the night? So give alms of a dinar for each one of them, for you have killed them in anger."

AN INVOCATION FOR ONE STRUCK BY THE JINN

Al-Muzaffar b. Muhammad b. 'Abd al-Rahman narrated from 'Abd al-Rahman b. Abu Najran from Sulayman b. Ja'far from Ibrahim b. Abu Yahya al-Madani who said: The Messenger of

Allah, blessings on him, said: 'Whoever is struck by a stone or by the jinn, let him take the stone which was thrown and return it to the place from which it came and say: "Sufficient for me is Allah and a protection. Allah hears the one who calls. There is no end before Allah."'

He, blessings of Allah on him and his family, said: "Keep many domestic animals (*al-dawajin*) in your houses so that the demons are occupied with them instead of with your children."

LOOKING AT THE AFFLICTED

'Abid b. 'Awn b. 'Abd Allah al-Madani narrated from Safwan b. Yahya Bayya' al-Sabiri from Muhammad b. Ibrahim from Hannan b. Ibrahim from Abu 'Abd Allah al-Sadiq, peace be upon him, who said: 'When you see the afflicted, say "Praise be to Allah who has protected me from that which afflicts you, and had He willed to do so, He would have done it. Praise be to Allah Who did not do so."'

From al-Baqir, peace be upon him, that he said: 'When you see the afflicted say: "Praise be to Allah who has protected me from that which afflicts you, and has favoured me by far over you and over many of those He created."'

FOR THE INSANE AND THOSE AFFLICTED WITH THE FALLING SICKNESS

Muhammad b. Ja'far b. Mihran narrated from Ahmad b. Hammad from Abu Jafar al-Baqir, peace be upon him, that he had prescribed cyclamen (*bukhur maryam*) for his bondmaid and said that it was beneficial for everything caused by the spirits such as possession (*al-mass*), mental disorder, madness, the falling sickness, ensnarement, etc. It is beneficial and has been proved, by the will of Allah, the Exalted.

He said: "Take storax or sanadarch (*sandarus*) and saliva (*bazaq*) from the mouth, Sandari false bdellium (*kur sandari*), the bark of the colocynth (*qushur al-hanzal*), *marmari*, white sulphur (*kibrit abyad*), a fragment inside the *muql* and Yamani sweet cyperus (*su'd Yamani*). Break into it three drops of myrrh and 'porcupine hair' (*sha'r qanfadh*) mixed with Syrian liquid pitch (*qitran shami*). Put it all together and create vapours (*bukhur*). It is good and beneficial, Allah the Exalted willing."

AN INVOCATION FOR SPELLS

Muhammad b. Ja'far al-Bursi narrated from Ahmad b. Yahya al-Armani from Muhammad b. Sayyar from Muhammad b. al-Fadl b. 'Umar from Abu 'Abd Allah, peace be upon him, who said: 'Amir al-Mu'minin, blessings of Allah on him, said that Jibra'il peace be upon him, came to the Prophet, blessings be on him, and said: "O Muhammad." He replied: "At your service, O Jibra'il." He said: "Such-and-such a Jew has bewitched you and put a spell in the well of Banu so-and-so. Therefore, send to it the most trustworthy of people in your opinion and the most important of them before you and the equal of you, so that he may bring you the spell."' He [Abu 'Abd Allah] said: 'The Prophet, blessings be on him, sent 'Ali b. Abu Talib, peace be upon him, and said: "Go to the well of Dharwan, for in it is a spell with which the Jew Labid b. A'sam has bewitched me, and bring it to me."

'Ali peace be upon him, said; "I set out at the request of the Messenger of Allah. I descended into it and there was the spring water as if it were water in a cistern because of the spell. I searched for it hurriedly until I came to the bottom of the well but I did not obtain it. Those who were with me said: 'There is nothing in it.' So I went up. But then I said: 'No, by Allah, he did not lie and nor do I, and I am not with him as you are,' meaning the Messenger of Allah. I searched for it again carefully, and brought it out, in truth.

"I went to the Prophet, and he said: 'Open it.' I opened it and there was, in truth, a piece of a palm branch inside it on which was tied twenty-one knots. Jibra'il had brought down that day to the Prophet the two suras of taking refuge (*al-Falaq* (113) and *al-Nas* (114)). The Prophet said: "O 'Ali, then recite over the string." Whenever Amir al-Mu'minin recited it, a knot opened, until he finished with all of them and Allah, the Mighty and Sublime, removed the spell from His Prophet and restored him to health.'

It is related that Jibra'il and Mika'il, peace be upon them, came to the Prophet, blessings of Allah on him and his family. One of them sat on his right and the other on his left. Then Jibra'il said to Mika'il: "What ails the man?" Mika'il replied: "He has been treated." Jibra'il, peace be upon him, asked: "Who has treated him?" He [Mika'il] replied: "Labid b. A'sam, the Jew." Then he related the *hadith* until the end.

ON THE TWO SURAS OF TAKING REFUGE (THE SURA AL-FALAQ AND THE SURA AL-NAS)

Ibrahim al-Baytar narrated from Muhammad b 'Isa, from Yunus b. 'Abd al-Rahman - and he is called Yunus al-Musalli because of the frequency of his prayers - from Ibn Muskan from Zarara, who said: "Abu Ja'far al-Baqir, peace be upon him, said that spells do not give power over an anything but the eyes."

From Abu 'Abd Allah al-Sadiq, peace be upon him, that he was asked about the two suras of taking refuge (al-Falaq (113) and al-Nas (114)) and whether they were part of the Qu'ran. Al-Sadiq replied: "Yes, they are of the Qur'an." The man said: "They are not of the Qur'an according to the reading of Ibn Mas'ud nor in his collection of the Qur'an." Abu 'Abd Allah replied: "Ibn Mas'ud erred," or he said: "Ibn Mas'ud lied, they are both of the Qur'an."

The man said: "Shall I read them, O son of the Messenger of Allah, as they are in the written text?" He said: "Yes, and do you know the meaning of the two suras and for what they wem revealed? Labid b. A'sam, the Jew, cast a spell on the Messenger of Allah, blessings of Allah on him and his family." Abu Basir said to Abu 'Abd Allah: "Was it possible that his spell would have an effect?" Abu 'Abd Allah, peace be upon him, replied: "Ycs indeed, the Prophet, blessings on him, thought that it was comprehensive, but it was not comprehensive. He was looking for the mode of the spell but did not see it until he touched it with his hand. Spells are a fact and they do not have power over anything except the eye and the genitals. Then Jibra'il came to him and informed him of that, so he called 'Ali, peace be upon him, and sent him to bring that out of the well of Dharwan." Then he narrated the *hadith* upto the end.

A SPELL FOR THE BEWITCHED

Sahl b. Muhammad b. Sahl narrated from 'Abd Rabbihi b. Muhammad b. Ibrahim from Ibn Aruma from lbn Muskan from al-Halabi, who said: I asked Abu 'Abd Allah, peace be upon him, about spells (*al-nashra*) for the bewitched. He said: "My father, peace be upon him, did not see any harm in it."

From Muhammad b. Muslim who said: Abu 'Abd Allah, peace be upon him, dictated this invocation to us saying that it was an inheritance and that it would neutralize spells. 'Write it on a paper and fasten it on to the bewitched person:

Musa said, What you have brought is spells. God will assuredly bring it to naught. God sets not right the work of those who do corruption. God verifies the truth by His words, though sinners be averse (10:81-2). What, are you stronger in constitution or the heaven He built? He lifted up its vault, and levelled it (79:28). So the truth came to pass, and false was proved what they were doing. So they were vanquished there, and they turned about, humbled. And the sorcerers were cast down, bowing themselves. They said, We believe in the Lord of all Being, the Lord of Musa and Harun (7:118-22).'

INVOCATION FOR ONE WHO WISHES TO VISIT THE RULER

Al-Ash'ath b. Abd Allah narrated from Muhammad b. 'Isa from Abu al-Hasan Al-Ridha', peace be upon him, from Musa b. Ja'far, peace be upon him, who said: 'When Abu al-Dawaniq [the caliph Abu Ja'far al-Mansur (d.136/754)] sent for Abu 'Abd Allah, peace be upon him, intending to kill him, the governor of Medina took him [Abu 'Abd Allah] to the caliph. Abu al-Dawaniq wanted him to be quick and, in his eagerness to kill him, found him slow to arrive.

'When he came before him, he laughed and greeted him and made him sit by his side. He said: "O son of the Messenger of Allah, by Allah, I sent for you determined to kill you, but I looked at you and conceived a great affection tor you. By Allah, I have not found anyone from my family more beloved than you, nor one more likeable. But, O Abu 'Abd Allah, what is this I hear about you disparaging us and speaking badly of us?" He replied: "O Amir al-Mu'minin [i.e. Abu al-Dawaniq], I have never spoken badly of you." He [the caliph] smiled and said: "By Allah, you are more true, in my view, than all those who slander you concerning this. My seat is before you, and my ring. So be cheerful, and do not be afraid of me in your affairs, great and small, for I will not hold you back from anything."

'Then he commanded him to leave and gave him presents and gifts, but he [Abu 'Abd Allah] refused to accept anything and said: "O Amir al-Mu'minin, I have wealth and sufficiency and much good. But if you are going to free me, you must [do the same] for those of my family who are left behind; remove from them the sentence of death." He replied: "I have accepted that, O Abu 'Abd Allah, and I have given orders for 100,000 dirhams [for you], so distribute it among them." He [Abu 'Abd Allah] said: "You have made close the ties of kinship, O Amir al-Mu'minin."

When he left his presence, there walked before him the elders and the youth of the Quraysh from every tribe. With him was 'Ayn Abu al-Dawaniq, who said to him: "O son of the Messenger of Allah, you gave a look of healing when you came into the presence of Amir al-Mu'minin, and he did not reproach you for anything except that your lips were moving with something, so what was that?" He replied: "When I looked at him, I said: 'O He Who is not wronged and is Eternal, and with Him is the making close of the ties of kinship, bless Muhammad and his family and protect me from his evil by Your Power and Your Might'. By Allah, I did not add on [anything] to what you have heard." Al-'Ayn returned to Abu al-Dawaniq and informed him of his account. He [Abu al-Dawaniq] said: "By Allah, he had not completed what he said when what was in my heart of evil wickedness was removed."'

ON THROBBING BLOOD-VESSELS

Ahmad b. Muhammad b. al-Jarud narrated from Muhammad b. 'Isa from Dawud b. Razin, who said: I complained to Abu 'Abd Allah al-Sadiq, peace be upon him, and said: 'O son of the Messenger of Allah, yesterday one of my blood vessels throbbed and I waited until it was morning and came to you seeking help.' He replied: 'Put your hand on the place which is throbbing and say three times: "Allah, Allah, Allah, my Lord in truth," and it will abate at once.'

From al-Mufaddal b. 'Umar al-Ju'fi from Abu 'Abd Allah al-Sadiq, peace be upon him, who said: 'Learn from me, O Mufaddal, an invocation for all pains from throbbing blood-vessels and other things. Say: "In the Name of Allah, and by Allah, how many are the blessings of Allah in a blood vessel which is quiet (*sakin*) and one which is not (*ghayr sakin*), on a grateful servant and an ungrateful one." Then take your beard (*al-lihya*) by your right hand after the obligatory prayer and say three times: "O Allah, remove my distress and hasten my recovery and take away my injury." Endeavour to accompany that with tears and weeping.'

ON SEEKING PROTECTION FROM THE JINN

'Abd Allah b. Yahya al-Bazzaz narrated from 'Ali b. Muskan from 'Abd Allah b. al-Mufaddal al-Nawfali from his father from al-Husayn b. 'Ali, peace be upon him, who said: 'When I say these words, I pay no attention to the jinn and human beings who gather against me: "In the Name of Allah, and by Allah, and to Allah, and in the path of Allah, and according to the creed of the Messenger or Allah, blessings be on him. O Allah, protect me by Your Strength and Your Might and Your Power from the evil of every evil-doer, and the plot of the wicked. Surely I love the righteous and chosen ones, and Allah bless Muhammad, the Prophet and his family."'

ON LONELINESS

'Ali b. Mahan narrated from Sarraj, the client of Al-Ridha', peace be upon him, from Ja'far b. Daylam from Ibrahim b. 'Abd al-Hamid from al-Halabi, who said: A man said to Abu 'Abd Allah at-Sadiq, peace be upon him, 'When I am on my own, loneliness (*al-wahsha*) and anxiety come upon me but when I mix with people, I feel nothing of that.'

Al-Sadiq said: 'Place your hand on your heart, and say: "In the Name of Allah, in the Name of Allah, in the Name of Allah." Then pass your hand over your heart and say "I take refuge in the Might of Allah. I take refuge in the Power of Allah. I take refuge in the Majesty of Allah, I take refuge in the Exaltedness of Allah, I take refuge in the force of Allah, I take refuge in the Messenger of Allah, I take refuge in the Names of Allah, from the evil of what I fear and from the evil of what I am afraid of for myself." Say that seven times.'

He [the man] said: I did that and Allah removed from me the loneliness and replaced it with tranquillity and security.

FOR TEMPTATION

Al-Husayn b. Bistam narrated from Muhammad b. Khalaf from Ibn 'Ali b. al-Washsha' from 'Abd Allah b. Sinan who said: A man complained to Abu 'Abdallah, peace be upon him, of an abundance of desire (*al-tammani*) and temptation. He [Abu 'Abd Allah] said: 'Pass your hand over your chest and say: "In the Name of Allah, and by Allah, Muhammad is the Messenger of Allah, and there is no power or strength except with Allah, the Most High, the Mighty. O Allah, remove from me what I fear." Then pass your hand over your belly and repeat it thrice Allah, the Exalted, will remove and turn it away from you.'

The man said: I would often break my prayer because of it being marred by desires and temptation. Then I did as my lord and master instructed me, three times, and Allah turned it away from me and cured me of it so that I did not experience it after that.

From al-Mufaddal b. 'Umar from Abu 'Abd Allah, peace be upon him, who said: 'Zayn al-'Abidin, peace be upon him, would protect his family with this invocation and teach it to his intimates. Place your hand on your mouth and say: "In the Name of Allah, in the Name of Allah, in the Name of Allah, and by *God's handiwork, who has created everything very well. He is Aware of the things you do (27:88).*"

Then say seven times: "Subside, O pain, I ask you by Allah, my Lord and your Lord and the Lord of everything in Whom trust what is in the night and the day, and He is the All-hearing, the All-knowing."'

ON INFLATION OF THE BELLY

'Umar b. 'Uthman al-Khazzaz narrated from 'Ali b. Isa from his uncle, who said: I complained to Musa b. Ja'far, peace be upon him, of inflation of the belly (*rih al-bahr*). He said: 'Say while prostrating: "O Allah, O Allah, O Allah, O Merciful, O Lord of lords, O Chief of chiefs, O God of gods, O Master of masters, O King of kings, heal me with Your healing from this illness and turn it away from me, for I am Your servant and the son of Your servant; I turn about in Your grasp."'

I left his [Musa b. Ja'far's] presence, and by Allah, Who honoured him with the Imamate, I prayed it only once in my prostration and did not experience it after that.

ON SEVERE AGONIES OF DEATH

Al-Ahwas b. Muhammad narrated from 'Abd al-Rahman b. Abu Najran from Ibn 'Isa from Hariz b. 'Abd Allah al-Sijistani on the authority of Abu Ja'far al-Baqir, peace be upon him, who said: 'When you visit a patient while he is suffering severe agonies of death, say to him: Pray this prayer seven times and Allah will make it easy for you: "I take refuge in Allah, the Mighty, Lord of the Mighty and Noble Throne, from every swelling blood-vessel *('irq nifar)* and from the evil of the heat of the fire." Then teach him the words of deliverance *(kalimat al-faraj)*.'

I said: 'O son of the Messenger of Allah, what are the words of deliverance?' He replied: 'Say "There is no god but Allah, the Wise. There is no god but Allah, the Most High, the Mighty. Glory be to Allah, the Lord of the seven heavens and the Lord of the seven earths, and what is in them and what is between them and what is under them and the Lord of the Mighty Throne. Praise be to Allah, the Lord of the Worlds." Then move him on to the place in which he would pray. He will find relief and his affair will be made easy, Allah, the Exalted, willing.'

A COMPREHENSIVE INVOCATION

Ibrahim b. 'Isa al-Za'farani narrated from Muhammad b. Habib al-Harithi — and he was the most knowledgeable and pious of the people of his time — from Ibn Sinan from al-Mufaddal b. 'Umar, who said: Abu 'Abd Allah, peace be upon him, said: 'If you are unable to pass the night until you have taken refuge in eleven ways, then do that.' I said: 'Inform me of them, O son of the Messenger of Allah.'

He said: 'Say: "I take refuge in the Might of Allah, I take refuge in the Power of Allah, I take refuge in the Majesty of Allah, I take refuge in the Beauty of Allah, I take refuge in the Sovereignty of Allah. I take refuge in the Defence of Allah, I take refuge in the Grace of Allah, 1 take refuge in the Force of Allah, I take refuge in the Dominion of Allah, I take refuge in the Perfection of Allah, I take refuge in the Messenger of Allah, blessings of Allah on him and his family and his Ahl al-Bayt, from the evil of what He originated and scattered and created." Take refuge in Him from whatever you wish, for neither reptile (*hawamm*) or jinn, human or demon, will harm you if Allah, the Exalted, wills.'

From Abu Hamza al-Thumali from Abu Ja'far al-Baqir, peace be upon him, that he said: 'Take refuge for yourself from reptiles with these words: "In the Name of Allah, the Merciful, the Compassionate, in the Name of Allah, and by Allah. Muhammad is the Messenger of Allah, blessings be on him. I take refuge in the Might of Allah. I take refuge in the Power of Allah over what He wills, from the evil of every reptile which creeps by night and day. Surely my Lord is on a straight path."'

AN INVOCATION FOR WEALTH AND CHILDREN

Salih b. Ahmad narrated from 'Abd Allah b. Jabala from al-'Ala' b. Razzin from Muhammad b. Muslim, who said: Abu 'Abd Allah, peace be upon him, said: 'Protect your wealth and your family, and guard them with these words to recite over them after the final evening prayer (*salat al-'isha'*): "I seek refuge for myself, my offspring, my family, and my wealth, by the Perfect Words of Allah, from every demon and reptile, and from every evil eye." This is the invocation by which Jibra'il, peace be upon him, sought protection for al-Hasan and al-Husayn, blessings of Allah on them.'

AN INVOCATION AGAINST THIEVES

Al-Khidr b. Muhammad narrated from [both] Ahmad b. 'Umar b. Muslim and Muhsin b. Ahmad from Yunus b. Ya'qub from Abu 'Abd Allah, peace be upon him, who said: Whoever says these words and uses this invocation every night, I guarantee him that no murdering thief (*sariq*) will kill him in the night or day, After the final evening prayer say: "I take refuge in the Might of Allah, I take refuge in the Power of Allah, I take refuge In the Forgiveness of Allah, I take refuge in the Mercy of Allah, I take refuge in the Sovereignty of Allah Who is Powerful over all things. I take refuge in the Nobility of Allah, I take refuge in the Force of Allah, from the evil of every obstinate tyrant (*jabbar*) and rebellious demon, and every murderer and thief and evil occurrence, from the evil of venomous vermin and the reptile and *al-'amma*, from the evil of every creature small and large, by night and day, from the evil of the ungodly, Arab and non-Arab (*al-'ajam*), and their immoral ones, from the evil of the ungodly jinn and men, and from the evil of every creature my Lord has '..*seized by its forelock, Surely my Lord is on a straight path. (11:56)*'"

THE LOUSE OF THE VULTURE

Muhammad b. al-Aswad al-'Attar narrated from Muhammad b. 'Isa from Faddala b. Ayyub from Ibrahim b. al-Husayn from his father al-Husayn b. Yahya, who said: The louse of a vulture (*qamla al-nasr*) bit me and entered my skin (*al-jild*). I was afflicted with a severe pain. So I complained of that to Abu 'Abd Allah, peace be upon him, who said: 'Put your hand on the place which pains you and rub it. Then put your hand on the place where you perform the prostration after you finish the morning prayer (*salat al-fajr*). Say: "In the Name of Allah, and by Allah. Muhammad is the Messenger of Allah, blessings and peace be on him." Then raise your hand and put it on the afflicted area and say seven times: "Heal me, O Healer, there is no healing but Yours, a healing which does not omit any illness."'

ON VISITING THE SICK

Ahmad b. Muhammad b. 'Abd Allah al-Kufi narrated from Ibrahim b. Maymun from Hammad b. 'Isa from Hariz from Abu 'Abd Allah al-Sadiq, peace be upon him, from his pure forefathers, on them be peace, that [one of them] said: 'There is not a believer who visits his fellow believer suffering from an illness and says to him: "I seek protection for you in Allah, the Mighty, the Lord of the Noble Throne, from the evil of every swelling blood-vessel and from the evil of the heat of the fire", except that Allah will relieve him of it, if there is a delay in his appointed time.'

AN INVOCATION FOR THE EVIL EYE

Muhammad b. Sulayman b Mihran narrated from Ziyad b. Harun al-'Abdi from 'Abd Allah b. Muhammad al-Bajali from al-Halabi from Abu 'Abd Allah, peace be upon him, who said: 'Whoever admires something of his fellow believer, let him say "Allah is Great" over it, for the evil eye is a fact (*haqq*).'

Muhammad b. Maymun al-Makki narrated from 'Uthman b. 'Isa from al-Hasan b. al-Mukhtar from Safwan al-Jammal from Abu 'Abd Allah al-Sadiq, peace be upon him, who said: 'If the graves were laid open for you, you would see that most of your dead have the evil eye; for the evil eye is a fact. Surely, the Messenger of Allah, blessings of Allah on him and his family, said: "The evil eye is a fact, so whoever admires something of his brother, let him invoke Allah concerning that. If he invokes Allah, it will not harm him."'

THE PRAYER OF THE DISTRESSED

Hakim b. Muhammad b, Muslim narrated from al Hasan b. 'Ali b. Yaqtin from Yunus from Ibn Sinan from Hafs b. 'Abd al-Hamid from Muhammad b. Muslim from Abu Ja'far Muhammad b. 'Ali, peace be upon him, that one of his children was ill. He went to him and kissed him and said: 'O my son, how do you find yourself?' He replied: 'I am suffering from a pain.' He said: 'When you complete your afternoon prayer (*salat al-zuhr*) say ten times "O Allah, O Allah, O Allah,"' for a distressed person (*makrub*) does not say it without the Lord, Blessed and Exalted, saying "Here I am, O my servant, what is your need?"'

From Abu 'Abd Allah, peace be upon him, who said: 'The prayer of a distressed person in the night is: "O Revealer of healing by night and day and Remover of illness by night and day, bring down on me Your Healing, a healing for all the illness in me."'

Al-Qasim b. Bahram narrated from Muhammad b. 'Isa from Abu Ishaq from al-Husayn b. al-Hasan al-Khurasani — and he was among the chosen ones — who said: I visited Abu 'Abd Allah al-Sadiq, peace be upon him, in the days of Abu al-Dawaniq, with a group of my brothers who had performed the Hajj. He [al-Sadiq] was asked about the prayer of the distressed. He replied: 'The prayer of the distressed is when one has completed the night prayer (salat al-layl). Put your hand on the place on which you perform the prostration and say: "In the Name of Allah, in the Name of Allah, Muhammad is the Messenger of Allah, 'Ali is the Imam of Allah on His earth, over all His servants. Heal me, O Healer. There is no healing but yours. A healing which does not leave out any illness from among every disease and illness."' Al-Khurasani said: I do not know whether he said to repeat it three times or seven times.

From him, that he said: "The prayer of the distressed and anxious, those at their wits' end, and those afflicted with trials:

There is no god but Thou. Glory be to Thee. I have been one of the oppressors (al-zalimin) (21:87).

It should be said on Thursday night when one has completed his obligatory evening prayer." He said: "I learnt it from Abu Ja'far al-Baqir, peace be upon him, who said he took it from 'Ali b. al-Husayn from al-Husayn b. 'Ali, who said he took it from Amir al-Mu'minin, who took it from the Messenger of Allah, who learnt it from Jibra'il who learnt it from Allah, the Mighty and Sublime."

THE PRAYER OF A MOTHER FOR A SON FROM ABOVE

'Ali b. Mihran b. al-Walid al-'Askari narrated from Muhammad b. Salim from al-Arqat — he was the son of the sister of Abu 'Abd Allah al-Sadiq, peace be upon him — who said: I was very ill and my mother sent for my maternal uncle. He came while my mother was outside the door of the house - and she was Umm Salama b. Muhammad b. 'Ali - saying: "Alas, my boy!" My uncle saw her and said: 'Gather your dress around you and go up to the roof of the house. Then remove your veil (*al-qina'*) so that you expose your hair to the sky and say: "My Lord, You gave me to him and You granted him to me. O Allah, renew Your grant today, surely You are Able and Powerful." Then prostrate yourself and do not raise your head until your son is restored to health.' She heard that and acted on it. He [al-Arqat] said: I rose at once and went out with my maternal uncle to the mosque.

[PROTECTION FROM] WHOEVER WISHES EVIL TO OTHERS

Sa'd b. Muhammad b. Sa'id narrated from Musa b. Qays al-Hannat from Muhammad b. Sa'id - he was the father of Sa'id b. Muhammad - from al-Sha'iri from Ja'far b. Muhammad al-Sadiq, peace be upon him, who said: The Messenger of Allah, blessings of Allah on him and his family, said: 'Whoever wishes a person evil and that person wishes Allah to make a barrier between the two of them, let him say when he sees him:

"I take refuge in the Might of Allah and His Strength, from the Might of His creation and its strength. *I take refuge with the Lord of the Daybreak, from the evil of what He created (113:1-2)."'*

Then say what Allah, the Mighty and Sublime, said to His Prophet: So, if they turn their backs, say: God is enough for me. There is no god but He. In Him I have put tny trust. He is the Lord of the Mighty Throne (9:129).

Allah will turn away from him the plot of every plotter, the deception of every cunning person and the envy of every envier. Do not say these words except to his face and Allah will protect him by His Might.

FOR CHARITY

Ibrahim b. Yasar narrated from Ja'far b. Muhammad b. Hakim from Ibrahim b. 'Abd al-Hamid fom Zarara b. Ayan from Abu Ja'far al-Baqir, peace be upon him, from his father from his grandfather from Amir al-Mu'minin, peace be upon him, who said: 'The Messenger of Allah, blessings on him, said, "Treat your sick with charity (*al-sadaqa*)."'

From him, blessings of Allah on him and his family: "Charity drives away inevitable affliction, so treat your sick with charity."

From him, blessings of Allah on him and his family: "Charity drives away an evil death from a person."

From Musa b. Ja' far, peace be upon him, that a man complained to him: "I have many dependants, all of whom are ill." Musa b. Ja'far, peace be upon him, replied: "Treat them with charity, for there is nothing more quick of response nor more beneficial for the patient than charity."

AN INVOCATION

Muhammad b. Yusuf al-Mu'adhdhin, who performed the call to prayer in the mosque in Samarra, narrated from Muhammad b. 'Abd Allah b. Zabad from Muhammad b. Bakr al-Azdi from Abu 'Abd Allah, peace be upon him, who recommended to his companions and followers who were ill to take a new pitcher and put water in it, having drawn the water themselves. They should recite the sura *al-Qadr* (97) slowly over the water thirty times, then drink from that, perform the ablution with it, and wipe themselves with it. Whenever it is used, there will be an increase in it, and that will not occur for three days without Allah, the Exalted, curing them of that illness.

FOR SERIOUS AFFLICTION

'Abd al-Wahhab b. Muhammad, who recited the Qur'an for the people of Mecca, narrated from Abu Zakariya Yahya b. Abu Zakariya from 'Abd Allah b. Abu al-Qasim from Sharif b. Sabiq al-Taflisi from al-Fadl b. Abu Qurra from Abu 'Abd Allah al-Sadiq, peace be upon him, who said: 'This invocation is for one who suffers from serious afflictions, like canker (*al-akila*) etc. Place your hand on the head of the afflicted person and say:

"In the Name of Allah, and by Allah, and from Allah, and to Allah, and what Allah wills. There is no might nor power except with Allah, Ibrahim the friend of Allah, Musa the spokesman of Allah, Nuh the confidant of Allah, 'Isa the Spirit of Allah, Muhammad the Messenger of Allah, blessings of Allah on them all, from every serious affliction and distressing affair, and from all wind, spirits, and pains decreed by Allah and His ordinances, for so-and-so, son of so-and-so, and that neither cankers nor other afflictions should come near him. I seek protection for him with the Perfect Words of Allah for which Adam, peace be upon him, asked his Lord, and He turned to him. Surely, He is Oft-returning, Compassionate. O clamouring pains and spirits, by the Will of Allah, by the Help of Allah, by the Power of Allah, surely to him belongs the creation and the affair. Blessed be Allah, the Lord of the Worlds."

Then recite the opening of the Book (the sura *al-Fatiha* (1)) and the verse of the Throne (2:255) and ten verses from the sura ***YaSin*** (36) and ask Him for healing, by the right of Muhammad and the family of Muhammad. He will be cured of every illness, Allah, the Exalted, willing.'

THE REMEDY OF 'THE HEALING'

Abu 'Atab 'Abd Allah b. Bistami narrated from Ibrahim b. al-Nadr from the son of Maytham al-Tammar of Qazwin, who said: We were in touch with the Imams, who gave this medication to their followers. It is the medication called 'the healing' (*al-shafiya*). It is different from the 'comprehensive medication'. This is for chroic and recent semi-paralysis, chronic and recent facial paralysis, chronic and recent ulcers (*al-dubayla*), chronic and recent coughs, tetanus (*al-kuzaz*), pestilence (*rih al-shauka*), pain of the (neck) eye [*sic*], and film covering the eye (*rih al-sabal*) – which causes hair to grow in the eye. [It is also] for pain of the legs from chronic *al-kham*, for weakness of the abdomen, for the winds which afflict children from flatulence, panic which afflicts a woman in her sleep during her pregnancy, consumption spread by breathing (*al-nafkh*) - and it is the yellow water (*al-ma' al-asfar*) in the belly - for leprosy, every sign of bile and phlegm, for bites (*al-nahsha*), and for those bitten by snakes and scorpions.

Jibra'il, the trusted Spirit, brought it down to Musa b. 'Imran, peace he upon him, when the Pharoah intended to poison the Banu Isra'il and made a day for them on Sunday. The Pharoah prepared many kinds of food for them and set up many tables and put the poison in the food. Musa went forth with the Banu Isra'il - and they were 600,000 – stopping with them at the place of entertainment. He sent back the women and children and advised the Banu Isra'il, saying:

"Do not eat of their food and drink of their drink until I return to you." Then he went among the people and gave them this medication to drink in the amount held by the head of a needle. He knew they would disobey his command and eat the Pharoah's food. Then he went forward, and they went with him. When they saw the tables set up, they hurried to the food and put their hands in it.

Some time earlier, the Pharoah had called Musa, Harun, Yusha' b. Nun, and the elite of the Banu Isra'il, and directed them to a table especially for them. He said: "I have resolved that none will cut the daman other than me or the distinguished people in my kingdom. So eat until you are full." The Pharoah put in the strongest poison time and again. When they finished eating, Musa and his companions left. He said to the Pharoah: "We have left the women and children and the belongings behind us and we are awaiting them." The Pharoah said: "Then the food will be brought back for them and we will honour them as we have honoured those with you. So bring them, and I will feed them as I fed your companions."

Musa went to the people and the Pharoah turned to his associates and said to them: "You claim that Musa and Harun have cast a spell on us and have shown us by this spell that they are eating something of our food. They have left, and their spell is gone, so gather whomever you are able to, for the remaining food today and tomorrow so that they are separated." They did that, and the Pharoah had ordered food for his companions without any poison in it. He gathered them, and among them were those whom he gave to eat and those whom he did not. Those whom he gave to eat of his food were saved. There perished among the companions of the Pharoah 70,000 men and 160,000 women besides the riding-beasts, dogs, etc. The Pharoah and his companions were amazed at the medicine called 'the healing' that Allah had ordered him [Musa] to give his companions.

Then Allah, the Exalted, revealed this medication to His Prophet, and Jibra'il, peace be upon him, brought down the copy of it: "Take one part of peeled garlic (*thum*). Crush it, but do not grind it finely, and put it into a saucepan or cooking pot, depending on the amount that has been prepared. Then light a low fire under it and pour over it the clarified butter from a cow - an amount enough to cover it. Cook it over a low fire until that butter is soaked up. Then pour it over it again and again until the garlic does not absorb anymore. Next pour over it fresh milk (*al-labn al-halib*), put it on a low fire, and do the same as you did with the fat— let the milk be that of a cow which has recently given birth - until it [the garlic] does not absorb any more milk. Then take honey from the comb (*al-shahd*) and squeeze it out of its comb. Boil it separately and do not let there be any of the comb in it. Pour it on to the garlic and put it on a low fire as you did with the fat and milk.

"Then take ten dirhams of fennel flower and grind it finely. Clean it but do not sift it. Take five dirhams of pepper and marjoram and grind it. Add them to it [the garlic] and make it into a jelly-like (*khabisa*) mixture on the fire. Put it into a clean, empty container, free of any odour. Put in the container some of the clarified butter from a cow and oil the container with it. Then bury it in barley (*sha'ir*) or ashes (*ramad*) for forty days, and the older it is, the better. When he is suffering severely, let the patient take the quantity of a chick-pea.

"One month after this medicine [has been prepared], it is beneficial for throbbing in the teeth and all that is caused by the phlegm, after a quantity equivalent to half a walnut is taken on an empty stomach. After two months, it is good for fever which is accompanied by shivering. The equivalent of half a walnut should be taken before sleep. It is very effective for digesting the food and for every ailment of the eye. After three months, it is good for the black and the yellow bile, excessively heated phlegm, and for the occurence of every illness resulting from the yellow bile. It should be taken on an empty stomach.

After four months, it is good for the darkness in the eye and the spirit which seizes a man when he is walking. It should be taken at night before he sleeps. After five months, violet oil or vinegar oil should be taken with the equivalent of half a lentil mixed with the oil. The person suffering from continual headache should inhale it. After six months, the equivalent of a lentil of it should be taken. The person suffering from migraine should inhale it, with violet oil, from the side on which his illness is. That should be done before breakfast, in the first part of the morning.

"After seven months, it is beneficial for wind which is in the ears. Put it drop by drop into the ear, taking the equivalent of a lentil of it with the oil of roses, at the first part of the morning when he is asleep. After eight months, it is beneficial for yellow bile and for the illness from which there is a fear of canker. It should be drunk with water and mixed with any oil you wish. That should be done before breakfast, at sunrise.

Tibb al-A'imma

"After nine months, it is beneficial, Allah willing, for vertigo (*al-sadar*), for excessive sleep, talking (*al-hadhayan*), trembling during sleep, dread (*al-wajal*), and panic. It should be taken with the oil of radish seeds (*bizr al-fujl*) on an empty stomach for anxiety (*al-balbala*), internal fever (*al-humma al-batina*), and confusion of the mind (*ikhtilat al-'aql*). Take the equivalent of a lentil of it with vinegar. For whiteness in the eye, drink it in any way you want on an empty stomach before sleeping.

"After eleven months, it is beneficial for the black bile which seizes the person with fear and temptation. Take the equivalent of a chick-pea with the oil of roses and drink it on an empty stomach, and drink the equivalent of a chick-pea of it without [any oil] before sleep. After twelve months, it is beneficial for recent and chronic semi-paralysis, when the equivalent of a chick-pea should be taken with marjoram water. Anoint the feet with olive oil and salt before sleeping and do the same thing the next night. Abstain from vinegar, milk, legumes, and fish. Eat with the [medication] whatever you wish.

"After thirteen months, it is beneficial for ulcers, laughing for no reason, and playing with one's beard. The equivalent of a chick-pea of it should be taken and mixed with rue water and drunk in the first part of the night. After fourteen months, it is beneficial for all poisons, even if the poison has been drunk. Take the seeds of egg-plant (*al-badinjan*) and grind it. Then boil it on the fire, strain it out, and drink it with the equivalent of a chick-pea of this medicine, once or twice or thrice or four times with tepid water. Do not take it more than four times and drink it at dawn.

"After fifteen months, it is beneficial for bewitchment, *al-hamma*, cold [in the belly], and winds. Take the equivalent of half a hazelnut, boil with pure water. Give it to drink when the person has gone to bed, and do not give it at night or the next day until he has eaten a lot of food. After sixteen months, he should take the equivalent of half a lentil and mix it with fresh rainwater which has fallen that day or night, or with hail. Apply it around the edges of the eyes of the person who has been blind for some time or become blind recently. Apply it in the early morning and late evening, and before sleeping, for four days; he will be cured. If not, apply it for eight days, and I have not seen it reaching eight days without the person being cured, by the will of Allah, the Mighty and Sublime.

"After seventeen months, it is beneficial Allah, the Mighty and Exalted, willing, for leprosy. Take the oil of the trotters (*al-akari'*) - the trotters of the cow, not of the sheep - with the equivalent of a hazelnut of the medicine. It is beneficial before bed and before breakfast. Take of it the quantity of one grain and anoint your body with it, rubbing vigorously. Take a little of it and inhale it with olive oil or the oil of roses. That should be done at the end of the day, in the bath.

"After eighteen rnonths, it is beneficial, Allah the Exalted willing, for leprosy (*al-bahaq*) which resembles vitiligo (*al-baras*), except that if the affected area is cut, it bleeds. Take of the medicine the equivalent of a chick-pea and mix it with walnut oil or bitter almond oil (*duhn lawz murr*) or pine-nut oil (*duhn sanaubar*). Drink it after dawn, and inhale a fair amount of it with that oil, and rub it on the body with salt."

He said: "These ingredients, which have been mentioned previously, should not be altered in their amount and application, because if they are contradicted they will disagree with the person and will not be beneficial at all.

"After nineteen months, take the seeds of a sweet pomegranate and squeeze out the juice, and take the quantity of one grain of colocynth (*al-hanzala*). Drink it for forgetfulness (*al-sahw*), amnesia (*al-nisyan*), excessively heated phlegm, and recent and chronic fever, on an empty stomach with hot water. After twenty months, it is beneficial, Allah willing, for deafness. It is beneficial with storax water. Extract its water and pour the equivalent of a small lentil into the ear; he will hear. If he still cannot hear, make him inhale of that water the equivalent of a lentil on the next day. Pour on the top of his head the remainder of the errhine (*al-sa'ut*). When a person suffering from pleurisy becomes very ill and his tongue is extended, take sour-grape seeds and give the patient this medicine to drink, for it will be beneficial and will relieve him of his illness. The older it is, the better, and a lesser amount of it should be taken."

A MEDICATION FOR ALL DISEASES AND MALADIES

Muhammad b. Ja'far b. 'Ali al-Bursi narrated from Muhammad b. Yahya al-Armani - and he was the means of access to al-Mufaddal b. 'Umar, and al-Mufaddal was the access to Abu 'Abd Allah al-Sadiq, peace be upon him - from Muhammad b. Sinan al-Sinani al-Zahiri Abu 'Abd Allah from al-Mufaddaal b. 'Umar from al-Sadiq, Ja'far b. Muhammad, peace be upon him, who said:

"This is the medication of Muhammad, blessings of Allah on him and his family, and it is similar to the medication which Jibra'il, the trusted Spirit, gave to Musa b. 'Imran, peace be upon him, except that this has qualities of treatment and more and less compared to that [previous medicine]. These medications are from the writings of the Prophets and the sages among the successors of the Prophets. If there is an increase or decrease in it, or if one grain is added or taken away from what has been stipulated, the original will be violated and the medication will be spoilt. It will not be successful, because when they contradict it they contradict them [the authorities].

"The medicine is: Put four *ratl* of peeled garlic in a saucepan and pour over it four *ratl* of cow's milk. Put it on a low fire until it absorbs the milk. Then pour over it four *ratl* of the clarified butter from a cow. When it [the garlic] absorbs it and is well cooked, pour over it four *ratl* of honey and put it on a low fire. Add to it the weight of two dirhams of *qurad* [a marine plant]. Stir it vigorously until it thickens. When it thickens and is well cooked, and mixed, transfer it while hot to a container. Fasten its top and bury it in barley or clean earth (*turab*) for the summer. In winter, take of it the equivalent of a large walnut every day in the early morning before breakfast. It is a comprehensive medication for all things big and small, significant and insignificant, and has been tried and is well known among the believers."

THE MEDICINE OF MUHAMMAD, BLESSINGS ON HIM

Ahmad b. Muhammad Abu 'Abd Allah narrated from Hammad b. 'Isa from Hariz from Abu 'Abd Allah, peace be upon him, concerning the medication of Muhammad, blessings of Allah on him and his family, which was not taken for anything except that it benefited the person who drank it, for all illnesses and winds. So use it and teach it to your fellow believers. For every believer who benefits from it, there will be for you freedom from the fire.

FOR THE LACK OF CHILDREN

Ahmad b. 'Imran b. Abu Layla narrated from 'Abd al-Rahman b. Abu Najran from Sulayman b. Ja'far al-Ja'fari from Abu Ja'far the first, al-Baqir b. 'Ali b. al-Husayn b. 'Ali, peace be upon him, that a man complained to him of lack of children. He had tried for a chiid from bondmaids and free-born women (*al-hara'ir*), but it was not granted to him and he was now sixty years old. He [al-Baqir] said: 'For three days after your obligatory evening prayer (*al-'isha'*) and after the morning prayer, recite: "Glory be to Allah," seventy times; "I ask for forgiveness from Allah", seventy times; and end it with the statement of Allah, the Mighty and Sublime:

Ask forgiveness of your Lord. Surely He is ever All-forgiving, and He will loose heaven upon you in torrents and will succour you with wealth and sons, and will appoint for you gardens, and will appoint for you rivers (71:10-12). Then have intercourse with your wife on the third night and you will be blessed, Allah willing, with a healthy boy.'

He [the man] said: 'I did that and the year was not over when I was blessed with a child.'

ON INTERCOURSE

Muhammad b. al-'Ays narrated from Ishaq b. 'Uthman from 'Uthman b. 'Isa from Muhammad b. Muslim who said: A man said to Abu 'Abd Allah, peace be upon him: "I have bought bondmaids and would like you to teach me something by which I may prevail over them." He [Abu 'Abd Allah] said: "Take a white onion (*basal*), cut it into small pieces, and fry it in olive oil. Then take an egg and break it into a bowl. Put some salt on it, and add it to the onion, then fry it and eat of it." He [the man] said: I did that and did not want anything of them without attaining it.

From him, peace be upon him, that he said to another: 'Prostrate yourself and say: "O Allah, make lasting in them my pleasure, increase in them my desire, and make my weakness strong over them, by Your Majesty, my Master."'

He said: "Kohl increases intercourse and henna also increases it." He, peace be upon him, said: "Fresh milk is beneficial for one whose semen (*al-ma'*) is reduced."

From Muhammad al-Baqir, peace be upon him, that he said: "Whoever does not have a child, let him eat eggs and eat them often, for it increases the progeny."

Al-Sadiq, peace be upon him, said: "Take endive, for it Increases the semen and improves the colour. It is hot and tender and increases the number of male children."

From al-Harith b. al-Mughira, who said: I said to Abu 'Abd Allah, peace be upon him, "I am from a family all of whom have passed away, and I do not have a child." He replied: "Pray to Allah, the Exalted, while prostrating and say: **Lord, give me of Thy goodness a goodly offspring. Yea, Thou hearest prayer (3:38). O my Lord, leave me not alone, though Thou art the best of inheritors (21:89).** Say that in the last *rak'a* of the evening prayer, then have intercourse with your wife that night." 'Al-Harith said: I did that and there were born to me 'Ali and al-Hasan.

ON DISAPPROVED TIMES FOR INTERCOURSE

Ahmad b. al-Khudayb al-Nisaburi narrated from al-Nadr b. Suwayd from Faddala b. Ayyub from 'Abd al-Rahman b. Salim, who said: I said to Abu Ja'far, peace be upon him, 'May I be your sacrifice, are there disapproved times for intercourse?' He replied: 'Yes. Even if it is lawful, it is disapproved of from the beginning of dawn to sunrise, and between sunset and nightfall; on the day when there is an eclipse of the sun; and on a night and day when there is an earthquake or a black wind or a red or yellow wind.

'The Messenger of Allah, blessings of Allah on him, spent the night of a moon eclipse with one of his wives and he did not do that night what he did on other nights. It was said to him: "O Messenger of Allah, this unkindness is hateful." He, blessings of

Allah on him, replied: "Do you not know that a sign appeared tonight? I dislike pleasure and diversion during it, and I would be like the people whom Allah rebuked in His, the Mighty and Exalted's, Book:

Even if they saw lumps falling from heaven, they would say, A massed cloud! (52:44). Then leave them alone to plunge and play, until they encounter that day of theirs which they are promised (43:83). And until they encounter their day in which they will he struck down (52:45).'"

Then Abu Ja'far, peace be upon him, said: "By Allah, after having knowledge of the times during which the Messenger of Allah forbad and disliked intercourse and diversion and pleasure, whoever has intercourse during those times disliked by the Messenger of Allah and is then blessed with a child, he will see in his child what he does not like. Know, O Ibn Salim, that whosoever does not avoid diversion and pleasure at the appearance of the signs is among those who makes a mockery of the signs of Allah."

ON INTERCOURSE ON THE NIGHT OF THE NEW MOON

'Abd Allah and al-Husayn, the sous of Bistam narrated from Muhammad b. Khalaf from 'Ali b. al-Husayn from Muhammad b. al-Jahm from Sa'd al-Mawla, who said: Abu 'Abd Allah al-Sadiq, peace be upon him, said to me: "Beware of having intercourse on the night the new moon (*al-hilal*) appears. If you do so and are then blessed with a child, it will be insane (*makhbut*)." I said: "May I be your sacrifice, why do you disapprove of that, O son of the Messenger of Allah?" He replied: "Do you not see the person afflicted with falling sickness? Most of them are not in a state of falling except on the first day of the new moon."

INTERCOURSE ON THE NIGHT OF THE MIDDLE OF THE MONTH

Ahmad b. al-Hasan al-Nisaburi narrated from al-Nadr b. Suwayd from Faddala b. Ayyub from 'Abd al-Rahman b. Salim, who said to Abu Ja'far al-Baqir, peace be upon him, "May I be your sacrifice, do you disapprove of intercourse at the start of the new moon and in the middle of the month?" He replied: "Because [sic] the person afflicted with falling sickness often has a fit at these times." He said: "O son of the Messenger of Allah, I understand about the beginning of the new moon, but what is wrong with the middle of the month?" He replied: "The crescent changes from one stage to another, and begins to wane. If you do that and are blessed with a child, it will be destitute, poor, weak, and subject to trials."

ON INTERCOURSE OF ONE WHO HAS HIS HAIR DYED

Muhammad b. Ja'far al-Bursi narrated from Muhammad b. Yahya al-Armani from Muhammad b. Sinan al-Zahiri from Yunus b. Zabyan from Isma'il b. Abu Zaynab that Abu 'Abd Allah, peace be upon him, said to one of his followers: "Do not have intercourse with your wife while you have your hair dyed, for if you are blessed with a child, it will be effeminate (*mukhannath*)."

ON INTERCOURSE ON THE NIGHT OF A JOURNEY

Muhammad b. Isma'il b. al-Qasim narrated from Ahmad b. Muhriz from Samr b. Abu al-Miqdam from Jabir al-Ju'fi from Abu Ja'far al-Baqir, peace be upon him, who said: 'Amir al-Mu'minin, peace be upon him, said: "The Messenger of Allah, blessings of Allah on him and his family, disapproved [of intercourse] on the night in whieh a person intended to travel and said that if he is blessed with a child, it will be squint-eyed (*ahwal*).'"

From al-Baqir, peace be upon him, who said: 'Al-Husayn b. 'Ali, peace be upon him, said to his companions: "Avoid intercourse on the night in which you intend to travel. If you do so and are blessed with a child, he will be squint-eyed.'"

ON INTERCOURSE IN FRONT OF CHILDREN

Ahmad b. al-Hasan b. al-Khalil narrated from Muhammad b. Isma'il b. al-Walid b. Marwan from al-Nu'man b. Ya'la from Jabir who said: Abu Ja'far al-Baqir, peace be upon him, said to me:

"Beware of having intercourse where a child who is able to describe your condition can see you." I said: "O son of the Messenger of Allah, is it [because of] a dislike of being seen?" He replied: "No, if you are blessed with a child, he will be renowned for dissoluteness (*al-fisq*) and immorality (*al-fujur*)."

Khalaf b. Ahmad narrated from Muhammad b. Marwan al-Za'farani from Ibn Abu 'Umayr from Salama Bayya' al-Sabiri from Abu Basir from Abu 'Abd Allah al-Sadiq, peace be upon him, that he said to him: "Beware of having intercourse with your wife while a child is watching you. The Messenger of Allah, blessings of Allah on him and his family, disliked that intensely."

ON INTERCOURSE WITH ONE FREE-BORN WOMAN BEFORE ANOTHER

Al-Mundhir b. Muhammad narrated from 'Allan b. Muhammad from Dharih from Abu 'Abd Allah, peace be upon him, who said that al-Baqir, peace be upon him, said: "Do not have intercourse with one free-born woman in front of another. As for [intercourse with] one bondmaid in front of another, there is no objection [to that]."

Tibb al-A'imma

AN INVOCATION FOR ANIMALS FOR THE EVIL EYE

Ahmad b. al-Harith narrated from Sulayman b. Ja'far from Abu al-Hasan Musa b. Ja'far al-Sadiq, peace be upon him, from one of his forefathers, peace be upon him, that regarding the invocation for animals (*al-hayawan*) he said: 'It is preserved with them. "In the Name of Allah, the Merciful, the Compassionate, In the Name of Allah, and by Allah, the evil eye *('ayn al-su')* departed from between its flesh, skin, bones, sinews, and blood vessels." Then Jibra'il and Mika'il, blessings of Allah be on them, met it and said: "Where are you going, O evil eye?" It replied: "I am going to the camel. I will drive it away from its train, and the riding-beast from its rein, the donkey from its bridle, and the child from his mother's lap. 1 will come upon the person fully dressed, from his feet."

They [Jibra'il and Mika'il] said to it: "Go, O evil eye, to the open country, for there is a snake with two eyes, one of water and the other of fire. Thus does Allah put a seal on the evil eye and a frowning face that obstructs, and a dry stone, and an envious eye, and one seeking fire. I return the evil eye, with Allah's help, to its people and within itself and to its side and to its most loving friends with the invocation of Allah and His words:

Have not the unbelievers then beheld that the heavens and the earth were a mass all sewn up, and then We unstitched them and of water fashioned every living thing? Will they not believe? (21- 30) Return thy gaze; seest thou any fissure?

Then return thy gaze again, and again, and thy gaze comes back to thee dazzled, aweary (67:3-4).

And Allah bless our master Muhammad and his pure family.'"

ON EATING THE PULP OF THE POMEGRANATE

Sulayman b. Muhammad, who performed the call to prayer at the mosque of the Messenger of Allah, blessings of Allah on him and his family, narrated from 'Uthman b. 'Isa al-Kilabi from Isma'il b. Jabir from Ja'far al-Sadiq, peace be upon him, from his pure forefathers from Amir al-Mu'minin, peace be upon him, who said: "Eat the pomegranate with its pulp, for it is an abdomenic (*dibagh*). Every grain of it which settles in the abdomen is life for the heart (*al-qalb*) and illumination for the soul, and the temptations of Satan are quelled for forty mornings. The pomegranate is among the fruits of Paradise. Allah, the Mighty and Exalted, has said:

Therein fruits, and palm trees, and pomegranates (55:68).

From Abu 'Abd Allah, peace be upon him, that he said: "Whoever cats pomegranate before sleeping is secure in himself until morning."

From al-Harith b. al-Mughira, that he said: I complained to Abu 'Abd Allah, peace be upon him, of a heaviness (*thiqal*) I felt in my heart (*al-fu'ad*) and of much indigestion after eating. He said: "Take of this sweet pomegranate and eat it with its pulp for it is good for the abdomen and will cure the indigestion and digest your food."

APPLES

Jabir b. 'Umar al-Saksaki narrated from Muhammad b. 'Isa from Ayyub b. Faddala from Muhammad b. Muslim, who said: Abu 'Abd Allah, peace be upon him, said: "If people knew what there was in apples, they would treat their sick only with it. Surely it is the quickest thing to benefit the heart, particularly its exudation (*al-nuduh*)."

From Abu Basir, he said: I heard al-Baqir, peace be upon him, say: "When you wish to eat apples, sniff them and then eat them, for if you do that every illness and danger will be expelled from your body and everything caused by winds will subside."

PEARS

Muhammad b. Ja'far al-Bursi narrated from Muhammad b. Yahya al-Armani from Muhammad b. Sinan al-Zahiri from Yunus b. Zabyan from al-Mufaddal b. 'Umar from Muhammad b. Isma'il b. Abu Zaynab from Jabir al-Ju'fi from Muhammad b. 'Ali al-Baqir, peace be upon him, from his forefathers that Amir al-Mu'minin, peace be upon him, said: "Eat pears (*al-kamathra*), for they burnish the heart (*al-qalb*)."

From Ziyad b. al-Jahm from al-Halabi, who said: Abu 'Abd Allah, peace be upon him, said to a man who complained to him of a pain he felt in his heart: "Eat pears."

CITRON

Abu Ghiyas 'Abd Allah b. Bistam narrated from 'Abd Allah b. Ibrahim from Muhammad b. al-Jahm from Ibrahim b. al-Hasan al-Ja'fari from Abu 'Abd Allah, peace be upon him, who said to his companions: "Tell me, with what do your physicians instruct you to eat citron (*al-utrujj*)?" He replied: "O son of the Messenger of Allah, they instruct us to eat it before meals." He said: "There is nothing more beneficial than it after a meal. Eat its preserves (*al-murabba*), for its pit has a fragrance like the fragrance of musk."

He, peace be upon him, said in another report: "It is good before meals but even better after meals." Then he said: "It causes harm before the meal and is beneficial after the meal. Dry cheese digests citron."

ON QUINCE

Al-Khidr b. Muhammad narrated from 'Ali b. al-'Abbas al-Khurrazi from Ibn Faddal from Abu Basir from al-Sadiq, peace be upon him, from his father from his grandfather from Amir al-Mu'minin who said: "eating quince increases a man's strength and removes his weakness."

Al-Ash'ath b. 'Abd Allah b. al-Ash'ath [narrated] from Ibn Muhammad al-Ash'ath b. Qays al-Kindi from Ibrahim b. al-Mukhtar from Ibn al-Mukhtar b. Abu 'Ubayda from Muhammad b. Sinan from Talha b. Zayd, who said: I asked Abu 'Abd Allah, peace be upon him, about cupping on a Saturday. He said: "It causes weakness." I said: "My illness is from my weakness and lack of strength." He said: "Then eat sweet quince with its seed, for it strengthens the weakness and makes fragrant and purifies the abdomen."

From him, peace be upon him, that he said: "In quince there is a quality not found in other fruits. I said: "And what is that?" He said: "It emboldens the coward from the knowledge of the prophets, blessings be upon all of them."

GALL

Ibrahim b. 'Abd al-Hamid al-Ansari narrated from Muhammad b. Marwan from Khalid b. Najih from 'Umar b. Shamr lrom Jabir b. Yazid al-Ju'fi from Abu Ja'far, peace be upon him, that he [Jabir] said: A man complained to Abu Ja'far of gall (*al-*

marar) which was inflamed in him until he was almost bent over. He [Abu Ja'far] said to him: "Make it subside with plums (*al-ijass*)."

From al-Azraq b. Sulayman, who said: I asked Abu 'Abd Allah, peace be upon him, about plums and he said: "They are beneficial for gall and relax the joints, but do not eat much of them for they will produce wind in your joints."

On his authority, he, peace be upon him, said: "Plums on an empty stomach calm the bile but stir up the wind."

From them, peace be upon them: "Eat mellowed (*al-'atiq*) plums, for the benefit of mellowed plums remain and the harm is removed. Eat them peeled, for they are beneficial for every [kind of] gall and heat, and the blaze stirred up from it."

ON EATING RAISINS

Muhammad b. Ja"ar al-Bursi narrated from Muhammad b. Yahya al-Armani from Muhammad b. Sinan al-Sinani from al-Mufaddal b. 'Umar al-Ju'fi from Abu 'Abd Allah al-Sadiq, peace be upon him, from his forefathers from Amir al-Mu'minin, peace be upon him, who said: "Whoever eats twenty-one red raisins ai the beginning of the day, Allah will repel front him every disease and illness."

From Hariz b. 'Abd Allah, who said: I said to Abu 'Abd Allah al-Sadiq, peace be upon him, "O son of the Messenger of Allah, the people relate a report from you regarding raisins. What is it?" He [al-Sadiq] replied: "Yes", and mentioned the hadith.

ON FIGS

Ahmad b. Muhammad b. 'Abd Allah al-Nisaburi narrated from Muhammad b. 'Arafa, who said: I was in Khurasan during the days of Al-Ridha', peace be upon him, and Ma'mun. I said to Al-Ridha': "O son of the Messenger of Allah, what do you say about eating figs (*al-tin*)?" He replied: "It is good for colic, so eat it."

From Abu Ja'far al-Baqir, peace he upon him, who said: 'Amir al-Mu'minin, blessings of Allah be on him, said: "Eat figs, for they are beneficial for colic. Eat less of fish, for its flesh wastes away the body and increases the phlegm and coarsens the soul.'"

From Amir al-Mu'minin, peace be upon him, he said: "eating figs relaxes obstructions (*al-sadad*) [in the body] and is beneficial for the wind of colic. So eat a lot of it during the day, and eat it at night but not too much."

ON ENDIVE

Muhammad b. Ja'far al-Bursi narrated from Muhammad b. Yahya al-Armani from Muhammad b. Sinan b. 'Abd Allah al-Sinani al-Zahiri from Yunus b. Zabyan from Muhammad b. Abu Zaynab from Ja'far b. Muhammad al-Sadiq, peace be upon him, from his forefathers from Amir al-Mu'minin, peace be upon him, that he said: "Eat endive, for there is not a morning when the drops of heaven do not fall on it."

From Muhammad b. Abu Nasr from his father from Abu 'Abd Allah, peace be upon him, that he [the father] said: I complained to him of a disturbance in my head and my teeth and a throbbing in my eye, so that my face was swollen from it. He, peace be upon him, said: "Take this endive and extract its juice. Take the juice and pour over it a lot of lump sugar. It will relieve it and drive away its harm." He [the father] said: I went to my house and treated it that night before I slept. I drank it and slept, and in the morning I was cured of it, praise be to Allah.

ON LOCUSTS

Hunan b. Ibrahim b. Muhammad al-Kirmani narrated from Muhammad b. Numayr b. Muhammad from al-Mubarak from his forefathers from Amir al-Mu'minin, blessings and peace be upon him, who said: "Eat locusts (*al-duban*). We Ahl al-Bayt love them."

From Dharih, that he said: I mentioned to Abu 'Abd Allah al-Sadiq, peace be upon him, the hadith related from Amir al-Mu'minin, peace upon him, regarding locusts, and that he said: "Eat locusts, for they increase the brain." Al-Sadiq, peace be upon him, replied: "Yes, and I say they are good for colic."

ON CLIPPING NAILS

Muhmmrnad b. Ja'far al-Bursi narrated from Muhammad b.Yahya al-Armani from Muhammad b Sinan al-Zahiri from al-Mufaddal b. 'Umar al-Ju'fi from Abu Zabyan from Jabir b. Yazid al-Ju'fi from Abu Ja'far Muhammad al-Baqir from his father from his grandfather, who said Amir al-Mu'minin, peace be upon him, said: "Clip your nails on Friday before the prayer, to ward off the greatest illness."

From him, peace be upon him, that he said: "Clipping nails on Friday keeps away every illness, and clipping on Thursday makes sustenance flow abundantly."

ON [EATING] FLESH

Muhammad b. al-Mundhir narrated from 'Ali, the brother of Ya'qub from Dawud from Harun from Ibn al-Jahm from Isma'il b. Abu Muslim al-Sakufi from Abu 'Abd Allah al-Sadiq, peace be upon him, that a man said to him: "O son of the Messenger of Allah, some Sunni scholars believe the Prophet, blessings of Allah on him and his family, said that Allah hates the butchers (*al-lahhamun*) and those who eat flesh (*al-lahm*) every day." He [al-Sadiq] said: "They have made a clear error. The Messenger of Allah only said that Allah hates those who eat the flesh of people in their houses, that is, who slander people. What is the matter with them? May Allah not have mercy on them. They go to what is lawful and make it unlawful by their numerous reports."

From Abu 'Abd Allah Ja'far b. Muhammad al-Sadiq, peace be upon him, who said: "Flesh produces flesh and increases the intellect. Whoever gives up eating it for some days, his intellect will be impaired."

And in another report, from him: "Whoever gives up eating flesh for forty days will become ill-natured and his intellect will be impaired. Whoever becomes ill-natured, call to him in his ear with the *iqama*.

ON EGG-PLANT

Abu al-Hasan al-Mu'alla Sajjada narrated from Abu al-Khayr al-Razi from Muhammad b. 'Isa from Muhammad b. Yaqtin from Sa'd b. Muslim from Abu al-'Azz al-Nahhas from Ibn Abu Ya'qub, who said Abu 'Abd Allah, peace be upon him, said: "Eat egg-plant. It is a cure for every illness."

On his authority, with the same chain of transmission, that he said: "Egg-plant is good for the black bile and is not harmful for the yellow bile."

From Al-Ridha', peace be upon him, he used to say to one of his stewards: "Give us egg-plant, for it is hot in the cold and cool in the heat, suitable at all times, and good in every condition." He said: I heard him say: "Mountain balm (*al-badharuj*) for us and watercress (*al-jirjir*) for the Banu Umayya; cupping on Monday for us and on Tuesday for the Banu Umayya."

ON LESIONS

Ahmad b. al-'Ays narrated from al-Nadr b. Suwayd from Musa b. Ja'far, peace be upon him, from his father Ja'far, peace be upon him, from his father Muhammad, peace be upon him, who said, concerning lesions (*al-jurh*): "Take fresh tar (*qir*) and an equivalent amount of the fresh fat of a goat (*ma'z*). Then take a new piece of cloth and a new container, coat the outside of it with the tar and place it on pieces of brick. Light a low fire under it from the morning till the afternoon.

Then take an old piece of flax and place it on your hand. Coat the tar over it and apply it over the lesion. If the lesion has a cavity, twist the flax together and pour the tar into the lesion.

Then insert the twisted flax into it."

ON THE EVIL EYE

Recite, write, and fasten to him the the sura *al-Hamd* (1), the two suras of taking refuge (*al-Falaq* (113) and *al-Nas* (114)), the sura *al-Ikhlas* (112), and the verse of the Throne (2:255), and: "O Allah, You are my Lord, there is no god but You. In You I trust, and You are the Lord of the Mighty Throne. There is no might nor power except with Allah, the Most High, the Mighty. Sufficient for me is Allah, and the best Protector. Whatever Allah has willed was, and whatever He did not will was not. I witness that Allah is Powerful over all things, and *that Allah encompasses everything in knowledge (65:12). He has numbered everything in numbers (72:28).*

O Allah, I take refuge in You from the evil in my self and from every creature you take by the forelock. Surely my Lord is on a straight path (11:56). So if they turn their backs, say: God is enough for me. There is no god hut He, In Him I have put my trust. He is the Lord of the Mighty Throne (9:129).

In the Name of Allah, the Lord of a frowning face and confining water and dry stone, I trust, and crushing water and searching meteor, from an envious eye and from the evil eye. I return the evil eye to him and to those most loved by him, in his liver (*al-kabd*) and his kidney, thin blood, heavily laden fat, delicate bone, in what he deserves. In the Name of Allah, the Merciful, the Compassionate, *and therein We wrote down for them: A life for a life, an eye for an eye, a nose for a nose, an ear for an ear, a tooth for a tooth, and for wounds retaliation (5:45).* Allah bless our master Muhammad and his family."

ANTS

Grind caraway (*al-karawiya*) and throw it into the hills of the ants (*al-naml*). Write [the following] on something and hang it at the corners of the house: "In the Name of Allah, the Merciful, the Compassionate. If you believe in Allah and the Last Day and the Prophets and what has been revealed to them, then I ask you by the right of Allah, and by the right of your Prophet and our Prophet, and what has been revealed to them, to move away from our dwelling.

INDEX OF AFFLICTIONS

abscesses, 140
Abu Murra [Satan], 48
aches, 7, 63
amnesia, 168
anger, 82, 138, 144, 145
ants, 185
anxiety, xxxiii, 125, 153, 167
barun, 96
bewitched, 50, 147, 149
bite, 111, 164
bleeding, 101, 102
blind, 37, 49, 51, 53, 168
blood, ix, xix, xxix, 21, 38, 41, 63, 65, 66, 67, 68, 69, 76, 89, 95, 101, 118, 130, 140, 143, 144, 151, 152, 155, 158, 176, 185
bowels, 78, 93, 94, 129
breath, 9, 96, 133, 164
caliph, ix, x, xi, 150
cankers, 163
cataract, 109
chapping, 93
childbirth, 35, 120, 121, 122
children, xli, 56, 111, 138, 145, 146, 159, 164, 170, 172
climate, xix, xxx, xxxi
clothes, xxviii, 25, 71, 100, 142
coldness, 33, 113
colic, xx, 39, 77, 181, 182

colour, 61, 96, 172
combing
  the beard, 9
confusion, xxi, 167
consumption, 38, 107, 164
coughing, 18, 108
crying, 91
cyst, 142
dampness, 79
deafness, 14, 168
death, xxiii, 26, 58
decay, 16
demons, 43, 51, 100, 146
desire, xxiii, xxviii, 17, 18, 20, 27, 49, 65, 71, 126, 153, 171
destiny, 82
devil, 47
diarrhea, 58
diarrhoea, xxviii
dirt, 103
disease, xvii, xx, xxiii, xxxiii, xxxiv, 6, 9, 23, 38, 44, 69, 81, 132, 133, 134, 135, 136, 159, 180
dissoluteness, 175
dissolves, 131, 136
dryness, 90
dumb, 127
dying, 19, 98
effeminate, 174
eggs, xxviii, 172
enchantment, 50

excess, xxviii, 18, 79, 90, 96, 103, 140, 144, 166, 167, 168
falling sickness, 117, 144, 146, 173, 174
fear, xxxiii, 14, 20, 29, 33, 34, 35, 42, 43, 51, 55, 60, 78, 93, 99, 106, 111, 116, 123, 129, 139, 143, 153, 166, 167
fever, xxxiii, 5, 40, 54, 56, 57, 58, 59, 60, 61, 62, 76, 93, 96, 120, 166, 167, 168
Fever, 57, 58, 62
fire, 17, 18, 30, 38, 41, 44, 53, 62, 63, 78, 79, 80, 87, 89, 90, 93, 95, 97, 101, 102, 128, 130, 131, 155, 158, 165, 166, 167, 169, 170, 176, 184
Fire, 51
flatulence, 96, 110, 164
food, xxviii, 25, 30, 33, 70, 71, 80, 87, 96, 100, 138, 164, 165, 166, 167, 177
forgetfulness, 20, 168
gall, 179, 180
ganglia, 33, 136, 137
gluttony, xxviii, xxx
grief, 19, 33, 100, 125
gripes, 83, 130, 131
head, 6, 7, 8, 15, 30, 54, 61, 63, 67, 85, 86, 88, 91, 92, 93, 96, 101, 103, 107, 110, 144, 160, 163, 164, 169, 181
headache, 10, 41, 166
heat, xxxi, 12, 38, 57, 59, 68, 69, 80, 93, 102, 155, 158, 180, 184
heaviness, 177
hemorrhoids, xxxi, 101, 102, 131
immorality, 21, 175
indigestion, 70, 96, 177

insanity, 124
itching, 65
jaundice, 88, 93, 96
jinn, xx, 41, 42, 45, 47, 48, 52, 116, 117, 123, 140, 143, 145, 152, 156, 157
laughing for no reason, 167
legumes, 93, 131, 167
leprosy, xx, 9, 81, 86, 135, 136, 137, 138, 164, 168
lesions, 184
loneliness, xxxiii, 153
louse of a vulture, 157
madness, 41, 124, 146
mental disorder, 124, 139, 146
migraine, 10, 11, 91, 166
milk, 74, 76, 90, 113, 132, 165, 167, 169, 170, 172
moisture, 111
obstructions, 181
odour, 65, 166
pale, 58, 84, 101
panic, 124, 140, 143, 164, 167
paralysis, 112, 163, 167
pebble, 13, 14
pestilence, 164
physician, xxiii, xxiv, xxix, xxxii, xxxiii, xxxix, xli, 72, 101
physicians, x, xxiii, xxvii, xxix, xxxii, xxxvi, 58, 101, 178
pleurisy, 93, 169
poison, 59, 67, 82, 103, 138, 164, 165, 167
possession, 123, 146
protection, xxxii, xxxiv, xxxv, 6, 8, 11, 13, 19, 27, 28, 29, 30, 39, 40, 42, 44, 45, 46, 47, 48, 55, 60, 66, 69, 105, 115, 117, 119, 122, 123,

135, 136, 137, 139, 140, 143, 145, 156, 158, 163
psychological, xxxiii, xxxiv, xxxvi
pus, 89
pustule, 39
relapse, xxix
rumbling, 82, 129, 130
saliva, 90, 146
Satan, xx, 48, 49, 50, 51, 81, 100, 119, 122, 124, 177
sciatica, 38, 94
scorpion, 54, 111
shivering, 166
sin, 3, 5
sleep, xxviii, 20, 27, 51, 77, 87, 107, 109, 139, 143, 164, 166, 167
sleeplessness, 5
sluggish, 41
smelling sweet scents, xxviii
snake, 55, 111, 176
soothsayer, 46
sores, 140
sorrow, xxxiii, 19, 29, 84, 116, 125, 126
spells, 34, 35, 51, 148, 149
Spells, 149
spirits, 144, 146, 163
stones, 87, 115, 128
stubborn, 36

swelling, 33, 143, 155, 158
talking, 130, 167
temptation, 153, 167
tetanus, 164
Thinness, 128
thirst, 90, 96
throbbing, 38, 84, 94, 151, 152, 166, 181
traps, 55
ulcers, 163, 167
urine, xix, 73, 74, 82, 93, 96, 133
vermin, 157
vertigo, 167
vinegar, 16, 78, 93, 103, 114, 131, 166, 167
vitiligo, 86, 135, 168
vomiting, xxviii, 64, 93
walking, 166
Walking, xxix
warts, 71, 141
weakness, 76, 100, 104, 111, 164, 171, 179
wild beasts, 45
wind, xxix, 42, 53, 57, 77, 85, 87, 96, 98, 109, 110, 115, 131, 163, 166, 172, 180, 181
worms, 78, 96
yellowness, 96

ANATOMICAL INDEX

abdomen, xxix, xxxi, 25, 84, 87, 113, 127, 164, 177, 179
arch of the foot, 94
arm, 26, 34, 143

back, 6, 15, 27, 62, 85, 98, 110
beard, 9, 103, 152, 167
belly, xxviii, 6, 15, 22, 23, 63, 77, 78, 82, 83, 91, 92, 93, 96, 98,

111, 115, 120, 122, 123, 128, 129, 153, 154, 164, 167
bile, ix, xix, xx, xxix, 79, 80, 93, 144, 164, 166, 167, 180, 184
Bile, xx
bladder, 27
Bladder, 26, 93, 96
body, x, xxvii, xxviii, xxix, xxx, xxxi, xxxiii, xxxiv, 6, 7, 18, 21, 56, 63, 70, 76, 77, 86, 108, 119, 120, 128, 132, 134, 143, 168, 178, 181
bone, 17, 62, 111, 176, 185
brain, 96, 182
breast, xxxiv, 9, 20, 21, 96
buttocks, 101, 102
cheek, 9, 142
chest, 62, 69, 134, 153
combing
   the eyebrows, 9
   the head, 9, 80
constituents, xx, xxix, xxx, 59, 144
ear, 13, 16, 89, 90, 183, 185
Ear, 12, 13
ears, 12, 36, 166
elements, x, xviii, xix, xxi, xxii, xxx
eyebrow, 92
eyelashes, 105
eyes, xxi, 12, 48, 85, 92, 96, 100, 103, 104, 105, 106, 107, 109, 112, 132, 134, 148, 168, 176
face, 41, 85, 144, 161, 181, 185
Face, 95, 116
faculties, x
feet, 5, 31, 49, 85, 93, 167, 176
finger, 14, 17, 39, 62, 82, 92, 105
flesh, 17, 63, 75, 105, 111, 176, 181, 183
Flesh, 183

gall, 179, 180
genitals, 28, 120, 122, 149
groin, 35, 125
gums, 16, 76
hair, 9, 21, 92, 135, 147, 160, 164, 174
Hair, 137
hamstring, 32
Hamstring, 32
hands, 37, 41, 51, 91, 93, 107, 164
head, 6, 7, 8, 15, 30, 54, 61, 63, 67, 85, 86, 88, 91, 92, 93, 96, 101, 103, 107, 110, 144, 160, 163, 164, 169, 181
hearing, xxxi, 6, 7, 13, 15, 17, 43, 45, 47, 84, 92, 98, 104, 122, 127, 128, 132, 154
Hearing, 43
heart, xv, 21, 22, 31, 48, 49, 76, 84, 96, 99, 113, 127, 128, 134, 139, 142, 145, 151, 153, 177, 178
hips, 68
humours, ix, xviii, xx
joints, 84, 87, 96, 109, 180
kidney, 185
kidneys, 96, 128
legs, 29, 164
limbs, 6, 15, 21, 76
lips, 134, 151
liver, 93, 185
mouth, 14, 15, 90, 104, 117, 146, 154
nails, 105, 182
navel, 23, 91
neck, 68, 69, 164
nerves, 21
nose, xxviii, 135, 137, 185
organs, xviii, 6
palm of my hand, 141

phlegm, ix, xix, xx, xxix, 9, 79, 80, 93, 144, 164, 166, 168, 181
privy parts, 28
qualities, x, xviii, xxx, xxxii, 169
shoulder, 59, 68, 78, 129
side, 11, 17, 52, 62, 85, 107, 114, 135, 136, 150, 166, 176
sight, 6, 15, 31, 43, 49, 51, 84, 92, 104, 105, 127, 128
Sight, 43
skin, xx, xxxiv, 21, 62, 92, 118, 157, 176
soul, xxvii, xxxiii, xxxiv, xxxv, 17, 20, 27, 47, 50, 100, 177, 181
spleen, xx, 25, 26, 114
Spleen, xx
teeth, 9, 15, 16, 54, 79, 109, 166, 181
temperaments, x, xviii
thighs, 28, 56
throat, 18
Throat, 113
tongue, 169
Urethra, 93
urine, xix, 73, 74, 82, 93, 96, 133
vein, 5, 6
waist, 24, 71, 94, 96
wombs, 127

INDEX OF ARABIC TERMS

'ajam, 157
'ala al-riq, 9, 78
'amma, 157
'anbar, 85
'aqd, 33
'aqir qarha, 9
'aqrab, 54
'araq, 58
'atash, 90
'atiq, 108, 180
'aura, 28
'ayn, 41, 91, 109
'Ayn, 151
'ayn al-su', 176
'urqub, 32
'uruqi, 21
'usr, 93
a'da, 6
abarfiyun, xxii, 107, 108, 111, 113

abhal, 30
abradhar, 102
ad'iya, xxxii
adas, 131
adim, 56
adras, 9
'adud, 26
afa'i, 75
afarbiyun, xxii
afitimun, 97
afsa, 88
afshuraj, 87
ahl al-bala', 137
ahwal, 174
ajwa, 78, 103
akari', 168
akhda'an, 69
akhlat, ix
akhras, 127

akila, 163
alban, 74
alban al-liqah, 132
al-firash, 120
alwa', 83
a'ma, 37
amlaj, 87
andarani, 109
anf, 135
anisun, 87
anjudan, 97
aruzz, 128
'asabi, 21
'asal, xxviii
asarawan, xxii, 96
asarun, xxii
Atibba, xxv
'ayn, 96
'azm, 17
badan, xxviii
badharuj, 184
badinjan, 167
bahaq, 86, 168
balabil, 21
balasan, 90
balbala, 167
balgham, xxix
balilaj, 87
ban, 118
banafsaj, 118
banj, 107
baql, 93
baras, 135
bard, xxviii
barni, 79
barun, 96
basal, 171
basar, 6
basbasa, 94

bashari, 21, 92
bathr, 39
batin hadr al-qadam, 94
bawasir, xxxi
bawl, 73
bayd, xxviii
bazaq, 146
billa, 111
birsam, 93
bizr al-fujl, 167
bizr qutuniya, 78
bukhur, 147
bukhur maryam, 146
bunduqa, 9
burr, 62
butn, xxviii, 78
da' al-khabith, 133
dabba, 36
dabib al-dawabb, 65
dam, xxix
dam al-muhtariq, 140
damamil, 140
dar filfil, 87
dar sini, 87
daras, 54
darban al-fu'ad, 96
dawa' al-jami', 111
dawajin, 146
dawam al-dam, 76
dhubab, 137
dhukran, 102
dibagh, 177
dimagh, 96
duban, 182
dubayla, 163
dud, 78
du'f, 76
duhn, 13
duhn al-ward, 87

duhn dhakar, 119
duhn lawz murr, 168
duhn sanaubar, 168
duhn zanbaq, 101
durraj, 138
fakhdhan, 28
falij, 112
faludhaj, 60
fam, 14
fanidh, 90, 95, 96, 97
faras, 125
farj, 28, 120
fasd, 140
faz', 124
filfil, 87
filfil al-abyad, 108
fiqh, xxvii
fisq, 175
fu'ad, 21, 177
fujur, 175
ghadad, 136
ghazal, 26
ghiswa al-'ayn, 105
habba, 108
habba a-sauda', 59
hadhayan, 167
hadith, xii, xiii, xv, xvi, xvii, xix, xx, xxv, xxvii, xxxvi, xxxvii, xxxviii, xl, xli, 66, 106, 108, 139, 148, 149, 180, 182
Hadith, xii
haff, 105
ha'id, 56
hajib, 92
hakka, 65
halilaj al-asfar, 108
halq, 18
hama, 91
hamam, 144

hamm, 125
hamma, 167
hammam, xxviii
hanzala, 168
haqq, 158
haqw, 35
hara'ir, 170
harmal, 81
harun, 36
hasah, 87
hashayan, 120
hasw al-laban, 113
hawamm, 156
hayajan, 65
hayawan, 176
hayya, 55
hilal, 173
hiltit, 111
hindiba', 94
hinna', 86
hinta, 16
hirz, 143
hujja, 102
hujjama, xxviii
humma, 40
humma al-batina, 167
humma al-ghabb al-ghaliba, 59
humma al-rib', 58
huqna, xxviii
ihlilaj, 58
ihlilaj al-aswad, 87
ihlilaj asfar, 9
ijass, 180
ikhtilat al-'aql, 167
'ilk rumi, 9
ima', 18
inath, 101
Injil, 46
iqlimiya al-dhahab, 109

irq al-'aqir, 33
irq al-madini, 5
'irq al-min al-judham, 136
irq al-nisa', 38
irq nuqqar, 38
ishal, xxviii
isnad, 28
ithmid, 103
jabbar, 157
jamal, 37
jami'a, 18
janaba, 56
janah, 138
janb, 114
jasad, 6
jawarih, 6
jawzat, 30
jibn 'atiq, 90
jild, 62, 157
jima', 96
jirjir, 184
jismi, 21
judham, 9
junun, 41
jurh, 184
juzbawwa, 87
kabd, 185
kafur, 104
kahil, 69
kahin, 46
kalima al-tawhid, 99
kalimat al-faraj, 155
kama', 103
kamathra, 178
kammun, 95
kanif, 141
karawiya, 185
kasal, 41
kashim, 24

katif, 78
kattan, 35
kays, 119
kayy, xxviii
khabisa, 166
khabitha, 73
khabl, 124
khafaqan, 113
khall, 93
khall al-khumr, 16
khaluq, 119
kham, 77, 164
khamr, 74
kharbaq abyad, 107
khardal, 9
khasira, 24
khauf, 34
khazaf abyad, 78
khinsir, 105
khiri, 131
khishkhash ahmar, 97
khiyar, 88
khiyar shanbar, 87
khubat, 124
khulanjan, 87
kibrit abyad, 147
kuhl, 100, 104, 109
kulyatan, 96
kundur, 9
kundur dhakar, 30
kundus, 77
kur, 87
kur sandari, 146
kurrath, 26
kuzaz, 164
kuzbara, 76
labn al-halib, 165
lahhamun, 183
lahm, 17, 76, 183

lahm al-da'n, 76
lahmiyya, xxix
laqwa, 112
lasa', 111
lauz azraq, 131
lift, 136
lihya, 152
litha, 16
luban, 79
lubna 'asal, 101
lusus, 37
ma' al-matar, 39
ma', xxxi, 172
ma' al-asfar, 164
ma' al-bi'r, 120
ma'ida, xxix, 25
ma'z, 184
mafasil, 84
maghs, 130
majnun, 55
makhbut, 173
ma'khudh, 50
makrub, 159
mann, 103
maq'ad, 101
maraq bi-lahm, 135
marar, 180
marham, 102
marmari, 147
marzanjush, 112
mashw, 94
masru', 117
mass, 146
mastaka, 58
mathana, 27
mawla, xl
Mawla, 92, 144, 173
milh, 95
milh hindi, 97

mirra, xxix
mirra al-ghaliba, 144
misk, 78
mu'alajun, xxxii
mu'ayyana, 68
muhaq, 141
mujami'a, 25
mukhannath, 174
muql, 131, 147
murabba, 178
murr, 104
mutaqaddima, 67
nabidh, 30
nafi'a, 68
nafkh, 164
nahal, 128
nahsha, 164
naml, 185
nankhwah, 9
narmishk, 90
nashr, 65
nashra, 55, 149
naz', 98
nazar wa, 91
nazara, 124
nifar, 155
nifas, 124
nifkha, 96
nisyan, 168
nuduh, 178
nura, xxviii
nushadir, 109
qada', 82
qadam, 94
qafa', 62
qaih, 89
qalb, 177, 178
qamla al-nasr, 157
qaqula, 87

qaqula murabban, 95
qaranful, 85
qaraqir, 82
qasim al-nar, 80
qawlanj, 39
qay', xxviii
qilqil, 87
qina', 160
qir, 184
qirfa al-qaranfal, 87
qitran shami, 147
qulama zufur, 94
qurad, 170
quruh, 140
qushur al-hanzal, 147
ra's, 6
rabw, 133
raha, 92
rak'a, 133
rak'a, 132, 142, 172
ramad, 12, 166
ratb al-'ayn, 103
raziqi, 108, 119
raziyanaj, 58
rih, xxix
rih al-bahr, 154
rih al-khabitha, 85
rih al-sabal, xxi, 164
rih al-shauka, 164
rih shabika, 85
rih umm al-sibyan, 110
rijl, 5
riq, 90
riyah, 96
rughwa, 88
rumman, 69
rumman al-hulw, 95
ruqqa, xxxii
rutuba, 79

sa'ut, 169
sab', 37
sabbaba, 39
sabir, 104
sadad, 181
sadaqa, 66, 161
sadar, 167
sadhab, 89
sadhaj, 95
sadr, 9
safar, 37
safarjal, 87
sahir, 46
sahw, 168
Sajzi fanidh, 90, 97
sakkarat, 69
salat al-fajr, 157
salat al-'isha', 156
salat al-layl, 35, 159
salat al-nahar, 35
salat al-zuhr, 159
saljam, 136
sam', 6
samam, 14
samgh 'arabi, 79
samm, 103
samn 'arabi, 26
samn baqr, 87
sandarus, 146
saqayn, 29
sar, 101, 102
sariq, 157
sa'tar, 9
sawiq, 80, 111
sha'ir, 166
shabath, 143
shafiya, 163
shahd, 165
shahm, 74

sha'irat, 141
sham', 101
shaqaqul, 87
shaqiqa, 10
sha'r qanfadh, 147
sha'ri, 21
sharib, 137
shausa, 112
shayatin, 43
shina, 95
shiraj, 30
shuniz, 9
Shuniz, 82
sihr, 34
sil'a, 142
silikha, 90, 97
sill, 38
simsim ghayr muqashshar, 13
sinam, 30
sirjin, 103
siwak, 79
soghmuniya, 90
su'al, 18
su'd, 16
su'd Yamani, 147
suda', 10
sufra al-'ayn, 96
sukkar, 57
sukkar al-tabarzad, 80
sultan, 34
summaq, 76
sunbula, 90
surra, 23
su'ut, xxviii
ta'widh, 56
taba'i', xxix
talq, 83
taly, 64
tama'im, 55

tammani, 153
tamr, 69
taqs, xxx
taqtir al-bawl, 83
tasrih al-ra's, 80
thabit, xxxi
thiqal, 177
thu'alil, 71
thum, 165
tibb, xxvii
Tibb, xxxix
Tibb al-Nabavi, xiii
Tibb al-Nabi, xxxix
Tibb-al-Nabbi, xiii
tihal, 25
tin, 54, 135, 181
tin al-Armani, 78
tin al-jir, 135
tiryaq, 75
tuffah, 61
tukham, 70
tumushshut, 80
turab, 170
turba, xxx, 136
tutiya hindi, 109
'udhat, xxxii
udhun, 12
umma, 4
'unq, 68
'urf, 37
'usr, 35
usul al-karafs, 114
utrujj, 178
utun, 74
waba', 9
wad', 125
wadah, 86
wahiya, 68
wahsha, 153

wahshiya, 125
wahy, xxxi
wajal, 167
wajh, 41
wajj, 87
waram, 33
wark, 94
wasakh kathir, 103
wasawis, 21
wasi, 84
wilada, 35
wudu', xxix
yaraqan, 88
yubs, 79
za'faran, 25
zabib, 72
zahir, 78
zahr, 6
zanbaq, xxii, 108, 110, 119
zanjabil, 87
zaybaq, xxii, 85
zayt, 89
zaytun, 16
zibd, 94
zirabaja, 93
zukam, 77

INDEX OF PERSONAL NAMES

'Abbas b. 'Asim al-Mu'adhdhin, 119
'Abbas b. 'Umar al-Kuludhani, xxxviii
'Abbas b. Muhammad, 98
'Abd al-'Ala', 30
'Abd al-Aziz, 62, 106, 134
'Abd al-Aziz b. 'Abd al-Jabbar, 132
'Abd al-Aziz b. al-Hassan, 138
'Abd al-Hamid b. 'Umar b. al-Hurr, 73
'Abd Allah al-Mufaddal al-Nawfali, 110
'Abd Allah b. 'Abd al-Rahman b. Abu Najran, 101
'Abd Allah b. 'Ammar al-Duhni, 40
'Abd Allah b. 'Ubayda, 65

'Abd Allah b. 'Uthman, 113
'Abd Allah b. Abu al-Qasim, 162
'Abd Allah b. al-'Abbas b. al-Mufaddal, 111
'Abd Allah b. al-'Ala al-Qazwini, 34
'Abd Allah b. al-Ajlah, 89
'Abd Allah b. al-Mufaddal al-Nawfali, 152
'Abd Allah b. al-Mughira, 109
'Abd Allah b. Bukayr, 56, 67, 68, 99
'Abd Allah b. Ghalib, 34
'Abd Allah b. Jabala, 156
'Abd Allah b. Mas'ud al-Yamani, 9
'Abd Allah b. Maymun al-Qaddah, 104

'Abd Allah b. Muhammad al-Bajali, 158
'Abd Allah b. Muhammad b. Mihran al-Kufi, 18
'Abd Allah b. Musa, xli, 105
'Abd Allah b. Musa al-Tabari, 68, 91
'Abd Allah b. Muskan, 65, 74
'Abd Allah b. Sinan, 3, 4, 5, 22, 54, 61, 71, 86, 117, 142, 153
'Abd Allah b. Yahya al-Bazzaz, 152
'Abd Allah b. Zuhayr al-'Abid, 110
'Abd Allah Shubr al-Kazimi, xxxix
'Abd al-Rahman Abu Najran, 62
'Abd al-Rahman al-Qusayr, 7
'Abd al-Rahman b. 'Abd al-Majid al-Qusayr, 76
'Abd al-Rahman b. Abu 'Abd Allah, 56
'Abd al-Rahman b. Abu Hashim, 117
'Abd al-Rahman b. Abu Najran, 75, 145, 154, 170
'Abd al-Rahman b. al-Hajjaj, 75
'Abd al-Rahman b. al-Jahm, 129
'Abd al-Rahman b. Salim, 172, 174
'Abd al-Rahman b. Yazid, 103
'Abd al-Rahman Sahl b. Mukhlid, 114
'Abd al-Wahhab b. Mahdi, 120
'Abd al-Wahhab b. Muhammad, 162
'Abd al-Wahid b. Maymun, 81
'Abd Rabbihi b. Muhammad b. Ibrahim, 149
'Abid b. 'Awn b. 'Abd Allah al-Madani, 146

'Asim b. Hamid, 63
'Abd Allah b. Ja'far b. al-Husayn b. Malik b. Jami' al-Humayri, xxxvii
Aban b. 'Uthman, 6, 40, 42, 55, 56
Aban b. 'Uthman, 27
Aban b. Abu al-'Ayyash, 35
Aban b. Taghlab, 30
'Abd Allah b. al-Fadl al-Nawfali, 61
'Abd Allah b. Ibrahim, xli, 178
Abu 'Abd Allah Ahmad b. Muhammad b. Sayyar al-Basri, xxxvii
Abu 'Abd Allah al-Husayn b. [Ahmad] Muhammad al-Khawatimi, 15
Abu 'Abd Allah al-Husayn b. 'Ali, 32
Abu 'Abd Allah al-Khawatimi, 23
Abu 'Abd Allah al-Sadiq, 5, 11, 21, 23, 27, 28, 36, 41, 55, 60, 73, 75, 79, 80, 81, 86, 98, 100, 104, 108, 110, 111, 134, 135, 136, 137, 140, 142, 143, 144, 146, 148, 151, 152, 158, 159, 160, 162, 169, 173, 175, 180, 182, 183
Abu 'Abd Allah Muhammad b. 'Ubayd Allah al-Jannabi al-Barqi, known as Majilawayh, xxxviii
Abu 'Abd Allah al-Husayn b. Bistam, 4
Abu 'Abd Allah al-Sadiq, 10
Abu 'Abd Allah al-Sadiq, 55
Abu al-'Abbas Ahmad b. 'Ali al-Najashi, xxiv

INDEX OF VERSES OF THE QURAN

1

1:2-7 44
10:57..xxxiv
10:81-2 ....34, 149
11:56....................................157, 185
112 15, 17, 39, 41, 62, 77, 123, 129, 184
112:3-4 44
113.....xxii, 17, 39, 41, 77, 123, 129, 140, 144, 148, 184
113:1..44
113:1-2 161
113:2-5 44
114.....xxii, 17, 39, 41, 77, 123, 129, 140, 144, 148, 184
114:1-2 44
12:111...121
12:18..100
12:21..49
12:24..65
13:12..48
14:20..54
14:26-9 53
15:16-17 47
16:69..59
16:78..84
16:78-9 127
16:9..126
17:110-11 26
17:82...........................xxxiv, 23, 55
18:11-12 36
18:16..126
18:27..29
19:18..43
19:22-34 127
19:23-5 84
19:62 70

2

2:106-7 27
2:112 29
2:137 49
2:157 100
2:16-18 53
2:164 52
2:166-7 51
2:171 53
2:178 49
2:185-6 126
2:255 ....43, 52, 62, 77, 163, 184
2:264 53
2:72-3 17
20:105-7 141
20:121 51
20:4-8 46
20:55 124
20:77 37
21:30 ....8, 28, 83, 121, 126
21:31 ....47, 48
21:69-70 17
21:83 20
21:87 160
21:89 172
22:1-2 35
22:31 53
23:108 43
23:115-18 ....24, 123
24:35 45

24:39-40	54
25:48	49
25:61	46
27:12	65
27:61	46
27:62	19
27:8	18
27:88	15, 98, 154
28:35	35

3

3:117	53
3:145	27
3:190	52
3:26-7	45
3:38	172
35:43	50
36	163
36:37-44	121
36:51	121
36:71-2	37
37:4-10	52
38:42	49
39:67	32

4

4:28	49
4:76	51
41:1-2	47
41:41-2	23
41:44	xxxv
42:11-12	45
42:1-3	47
43:83	173
46:16	21
46:35	120, 122
48:1-7	32
48:28	54

5

5:45	185
52:44	173
52:45	173
55:68	177
56:1-6	141
56:75-6	40
59:16-17	51
59:19	50
59:21	55, 123
59:21-3	14
59:21-4	33, 143
59:22-4	52

6

6:13	17
6:73	45
6:7-9	51
65:12	45, 185
67:3-4	176

7

7:117	50
7:118-19	34, 54
7:118-22	150
7:13	50
7:158	77
7:18	50
7:188	65
7:31	xxviii
7:54	52
7:54-6	46
71:10-12	171
72:28	45, 185

72:8-9 122	*8:66* 49
76:13 59	80:20 126
78:7 47	
79:28 150	**9**
79:46 ....120, 122	9:129 .... 116, 124, 161, 185
	9:33 54
8	94:5-6 126
8:11 49	97 16, 27, 62, 122, 162

INDEX OF REMEDIES

abstaining from certain foods, xviii, xxxii, xxxiv
Abstaining from certain foods, xxxi
Abstaining From Certain Foods, 88
Accustom (the body) to what you are used to, xxxi
adhan, 77, 113
almond, 215
    almonds, 118, 169
alms, 84, 104, 163, 186
Aloe, 134
ambergris, 108, 142
amulet, 183
amulets, 69, 70
angels, xxxvii, 26, 59, 62, 159
animals, 46, 162, 186, 224
anise, 111
antimony, 133, 141
apples, 77, 88, 95, 226, 227
asafetida water, 144
asarabacca, xxi
ashes, 181, 211

balm, 114, 124, 234
barley, 102, 211, 217
barleycorn, 181
barleycorns, 181
bdellium, 111, 122, 188
beeswax, 130, 131
ben tree, 153
bishop's weed, 10, 122, 124
bread, 38, 185
brick, 131, 235
broth of meat, 173
butter, 33, 111, 120, 123, 210, 211, 217
camphor, 134
caraway, 236
cardamom, 110, 114, 119, 122, 124, 138, 139, 144, 146
carding, 101
Cassia fistula, 110, 119
Cassia spuria, 114, 124
Cassia tona, 110
cauterization, xviii, xxx, 80, 81, 82

201

celery root, 147
charity, 206
Charity, 205, 206
charms, xxxv, xliv, 68, 69, 71
cheese, 38, 114, 228
chew, xxix, 31, 90
cinnamon, 110, 111, 115, 119, 120, 122, 123, 124
citron, xxiv, 228
clay, xxi, 81, 96, 99, 100, 108, 122, 173
clothing, 172
clove, 108, 119
cloves, 108
clyster, 80
clysters, xxix, 81, 82, 85
colocynth, 188, 215
combing
   combing, 10
   the hair on the cheeks, 10
comprehensive, xxviii, 23, 54, 117, 143, 145, 146, 147, 148, 191, 208, 217
coriander, 96, 167
cotton, 16, 20
cucumber, 112, 119
cumin, 75, 104, 122, 147, 167
cupping, xviii, xxix, 81, 82, 83, 84, 85, 86, 87, 88, 228, 234
cyclamen, 187
cyperus, 188
Cyperus rotundus, 20
darnel, 88
dates, 88, 99, 100, 101, 106, 118, 133, 137, 163
declaration, 127, 129
dill water, 184
dodder, 125
drugs, xx, xxxvii
earth, xxxi, 8, 9, 12, 15, 17, 33, 35, 39, 40, 41, 42, 45, 49, 55, 56, 57, 58, 59, 60, 62, 65, 66, 67, 78, 103, 105, 116, 117, 127, 129, 130, 132, 150, 156, 159, 160, 162, 182, 198, 203, 217, 225
eating, xxix, xxx, xxxii, 31, 39, 88, 90, 100, 142, 164, 175, 209, 210, 226, 228, 230, 231, 233
egg-plant, 214, 234
Egg-plant, 234
endive, 119, 219, 231, 232
errhine, 216
euphorbium, xxi
fasting, 27
fat, 38, 93, 94, 135, 164, 165, 211
fennel, 11, 73, 75, 97, 122, 139, 211
figs, 230, 231
flax, 45, 130, 131, 235
fleawort, 99
flies, 57, 177
francolin, 178
Francolin, 178
frankincense, 10, 103
galanga, 111, 123
ganglia
   Beware of eating, 175
garlic, 210, 211, 217
garment, 15, 71, 72, 132, 160, 182
gilliflower, 169
ginger, 110, 111, 119, 120, 121, 123, 124
grape, 216
gum Arabic, 100
gum mastic, 73
gypsum, 173
haff, 135
hail, 214
healing
   the, xx, 208, 210
heelweed, 121
hellebore
   white, 138, 139, 144, 146

henbane, 138, 139, 144, 146
henna, 109, 219
honey, xviii, xxiii, xxx, xxxiii, 11, 28, 75, 82, 91, 101, 110, 111, 115, 119, 120, 123, 125, 138, 139, 144, 146, 167, 174, 184, 211, 217
inhaling medications, xxx, 81, 82, 85
intercourse, 31, 71, 90, 123, 218, 219, 220, 221, 222, 223, 224
Intercourse, 154
invocation, xix, xxiii, xxxiv, xxxv, xxxvii, xxxix, xliv, 6, 12, 13, 15, 19, 21, 27, 30, 36, 37, 39, 40, 43, 48, 51, 53, 54, 55, 66, 68, 69, 70, 71, 83, 91, 105, 116, 117, 136, 149, 151, 157, 159, 160, 161, 162, 179, 191, 194, 196, 199, 200, 207, 224, 225
Invocation, 11, 12, 14, 15, 16, 17, 18, 19, 21, 22, 26, 28, 30, 31, 33, 34, 35, 36, 37, 39, 40, 41, 42, 44, 45, 46, 47, 48, 49, 50, 54, 55, 56, 58, 59, 60, 61, 62, 63, 68, 70, 74, 82, 112, 117, 134, 136, 149, 151, 155, 156, 159, 162, 178, 186, 188, 192, 198, 199, 200, 202, 206, 224
iqama, 77, 113, 234
iron, 16, 42
ithmid, 133
jasmine, xxi, 130, 131, 142, 154
Jasmine, 139, 154
kays, 154
knife, 42
kohl, 135
Kohl, 135, 219
kuhl, 134
laxative, 120
leather, 71

leek, 33, 38, 169
lentils, 169
lime, xxx, 82, 85, 109
locusts, 232
lovage, 31, 90
mace, 120
male oil, 153
manna, 133
marjoram, 145, 211, 213
marmari, 188
massage, xxxii
mastic
    byzantine, 10, 115, 124
meat, 96
medicine of Al-Ridha, 143, 144
mercury, xxi, 108
moustache, 176
muql, 169, 188
musk, 98, 142, 155, 157, 160, 179, 228
mustard, 11, 16
mutton, 97
myrobalan, 111, 122, 124, 141, 169
myrrh, 134, 188
myrtle, 132, 148
Names of Allah, xxxvi, xxxviii, 20, 195
nard, 114, 124, 138, 139, 144, 146
nutmeg, 110, 119
olive oil, 113, 121, 213, 215, 219
onion, 219
oxide of zinc, 141
parchment of a gazelle, 32, 43, 44, 161
pears, 227
pepper, 110, 111, 119, 120, 121, 122, 123, 124, 138, 140, 144, 146, 211
pillows, 121
pine-nut oil, 215
pitch

syrian liquid, 188
plums, 229
Plums, 229
pomegranate, 88, 122, 215, 225, 226
poppy
   red-seeds, 124
porcupine, 188
pray, xix, xxiii, xxxv, xxxviii, xxxix, xlvi, 3, 4, 9, 13, 21, 23, 25, 27, 30, 32, 40, 44, 56, 72, 77, 78, 108, 111, 116, 117, 126, 128, 134, 141, 142, 157, 163, 166, 167, 168, 169, 172, 178, 179, 182, 183, 186, 190, 194, 196, 197, 198, 199, 200, 201, 202, 203, 204, 206, 218, 220, 225, 233
Pray, xxxix, 4, 32, 104, 171, 197, 220
prodigal, xxix
pyrethrum, 11, 115, 124, 138, 144, 146
quince, 110, 119, 228, 229
Qur'an, x, xvii, xix, xxii, xxxviii, xxxix, 17, 41, 69, 70, 98, 101, 190, 207
qurad, 217
Qur'an, xxii, xxix, xxxvii, xxxviii, 27, 69, 70, 71, 100, 158, 166, 182, 190
radish, 148, 213
rainwater, 50, 98, 108, 141, 160, 166, 173, 214
raisins, xxiii, 91, 230
raziqi, 139, 154
reliev, 8, 13, 18, 32
relieve, xxix, 12, 161, 201, 216, 232
remedies, xix, xx, xxiii, xxviii, 30, 77, 80, 85, 130
respiration, xxxii
rest, xxxii, xxxvii, 115, 128, 152, 170

rice, 120, 164, 165
roses, 110, 119, 212, 213, 215
rue, 103, 105, 113, 148, 149, 213
saffron, 32, 75, 98, 138, 139, 142, 144, 145, 146, 155, 157, 160, 179
Sajzi fanidh, 115, 125
salammoniac, 140
salt, 121, 124, 141, 213, 215, 219
Salt, 9
sanadarch, 188
sar, 130, 131
savin, 38
sawiq, 102, 143
scammony, 114, 115, 124, 125
scoria, 141
sea water, 141
secacul, 111, 114, 124
sesame, 16, 38, 39, 118, 132, 169
silk, 125, 138, 139, 144, 146, 169
silver container, 149
siwak, 100
sleeping, 11, 60, 99, 125, 133, 135, 138, 139, 213, 214, 226
sneezewort, xxi
soapwort, xxi
soil, xviii, xxxii, xxxiv, 58, 67, 68, 76, 174
spring, 32, 155, 189
starch, 115
steam, xxx, 81, 82, 85, 87, 100, 109, 110, 165
storax, 38, 100, 101, 103, 125, 130, 131, 188, 215
sugar, xviii, 73, 74, 102, 115, 118, 120, 232
sulphur, 188
sumac, 96, 130, 167
sun, 59, 66, 74, 108, 156, 185, 220
supplications, xix, xxiii, xxxv, 169, 171

sweat, 73
sweet asa, 125
sweet flag, 111
sweet flummery, 75
tar, 235
theriac, 95
thyme
   wild, 10
treatment, xxiii, xxxi, xxxii, xxxiii, xxxv, xxxvi, xxxvii, xxxix, xliii, 80, 146, 165, 181, 216
trotters, 214
Truffles, 133
turnips, 174, 175
vapours, 188
violets, 152
vomit, 73, 102
walnuts, 38
wash, 38, 70, 98, 105, 123, 132, 140, 142, 155, 165, 166
Wash, 157
water, xviii, xxxiii, 9, 28, 32, 35, 44, 61, 62, 65, 67, 70, 72, 73, 74, 76, 87, 88, 91, 101, 105, 110, 112, 119, 120, 122, 125, 132, 133, 138, 139, 140, 142, 145, 147, 148, 149, 155, 156, 157, 162, 169, 184, 185, 189, 206, 209, 212, 213, 214, 215, 216, 225, 236
watercress, 234
wheat, 20
wine, 38, 92, 93, 94, 99, 132
Wine, 20
words of deliverance, 198
Zamzam, xviii, 32, 76
zirabaja, 118

www.ingramcontent.com/pod-product-compliance
Lightning Source LLC
LaVergne TN
LVHW041917070526
838199LV00051BA/2645